What about

"Se and adults
will re ices."

lling series
d *The One*

"Tl his book
will g

founder of

"I apter has
comp I mean it:
a com

"Se enges for
teens

from Venus

"In ible feats:
he gr clarity to
their rabs hold
of you

ing of Age

"Fi ools they
need nect with
the he tor, I feel
strong *Important*
Decisi up in one
word, 'AWESOME.' "

—MURIEL THOMAS SUMMERS, principal, A. B. Combs Leadership Elementary School,
National Blue Ribbon School of Excellence, the National School of Character 2004

"How we live our lives is based on the values we choose. This book will help teens choose their values today in order to make the decisions that create a better tomorrow."

—A. C. GREEN, founder of A. C. Green Youth Foundation, former Los Angeles Laker and NBA "Ironman"

"This is brilliant! Having teenagers put their input into this book has a great effect. I was thinking *wow!* These are people I can relate to, teenagers like me with the same problems. Maybe I am not so alone."

—KRISTI MARCHESI, age 15, Queensland, Australia

"In a world where our teens are bombarded with mixed messages about sex, drugs, and image, Sean Covey's ability to 'tell it like it is' is a rare blessing. I highly recommend this book."

—RICHARD PAUL EVANS, author of the #1 *New York Times* bestseller *The Christmas Box*

"This book reinforces the importance of family communication and healthy relationships by encouraging teens to be proactive in these six areas of their lives. This message of choice and consequence is one that our children, neighborhoods, and communities need to hear again and again."

—MIKE CRAPO, United States senator

"If teenagers do not stand for something, they will fall for anything. *The 6 Most Important Decisions You'll Ever Make* empowers teenagers to be themselves and to stand up for what's right."

—DR. RANDAL PINKETT, winner of NBC's *The Apprentice* and president and CEO of BCT Partners

"This book helped me understand that I have the power to decide for myself who and what I want to be and do."

—ALEXANDER IAN KENNEY, age 16, Copenhagen, Denmark

"Sean Covey has done an outstanding job of understanding the complicated and dynamic needs of today's young people. Sean is one of the leading authorities in writing to teens. It is a pleasure to know and support Sean in this great work."

—STEDMAN GRAHAM, author of *Teens Can Make It Happen* and founder of AAD Education, Health and Sports

"If the decisions of tomorrow reflect the choices we make today, then I can think of no better way to start than with Sean Covey's *The 6 Most Important Decisions You'll Ever Make*. Its powerful message will change lives. With the help of Sean Covey, I realize now I have the power to create a great future starting today."

—CARLY HAYNIE, 100M breaststroke bronze medalist, Paralympic Games, Athens, Greece, 2004

"We first knew Sean Covey as Stephen's son and as a gutsy football quarterback. Good as his passes were, he has proven to be even better at speaking to the heart of a teenager. The wise plays he recommends in this book will make the teenage years a winning season."

—LINDA and RICHARD EYRE, *New York Times* #1 bestselling authors and founders of valuesparenting.com

"Sean Covey has a genuine understanding of the challenges and needs of teenagers. He demonstrated it in his first book, *The 7 Habits of Highly Effective Teens*, and he demonstrates it again in this terrific new book. What a valuable guide and resource for our young people! I hope every teenager in the world reads it."

—HAL URBAN, Ph.D., author of *Life's Greatest Lessons*

"This book has many motivational stories and effective strategies to help teenagers find answers before they have to make the decisions that will impact every facet of their future lives. You gotta read this if you want to succeed!"

—BRENT SINGLETON, age 18, winner of the 2005 U.S. Government National Clean Air Excellence Award and National President's Environmental Youth Award

"It's a rare opportunity to find a creative and inspirational book without the author appearing to be looking down on the reader. Sean Covey has created a conversational guide for teenagers all over the world as they face the significant challenges placed before them in today's world. More important, this excellent work provides a solid road map to the world of tomorrow."

—DOUGLAS SPOTTED EAGLE, international Grammy and Emmy award–winning recording artist, producer, and author

"This is a highly entertaining, straight-talk book that helps teens understand both the what and the why of making good choices in the critical areas of their lives. It's a 'must read' for teens and everyone who cares about them."

—A. ROGER and REBECCA MERRILL, parents of seven children, coauthors of *First Things First*, and authors of *Life Matters*

"The timing of this book could not have been better. I have a fifteen-year-old son, and Sean Covey advises with the expertise of a friend who cares. Any teenager willing to listen just might find her- or himself inspired to be greater and do better."

—ANSON DORRANCE, soccer coach of the eighteen-time National Champion University of North Carolina women's soccer team

"I love the way this book deals with the important things that matter to me and my friends."

—DANIEL ARIAS, age 13, Costa Rica

"There are a hundred good reasons to read this book—great stories, inspiring quotes, tons of tips on how to take 'the high road' in everything you do—but the chapter you're likely to read first and remember most is Dating & Sex. Covey shows us how to make the choices that will protect our health, heart, and happiness."

—THOMAS LICKONA, Ph.D., developmental psychologist and Professor of Education at the State University of New York at Cortland

"This book is an investment in the future of the world and is essential for the success of your teen. I love this book!"

—JULIE MORGENSTERN, author of *Organizing from the Inside Out for Teens*

"Sean's book is more of a primer for success than anything I've read, targeted to young people. Filled with practical yet timeless truths, it will help instill both the motivation and the guidance for anyone, young or old, to take charge of their future by understanding the power of today's choices."

—BOB GOODWIN, president and CEO of Points of Light Foundation

"Powerful stuff!! I have never seen some of the kids I work with so enthusiastic about a book—especially those who read little! There is no doubt that Sean's material gets through to teens and has a real positive impact on their lives."

—LUISON LASSALA, youth leader at Anchor Educational Youth Centre and teacher at Rockbrook Park School, Dublin, Ireland

"Through the inspiring and poignant stories of real teens and sound principles, this book brings wisdom and guidance to young people who face so many life-changing decisions and challenges. Written in a humorous and approachable style, this is a comprehensive handbook to life for the fortunate teens who read it."

—CHERI J. MEINERS, M.Ed., author of the children's series Learning to Get Along

"Parents, get your teens to read this! Nag them, pay them, or do whatever you have to. It is a simple and far-reaching message that can influence both today and tomorrow."

—DR. HENRY CLOUD, Ph.D., cohost of the radio program, *New Life Live*, and author of the million-seller Boundaries series

"It's the first time I've had the opportunity to read a book that mentions our main concerns focused on our feelings."

—EMILIO ALFONSO CANALES MARTÍNEZ, age 17, Nicaragua

"This is a great guidebook for young men and women on their own journey into a bright future. Simple, powerful messages from other teens 'illuminate' the pages of *The 6 Most Important Decisions You'll Ever Make* with real, live advice and make this the indispensable companion for the journey."

—FRANCES HESSELBEIN, chairman, Leader to Leader Institute

"This book does not just guide you but it makes you understand the true meaning of how teenagers live. After I finished the book I was not the same old me anymore. Not only has it changed my thoughts, it made me understand why these certain things are happening to me and how to overcome them."

—M. MANDAKH, age 19, Ulaanbaatar, Mongolia

"Sean Covey takes universal decisions and applies them individually. While teenagers will probably uncover many thought-provoking ideas and a wide variety of useful advice within the pages of this book, I'm sure the most important discovery will be within themselves."

—JON M. HUNTSMAN, JR., governor of Utah

"When I read this book, I felt like I was listening to advice from my best friend. By the time I finished this book, I could see that many good things will happen in my future if I listen to Sean's advice and make the right decisions today."

—STELLA SAPUTRA, age 19, Jakarta, Indonesia

"Any success I've had is attributable to the same guidelines Sean Covey lays out in this book. I've surrounded myself with the right people, people I truly want to be like, believers in me, not naysayers. My parents and family have been my biggest support system. For those teens that plain and simply just don't have any real support system, I only hope they listen to Sean."

—ERIK WEIHENMAYER, blind climber of Mount Everest

"Life is all about making choices. Learning to make the right choices is the essence of life. Here is a sensitively written book that every young person must read to gain the ability to make their lives worthy of pride and emulation."

—ARUN GANDHI, president, M. K. Gandhi Institute for Nonviolence

"I felt as if this book was made for me. It touched some nerves. It broadened my expectations and it gave me direction."

—SHERILYNNE WILLIAMS, age 17, Durban, South Africa

"When my daughter (and coauthor) Jenny and I were growing up as father and daughter, she referred to my discourses on life as the 'Lectures.' In *The 6 Most Important Decisions You'll Ever Make,* Sean Covey has taken all those life lectures and made them fun, easy to read, and most important, friendly to the teenage ear."

—BILL GOOD, coauthor of *A Very Good Guide to Raising a Daughter*

"The 6 Most Important Decisions You'll Ever Make is an engaging, sensible, and right-on read for young people as they try to make good decisions. Parents, get two copies...you'll want one for your own, too! Covey has penned another winner."

—JOHN HARRINGTON, hockey coach of Saint John's University and member of the gold-medal-winning 1980 U.S. Olympic Hockey Team

"If the decisions of tomorrow reflect the choices we make today, then I can think of no better way for our youth to start life than with Sean Covey's *The 6 Most Important Decisions You'll Ever Make*. Sean Covey's message offers the blueprints to a successful life, and he gives teens all the tools they need to build characters fitting of such a life."

—PAULO KRETLY, author of the Brazilian bestseller *Figura de Transição* and noted Brazilian leadership speaker

"Sean Covey's book provides an easy to read road map to a successful and fulfilling life where what matters most is who you are, not what you are or what you have. This book is engaging, interesting, and powerful. Dare yourself to read it!"

—NORM DEAN, assistant regional director, Western Metropolitan Region, Department of Education & Training, Victoria, Australia

"This book speaks directly to teenage concerns such as taking responsibility for one's life. I certainly wish I had learned to apply these principles when I was a teen. I have no doubt this book will be an absolute hit with me and my students."

—DR. HELEN EFTHIMIADIS-KEITH, life-skills coordinator, University of Limpopo (Turfloop campus), South Africa

"Thanks to *The 6 Decisions* book, I am overcoming my identity crisis. I used to think I was just like everyone else. Now, I know I'm one of a kind."

—PENGUIN, age 2, Antarctica

The 6 Most Important DECISIONS You'll Ever Make

A Guide for Teens

SEAN COVEY

A FIRESIDE BOOK

Published by Simon & Schuster

NEW YORK   LONDON   TORONTO   SYDNEY

FIRESIDE
Rockefeller Center
1230 Avenue of the Ameri<
New York, NY 10020

FIRESIDE and colophon are registered trademarks
of Simon & Schuster, Inc.

"The Paradoxical Commandments" are reprinted by permission of the author.
Copyright © 1968 by Kent M. Keith, renewed 2001

For information regarding special discounts for bulk purchases, please contact
Simon & Schuster Special Sales at 1-800-456-6798
or business@simonandschuster.com.

Designed by The FaQtory www.TheFaQtory.ca
Illustrated by The FaQtory and Mark Pett www.MarkPett.com

Manufactured in the United States of America

20   19   18   17   16   15   14

ISBN-13: 978-0-7432-6504-1
ISBN-10:   0-7432-6504-1

The stories in this book are based on interviews, letters, or previously published
materials. In some cases, names and other identifying details have been
changed.

To teens everywhere,
who are striving to choose the higher road

and

To my son, Michael Sean,
who has shown great courage in hard moments

Two roads diverged in a wood, and I—

I took the one less traveled by,

And that has made all the difference.

—Robert Frost

The **6** BIG ONES

The Choice Is Yours

Call me Sean.

I'm the author and I'm glad you're here. Don't worry. This won't be another boring book. This one's different. It's written just for teens and deals with your life, your problems, your stuff. It also has a lot of great cartoons. (I had to hire several artists and pay them a fortune because I can't draw worth squat.)

This book is about one idea. I'll get straight to the point.

```
There are six key decisions you make during
your teen years that can make or break your
future. So, choose wisely, and don't blow it.
```

If you do happen to blow it, however, it's not the end of the world. Just get back on track quickly and start making smarter choices.

Being a teen today is tougher than ever. While your grandparents may have had to walk uphill to school in the snow, you have a different set of challenges to navigate: like media overload, party drugs, Internet porn, date rape, terrorism, global competition, depression, and heavy peer pressure. It's a totally different world!

Although I still shoot spit wads, I'm no longer a teen, but I vividly remember the ups and downs I went through. Most of my problems began at birth. My dad said, "Sean, when you were born your cheeks were so fat the doctor didn't know which end to spank." He wasn't kidding. You should see my baby pictures. My cheeks hung off my face like water balloons. You can imagine how often I was teased.

Once I was with all the neighborhood kids jumping on our trampoline. We were playing a game of add-on and it was my turn. Susan, my neighbor, couldn't resist saying what everyone was thinking: "Man, look at Sean's bouncing cheeks. They're so fat."

David, my younger brother, in an effort to defend me, said, "They're not fat. They're muscle."

His valiant effort backfired, and everyone got a kick out of my new nickname, "Muscle Cheeks."

My problems continued into junior high school. I hated seventh grade and have chosen to forget most of it. I do remember that I still had fat cheeks and an eighth grader named Scott kept trying to pick a fight with me. I don't know why he picked on me. I'd never met the guy. Maybe it was because he was confident he could pound me. He'd wait in the hallway with a couple of his friends and challenge me to a fight every day after my algebra class. I was petrified and tried to stay away from him.

One day he cornered me.

"Hey, Covey. You big fat sissy. Why don't you fight me?"

"I dunno."

He then slugged me in the stomach real hard, knocking my breath out. I was too scared to fight back. He left me alone after that. But I was humiliated and felt like a loser. (By the way, I'm bigger than Scott now and I'm still looking for him. Kidding!)

As I began high school, to my pleasant surprise, my face grew into my cheeks, but a new set of problems arose. Suddenly I had to make a lot of important decisions that I wasn't ready for. During the first week, I was invited to join a club with seniors who drank a lot. I didn't want to join but I also didn't want to offend them. I started to make new friends. Then, there were all these new girls. One even started liking me. She was pretty and aggressive and it was exciting and scary all at once. I had so many questions. Should I like this girl? Who should I hang out with? What classes should I take? Should I go to that party? How can I juggle school, sports, and friends?

I didn't realize it at the time, but these were some of the most important decisions I'd ever make in my life.

The idea for this book started when I sent out surveys to hundreds of teens from all over and asked, "What are your biggest challenges?" Here's what a few of them said:

"Stress. Trying to fit everything in is my number one challenge because I have a lot on my plate."

"Parents. I have to deal with them every day and it's exhausting."

"School and grades. My mom screams at me."

"Dealing with sexuality. I have to be able to make the right choices now so that I don't have to live with my mistakes later. It seems like if you're not having sex when you're a teenager, then you're a prude or something."

"Preparing for college. It's right around the corner and I haven't really given it much thought. Every time I try to think about it, I just end up getting a huge headache, so I don't."

"Divorce of my parents. They always fight over who gets visitation."

"High school drama. Who's going out with who? Popularity. Best hair. Most athletic. Who's got money? Who said this about them? It's ridiculous!"

"Money. Barely enough money to live."

"Peer pressure is a major problem. I give in really easy, with the right people."

"Friends. They are just bugging the heck out of me. I don't relate to them anymore. They ignore me and stay in their little cliques. I feel excluded, so lately I have just been staying away from them."

"I worry about the safety of my family because you can walk the streets and get killed. Most people are not going to school just to do drugs. I fear for my lil' brother and sister."

"Dating. I don't date whatsoever and here I am 17. My friends dog me and make me feel like I'm not doing something I should."

"Body and appearance. I struggle with my weight all the time."

I carefully studied all the surveys I got back. I also interviewed numerous teens from various locations over a three-year period. And a pattern began to emerge. Out of the 999 different challenges that were mentioned, six stood out above all the rest.

As I looked deeper, I discovered that with each challenge there was a choice (or series of choices) to be made. Some teens I interviewed had made smart choices; others, dumb ones. As a result, some were happy and some messed up. These challenges represented fork-in-the-road decisions and the consequences were huge. It became clear that what you do about these challenges are the six most important decisions you'll ever make as a teen!

THE SIX MOST IMPORTANT DECISIONS YOU'LL EVER MAKE

 School. What are you going to do about your education?

 Friends. What type of friends will you choose and what kind of friend will you be?

 Parents. Are you going to get along with your parents?

 Dating & Sex. Who will you date and what will you do about sex?

 Addictions. What will you do about smoking, drinking, drugs, and other addictive stuff?

 Self-Worth. Will you choose to like yourself?

You may not have thought much about these decisions. Or you may be struggling with one of them or all of them. Whatever your situation, you need to learn all you can about each decision, the ins and outs, the good and bad, so that you can make *informed* decisions, with your eyes wide open. You don't want to get down the road and find yourself saying, "If only I'd known better."

Many decisions you make as a teen can impact your life forever. In his book *Standing for Something*, religious leader Gordon B. Hinckley tells this story about when he was young:

While working in a Denver railroad office, I was in charge of the baggage and express traffic carried in passenger trains. One day I received a call from my counterpart in New Jersey who said that a passenger train had arrived without its baggage car. Three hundred patrons were angry, as well they had a right to be.

We discovered that the train had traveled from Oakland, California, to St. Louis, where a switchman had mistakenly moved a piece of steel just three inches. That

piece of steel was a switch point, and the baggage car that should have been in Newark was in New Orleans, fourteen hundred miles away.

Prisons all over the world are filled with people who made unwise and even destructive choices, individuals who moved a switch point in their lives just a little and were soon on the wrong track going to the wrong place.

Each of these six decisions is like a switch point, a small three-inch piece of steel that will lead us down the right or wrong track for hundreds of miles.

A TALE OF TWO TEENS

Imagine two 19-year-old girls about to graduate from teen-agehood. At age 13, they were in similar situations. At 19, they are in very different places, because of their choices.

MEET ALLIE. She smiles a lot. She is attending a local university and has two great roommates; they have a riot together. Allie has a tuition scholarship, and also works part-time as a teacher's assistant. She plans to graduate in two years with a degree in English and become a teacher. Allie is dating two different guys right now, but isn't really serious with either yet. Throughout her teen years, she didn't date much and felt a little insecure about it, but she's proud that she didn't sleep around with every other guy. She hopes to meet a wonderful guy and get married someday.

At fifteen, Allie tried drugs once but afterward realized how stupid it was. Since then, except for an occasional glass of wine, Allie doesn't drink, smoke, or do drugs. She's free of addictions. Every Sunday night, Allie calls her mom, whom she calls her "best friend." Although she has problems, overall, she is confident, goal-driven, and happy with herself.

MEET DESIREE. She is strikingly beautiful but suffers from low self-esteem. When asked why, she replies, "I don't know. It's just that I'm always thinking I'm fat and ugly."

Desiree started smoking when she was fourteen and smokes two packs a day now. She claims she could quit tomorrow.

She works full-time at a grocery store making minimum wage. Although she completed high school, she never really tried in school and doesn't see a need to get more education. She lives in an apartment by herself and has various live-in boyfriends. During high school, she fooled around with lots of guys and was involved in many abusive relationships. "I always seemed to pick losers," she says.

Desiree doesn't have much of a relationship with her parents. And she has little contact with any of her best friends from high school. She doesn't know what she wants to do with her future and often gets depressed.

Two girls. Two totally different outcomes. Why? Because of their choices. Can you begin to see why making smart choices about school, friends, parents, dating, sex, addictions, and self-esteem is so huge?

THE TEN-YEAR EXPERIMENT

Before going any further, try this little experiment:

Your job is to introduce yourself to some-one as you were exactly ten years ago today and tell them a few things about yourself.

If your name is Jeremie and you're seventeen, you would say something like: "Hi, my name is Jeremie. I'm seven years old and I live in Toronto, Canada, with my parents and my younger brother, who is four. I just finished first grade. I have a goldfish named Spot and I love to color and play soccer. I feel happy inside."

If you're reading this book and you're near someone, try this experiment with them. Tell them it's part of a book assignment, so they don't think you've gone psycho. Introduce yourself as you were ten years ago, then have them do the same. If no one's around or you're too embarrassed (no big deal), just fill in the blanks below.

The date ten years ago today is:

My name is:

I am _____ years old.

I live in:

I live with:

My favorite things to do are:

I feel:

Now, shift gears. Your job is to introduce yourself to the same person as you would like to be ten years into the future. Tell them what you're doing and a little about yourself. Remember, this is how *you would like to be* ten years from now. So, Jeremie would say something like:

"Hi. I'm Jeremie. I'm 27 years old and I live in Vancouver, Canada. I just got married to a wonderful woman named Jasmine. A few years ago I graduated in music from the University of Toronto and I now teach piano at a private music school. I love my family and I hang out with them a lot. I'm feelin' really good about where I'm headed with my life."

The date ten years from now is:

My name is:

I am _____ years old.

I live in:

I live with:

Over the past ten years I have:

I feel:

You just practiced time travel. When you went back ten years, what memories surfaced? Were you in a good spot or a bad one?

And what about the future? What did you see ten years from now? What do you want to do and who do you want to become over the next decade?

FREE TO CHOOSE

The good news is, where you end up ten years from now is up to you. You are free to choose what you want to make of your life. It's called *free agency* or *free will* and it's your birthright. What's more, you can turn it on instantly! At any moment, you can choose to start showing more respect for yourself or stop hanging out with friends who bring you down. Ultimately, you choose to be happy or miserable.

The reality is that although you are free to choose, you can't choose the consequences of your choices. They're preloaded. It's a package deal. As the old saying goes, "If you pick up one end of the stick, you pick up the other." Choice and consequence go together like mashed potatoes and gravy. For example, if you decide to do poorly in school and not go to college, you'll suffer the natural consequences of finding it hard even to get an interview for a high-paying job. Likewise, if you date intelligently and avoid casual intimacy, you'll enjoy the consequences of having a good reputation and not worrying about STDs and pregnancy.

The word *decision* comes from the Latin root meaning "to cut off from." Saying "yes" to one thing means saying "no" to another. That's why decisions can be hard sometimes.

You're always better off making a decision once and being done with it instead of making it again and again. For example, as a teen, I decided I wasn't going to smoke, or drink, or do drugs. (Now, I'm not making myself out be a hero, because I made lots of mistakes as a teen, as I'll show you later. But I did do this one thing right.) So, I avoided parties where everyone got plastered. I chose not to hang out with guys who did drugs. I never felt peer pressure to do this stuff because I'd already made up my mind once and didn't have to keep making that decision over and over.

Some might say that I missed out on a lot of fun. Maybe so. To me, it gave me freedom: freedom from getting stoned and doing something stupid; freedom from a drunk driving offense; freedom from forming an addiction.

A QUICK OVERVIEW

There are different ways in which you can read this book. You can read it from start to finish (probably the best way), or skip around and go to the chapters that interest you the most. If you're really lazy, just look at the cartoons. Here is a quick overview of the chapters.

SCHOOL—I'm Totally Stressed Out!

Of all your challenges, school ranks #1. Why? It's the stress! As one teen put it, "School...Argh! People put pressure on students that school is everything and it stresses me out!"

You have to deal with gossip and grades, teachers and tests, labels and lunch ladies. Yikes! You have to cope with parents who actually expect you to try your best in school, for crying out loud. On top of that, you have to worry about preparing to get a real job someday.

Why is what you choose to do about education such a big decision? Probably because what you do about it will open doors of opportunity or slam them shut for a very long time.

In the chapter on school, we'll hit many important topics like:

- *How dropping out of school wrecks your money-making potential*
- *Finding motivation when you have none*
- *The 7 secrets to getting good grades*
- *Rising above a learning disability*
- *Preparing and paying for college*
- *Finding your voice (we're not talking choir here; we're talking about discovering what you're good at)*

FRIENDS—So Fun...So Fickle

Some teens find it easy to make good friends. For many, though, it's a struggle. We don't fit in. Or we're judged because we don't have a perfect body or wear the right clothes. It's especially hard when your family has to move and, suddenly, you're the new kid at school trying to break into established cliques. Many of us have had times when we've not had any friends at all. Or we have such a great need to be accepted we become friends with anyone willing to accept us even if they bring us down.

And then there's all the drama. It is the weirdest thing, but virtually every girl I've spoken to tells me, "Any two girls get along fine, but three never works." Us guys have a different set of challenges, like punching each other and dating each other's girlfriends.

Who you choose as friends and the kind of friend you choose to be is a huge decision. In this chapter, we'll talk about lots of interesting stuff such as:

DON'T YOU THINK TAMMY IS A TOTAL GOSSIP?

- *Surviving the popularity game*
- *What to do when you don't have any friends*
- *Being the kind of friend you'd like to have*
- *Surviving the catfights*
- *What you need to know about gangs*
- *Standing up to peer pressure*

 ## PARENTS—How Embarrassing!

"My mom is OK. She tries to understand me. But it's like the more she tries the more she annoys me. And then my dad is just crazy. And I just can't relate to him at all."

This is Sabrina. She's pretty normal. She loves her parents but can't figure them out half the time. Part of the problem with parents is how we see them. When I was in grade school, my parents were cool. But when I turned 13, they morphed into nerds and became so embarrassing. Suddenly, they forgot how to dress, talk, or walk upright. I'll never forget the time in eighth grade when I was on the sidelines during a football game and I felt a tap on my shoulder.

"Hey, Sean. It's me. Dad. Do you and your buddies want a piece?"

I was shocked. There stood my dad on the sidelines, where he wasn't supposed to be, with a 16-inch pizza, during the middle of my football game, asking me if I wanted a piece of freaking pizza.

I was horrified. And, in front of all my teammates, I denied that I even knew him.

But, trust me, when you get a little older you'll find that your parents will instantly mature and become cool again and your friends will start saying things like, "Dude, your mom is awesome."

The quality of the relationship you want to have with your mom and dad is a choice, and it's one of the most important decisions you'll ever make. In this chapter, we'll discuss many vital issues, including:

- *How to build an awesome relationship with your mom and dad*
- *Disarming your parents in one line or less*

- *Four magical expressions to use with your parents that work every time*
- *Surviving a divorce*
- *Coping with the "Why can't you be like your brother?" syndrome*
- *What to do when your parents are really messed up and you have to raise them*

DECISION 4 — DATING & SEX—Do We Have to Talk About This?

I wish we didn't have to talk about it, but we do. If we didn't, I'd be irresponsible, because it's one of the most important decisions you'll ever make. Perhaps the *most* important. (Parents, if you're secretly reading your teen's book right now to see what I have to say about this topic, just relax and trust me. I won't botch it.)

When I was a boy, my parents never talked about the birds and the bees. My dad would turn red in the face if he even thought about it. So, I learned all about it from the neighborhood boys that were in the know. But times have changed and you'd better get real clear on what kind of people you're going to date and what you're going to do about sex. If you don't, someone else will make the decision for you and you don't want that. In this chapter we'll get into stuff like:

- *Dating intelligently*
- *So you don't date...so what?*
- *The problem with centering your life on a girlfriend or boyfriend*
- *Spotting red flags in a relationship*
- *What are STDs and why should I care?*
- *Debunking the four great myths about teens and sex*

ADDICTIONS—It's Not Hard to Quit...
I've Done It a Dozen Times

I admit it. I picked up an addiction in high school—to nachos. I couldn't get enough of them. I couldn't watch a movie without nachos. I couldn't pass a 7-Eleven without getting my nacho fix. I'm still hooked. I've never stopped to think about what goes into that greasy, cheesy stuff, but I'm sure it ain't cheese.

I'm so lucky I didn't pick up any other addictions during my teens. I feel bad for a coworker who has to go outside every two hours in the rain or heat to have his smoke. I feel bad for a family friend who messed up his brain so bad from drugs that he's just not in there anymore. Clearly, the decisions you make around this challenge often stick with you for life.

Today, there's pressure to binge-drink, smoke, do drugs, take steroids, sniff glue, and do a number of other enticing things. As a couple of teens put it:
"A ton of people do it, so it's hard to stay away from it."
"I've stopped, but I still want it."

You won't want to miss this section. Your peers have some really good stories to share. We'll chat about:

- *The three brutal realities of addiction*
- *The truth about alcohol, tobacco, meth, ecstasy, 'roids, cocaine, prescriptions, inhalants, and more*
- *This is not your parents' marijuana!*
- *Conquering an addiction*
- *The drug of the twenty-first century*
- *Where to get great nachos*

DECISION **6** SELF-WORTH—If Only I Were
Better Looking

One girl said, "My biggest challenge is self-esteem. There are too many beautiful people. I feel ugly." If you ever feel this way, you're not alone. Compared to the models we see plastered in *Cosmopolitan* and *GQ,* we all feel ugly.

There's nothing wrong with wanting to look your best. But if your self-confidence or lack of it comes from how you stack up on the good-looks gauge, you've got serious problems.

The fact is, there are lots of kids with big noses and dorky clothes that are full of self-confidence. And there are loads of well-dressed, popular kids who have no self-confidence at all. Obviously, there's so much more to healthy self-worth than beauty and biceps.

When all is said and done, learning to like yourself is a choice. It may not seem that way, but it is. It's a matter of learning to get your security from within, not from without—or from what others say about you. This chapter will cover:

- *The one true mirror you should always look to*
- *Why fixating on other people's opinions of you is stupid*
- *Character and competence: the foundation stones of healthy self-worth*
- *What to do when you're depressed and can't pull out of it*
- *Developing your unique talents and skills*
- *Mining your own fields for diamonds*

THE 7 HABITS CRASH COURSE—They Make You or Break You

In addition to a chapter on each of the six decisions, there's a short chapter called The 7 Habits Crash Course. It's up next. A few years ago, I wrote a book called *The 7 Habits of Highly Effective Teens*. If you've already read that book, the chapter will serve as a good review of the habits. If you haven't read it, the crash course will get you up to speed. It doesn't really matter in which order you read these books. It's sort of like the *Star Wars* movies. They all go together but it doesn't really matter which one you watch first.

In this book, we'll use the 7 Habits as a tool kit to help you make these big decisions. So just what are the 7 habits of highly effective teens? Simply put, they are the habits that successful and happy teenagers from Africa to Alaska have in common. Don't leave home without them!

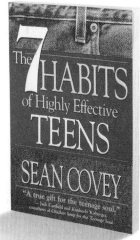

READY FOR TOMORROW

My purpose in writing this book is simple: I want to help you make smart choices around each of the six decisions so you can be happy and healthy today, and ready for tomorrow—a future so bright you'll have to wear shades. When you turn twenty and retire from being a teen, I want you to be able to say:

- *I have a solid education!*
- *I have good friends that bring out the best in me!*
- *I have good relationships with my parents!*

- *I don't have an STD, am not pregnant (nor gotten anyone pregnant), and have made smart choices about dating and sex!*
- *I am addiction-free!*
- *I like myself and am OK with who I am!*

Of course, you'll make mistakes during your teen years, face many struggles, and have many highs and lows. No one expects you to be perfect. But please don't make it harder than it has to be. By simply making smarter choices starting today your teenage journey can be so much smoother.

I like what the poet Robert Frost had to say about the importance of decisions.

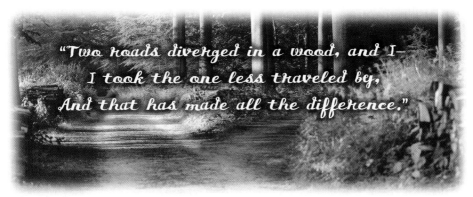

"Two roads diverged in a wood, and I—
I took the one less traveled by,
And that has made all the difference."

P.S.

Oh, by the way, I encourage you to personalize your book. A teen named Carol said, "I come from a book-oriented family. I've been reading since the age of three, and writing anything in a book is a *sin.*" I was raised this way too. But let's change that rule, right now. The new rule is: Mark up your book! Get out your pen, colored pencils, highlighter—whatever—and go to town. Scribble. Doodle. Have some fun with it. Write in the margins. Circle quotes you want to remember. Highlight stories that inspire you. Record insights as they come. You'll get a lot more out of this book if you make it your own.

Write in the margins°

● ● ● COMING ATTRACTIONS ● ● ●

Up next, we'll talk about who this guy they call "the man" really is. If you're curious, keep reading!

The 7 HABITS
CRASH COURSE

They Make You or Break You

On the next page is a chart with numbers from 1 to 54. Your challenge is to find each number on the chart, starting at 1, then 2, then 3, and so on, all the way to 54. Take 1 1/2 minutes and see how many numbers you can find. There are no missing numbers or tricks. Are you ready? On your mark, get set, go.

How far did you get? Most people get to about number 30. Now, I want you to try it again, but this time I'm going to teach you a method to help you locate the numbers. Go to page 32 and everything will be explained there.

Welcome back. So, how far did you get this time? Perhaps you got all the way to 54. What was the difference? The only difference is that I gave you a way of thinking—a framework—to help you find the numbers. Once you knew where to look, you could move at three times the speed.

That's exactly what the 7 Habits are. *They are a framework or a way of thinking that can help you solve your problems better and faster.* They will be vitally important in helping you make smart choices for these six most important decisions. So, throughout the book, I will refer to them from time to time.

To get you started, I'm going to give you a quick crash course on the 7 Habits. Before diving into the Habits, you need to understand two quick concepts: paradigms and principles.

WHAT'S A PARADIGM?

A *paradigm* is your perception, point of view, or the way you see the world. My brother-in-law Kameron once worked hard for several weeks building a wall made of railroad ties in his backyard. When he was almost finished, his neighbor regretfully asked Kameron if he could please take out the railroad ties and use rocks instead. She simply explained that her husband didn't want to look at a railroad tie wall for the rest of his life.

Kameron's workmates couldn't believe the nerve of this neighbor to ask such a thing when the wall was almost finished. Although Kameron didn't fully understand her reasoning, he knew they'd be neighbors for a long time, and, although it cost him another week of extra work, he did what she requested and replaced the railroad ties with rocks.

The next week, Kam's neighbor came over and expressed appreciation for rebuilding the wall for her husband's sake. "You see," she explained, "he'd never tell you this, but when my husband was a teenager, he was imprisoned in a labor camp for eighteen months in Germany after the war. During all those months he had to carry railroad ties, and, to this day, he gets sick to his stomach when he even looks at one."

Can you see how a little understanding immediately changed Kameron's perception? His anger turned to compassion in an instant. That's called a *paradigm shift.* Sometimes our paradigms or perceptions are way off and need to be fixed. That's why we shouldn't judge other people. We seldom know the whole story.

This book will challenge many of the paradigms you have about yourself and life in general. You may, for example, believe that you and your mom could never get along. Or you may be convinced that you could never do well in school. Or you may feel that it's unrealistic to refrain from having sex as a teen. In reality, it may be that your paradigm is messed up, and that with a little more information, you'd feel differently, just as Kameron did. Remember, the key to changing yourself is to first change your perspective or paradigm.

WHAT'S A PRINCIPLE?

Principles are natural laws. Gravity is a principle. If you toss an apple into the air, it will come down, regardless of whether you live in New York or New Delhi, or whether you're alive today or in 2,000 B.C.

Just as there are principles that govern the physical world, there are principles that govern human inter-action. Honesty, for example, is a principle. If you are honest with other people, you will earn their trust. If you are dishonest, you may fool people for some time but you'll eventually be found out—always. Other examples of principles are hard work, respect, service, focus, patience, responsibility, love, renewal, choice, and justice. There are dozens more.

The following is a transcript of an apocryphal radio conversation between a U.S. naval ship and Canadian authorities off the coast of Newfoundland. It illustrates what I mean by principles.

Americans: *"Please divert your course 15 degrees to the north to avoid a collision."*

Canadians: *"Recommend you divert your course 15 degrees to the south to avoid a collision."*

Americans: *"This is the captain of a U.S. Navy ship. I say again, divert YOUR course."*

Canadians: *"No, I say again, you divert YOUR course."*

Americans: *"This is the aircraft carrier USS* Abraham Lincoln, *the second largest ship in the United States Atlantic fleet. We are accompanied by three destroyers, three cruisers, and numerous support vessels. I demand that you change your course 15 degrees north. That's one-five degrees north, or countermeasures will be taken to ensure the safety of this ship."*

Canadians: *"This is a lighthouse. Your call."*

Principles are like lighthouses. They're timeless, universal, and self-evident. You can't break principles; you can only break yourself against them, no matter who you are.

Since principles can never fail us, they are the best possible things to center our lives on. By centering on principles, all the other important aspects of our lives—friends, boyfriends and girlfriends, school, and family—find their proper place. Ironically, putting principles first is the key to doing better in all these other areas.

Each of the 7 Habits is based upon a timeless principle that never goes out of style. Throughout the book I'll show you the havoc that's created when you center your life on anything other than principles.

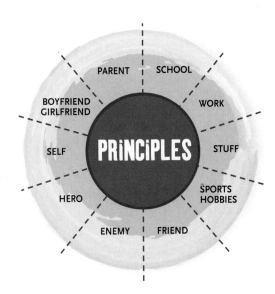

THE 7 HABITS

The 7 habits of highly effective teens are the 7 characteristics that happy and successful teens the world over have in common. Here's a list of the habits and quick explanations.

HABIT 1 BE PROACTIVE
Take responsibility for your life.

HABIT 2 BEGIN WITH THE END IN MIND
Define your mission and goals in life.

HABIT 3 PUT FIRST THINGS FIRST
Prioritize, and do the most important things first.

HABIT 4 THINK WIN-WIN
Have an everyone-can-win attitude.

HABIT 5 SEEK FIRST TO UNDERSTAND,
THEN TO BE UNDERSTOOD
Listen to people sincerely.

HABIT 6 SYNERGIZE
Work together to achieve more.

HABIT 7 SHARPEN THE SAW
Renew yourself regularly.

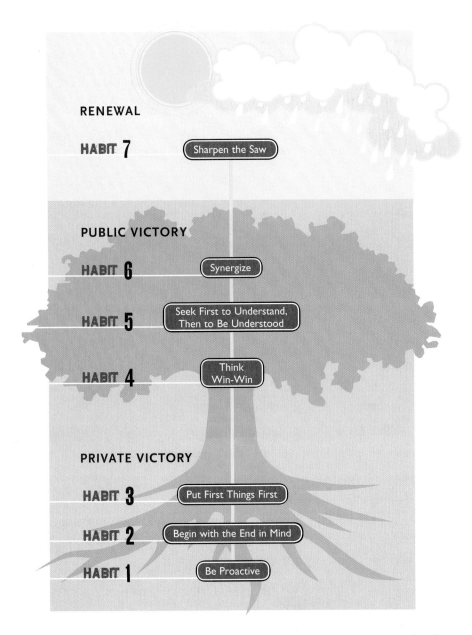

RENEWAL

HABIT 7 — Sharpen the Saw

PUBLIC VICTORY

HABIT 6 — Synergize

HABIT 5 — Seek First to Understand, Then to Be Understood

HABIT 4 — Think Win-Win

PRIVATE VICTORY

HABIT 3 — Put First Things First

HABIT 2 — Begin with the End in Mind

HABIT 1 — Be Proactive

As the above diagram shows, the habits build upon each other. The first three habits, numbers 1, 2, and 3, form the root structure. These habits deal with getting your own act together. We call it the Private Victory. It's all underground because nobody but you really knows what's going on. Too often, we try to change other people before changing ourselves but, as we all know, it doesn't work that way. All change starts at the roots, with you.

The next three habits, numbers 4, 5, and 6, form the trunk and branches, the stuff that everyone sees. These habits deal with getting along with other people. We call it the Public Victory. If you haven't won the Private Victory to some degree, it will be impossible to win the public one. The key to good relationships is to make peace with yourself first. It's inside out, not outside in.

Above the tree are the things that nurture the tree from the roots to the leaf tops, like rain and sunshine. This is Habit 7, or the habit of Renewal. It breathes life and vitality into all the other habits.

Let me give you an image for each habit to help you remember them.

HABIT 1 BE PROACTIVE

For Habit 1, picture a remote control.

Habit 1 is all about taking responsibility for your life and being the captain of your own ship. As my friend, author John Bytheway, puts it, proactive people carry the remote control to their lives. They choose their channel or mood. Reactive people allow other people or things to control them, as if they've given their remote to other people or things that can change their moods at the push of a button. They allow a rude comment by a friend to ruin their whole day.

Reactive people say stuff like:

- *"My boyfriend is making my life miserable."*
- *"I can't get good grades as long as he's my teacher."*
- *"Mom, you're messing up my life."*
- *"If I had her looks, I'd be popular too."*

In the movie *The School of Rock* there's a great scene in which the substitute teacher, Dewey, is sarcastically trying to teach the kids about how we too easily become victims to "the man," or that imaginary force that is out to get us.

Dewey: *What, you want me to teach you something? You want to learn something? All right, here's a useful lesson for you. Give up. Just quit. Because in this life, you can't win. Yeah, you can try, but in the end, you're just gonna lose, big-time, because the world is run by the Man.*

Frankie: *Who?*

Dewey: *The Man. Oh, you don't know the Man? Oh, well, he's everywhere. In the White House, down the hall. Miss Mullins, she's the Man. And the Man ruined the ozone, and he's burning down the Amazon, and he kidnapped Shamu and put her in a chlorine tank. Okay? And there used to* *be a way to stick it to the Man. It was called rock 'n' roll. But guess what. Oh, no. The Man ruined that too with a little thing called MTV! So don't waste your time trying to make anything cool or pure or awesome. 'Cause the Man's just gonna call you a fat, washed-up loser and crush your soul. So do yourselves a favor and just give up!*

The point is, when you play the victim, you give up control, and you hand over your remote to the Man, whether it be your parents, a teacher, a girlfriend or boyfriend, a boss, or fate itself. Habit 1 is all about taking back the remote and taking responsibility for your life.

For example, Jen told me how she used to let little comments at school make her miserable. After learning about Habit 1, however, she took back her remote. Jen said,

"It doesn't intimidate me to say 'hi' to people in the halls anymore. When something bad happens, I smile through it. It's kind of amazing how happy I am, and how I consider most days good when I used to consider the same days bad. And when he doesn't say 'hi' to me, I say 'hi' to someone hotter and make my own day."

As you'll see, Habit 1 plays a key role in every one of the important decisions.

HABIT 2 BEGIN WITH THE END IN MIND

For Habit 2, think of a road map.

Think about the last long road trip you went on. Without a map, how hard would it have been to find your destination? Pretty difficult. You might have eventually found it, but you would have wasted a lot of time and energy in the process. So it is with us. If we aren't clear about our end in mind, about our goals and what we stand for, we'll wander, waste time, and be tossed to and fro by the opinions of others.

To help you define where you want to go in life, I recommend writing a personal mission statement or a clear set of goals or both. Think of it as your personal road map.

WELCOME KINDERGARTNERS

Here's a mission statement shared by Ayesha Johnson from Hunter's Lane High School.

MY MISSION STATEMENT IS...

...To be the best I can be.

...To continue to be a role model to my younger cousins.

...To graduate from high school and college.

...To continue to help people with their situations.

...To be a good student.

...To be a wife and mother later in life.

...To be a successful business woman/owner.

...To one day save a lot of money and help the needy.

...To donate my organs to someone who needs them when I die.

...To most of all believe that through God all things are possible, if you just believe.

Imagine how much this mission statement directs Ayesha's life day to day. Mission statements come in all kinds of forms, some long, some short, in poetry or art form. Here's yet another mission statement by Peter Parker.

Whatever life holds in store for me, I will never forget these words: "With great power comes great responsibility." This is my gift, my curse. Who am I? I'm Spider-Man.

Throughout the book, I'll share mission statements from teens and encourage you to write your own.*

HABIT 3 PUT FIRST THINGS FIRST

For Habit 3, imagine a 13-hour clock.

When you put first things first, it expands your time. It's almost like having a 13-hour clock. The Time Quadrants is an amazing model that can help you find more time. It is made of two ingredients:

Important:
your most important things;
stuff that **really matters.**

Urgent: things that are in your
face and demand your **immediate attention.**

---

* For help building your own mission statement, go to www.6decisions.com.

THE TIME QUADRANTS

URGENT	NOT URGENT
1 • Exam tomorrow • Friend gets injured • Late for work • Project due today • Car breaks down **THE PROCRASTINATOR**	**2** • Planning, goal setting • Essay due in a week • Exercise • Relationships • Relaxation **THE PRIORITIZER**
3 • Unimportant phone calls, e-mails • Interruptions • Other people's small problems • Peer pressure • Too many clubs, activities, hobbies **THE YES-MAN**	**4** • Too much TV • Endless phone calls • Excessive computer games, Internet, messaging • Mall marathons • Personal time wasters (PTWs) GILLIGAN! **THE SLACKER**

(Left side labels: **IMPORTANT** for top row, **NOT IMPORTANT** for bottom row)

Quadrant 1 are things that are both important and urgent. This includes stuff like getting to work on time, a car breaking down, the big test tomorrow. These things are important and they have to be taken care of now. Sometimes crises just pop up; in fact, they always will. Too often, however, we create them because we procrastinate. That's why Quadrant 1 is the home of The Procrastinator. A Q1 lifestyle leads to burnout and high stress. Spend less time here.

Quadrant 2 includes things that are important but not urgent. So what is important but not urgent? How about exercise? Is that important? Yes. Is it urgent? No. Not really. You're not going to die if you don't exercise today. So, it belongs in Quadrant 2. What about a paper that is due in a week. Is it important? Yes. Is it urgent? No. Not yet. But if you procrastinate too long then suddenly it turns into a Q1 crisis. So, it also belongs in Q2. Quadrant 2 is where The Prioritizer lives. It's the place you want to be. Time spent here leads to a balanced life and high performance.

Quadrant 3 represents stuff that is urgent, but not important, such as many phone calls and e-mails, interruptions, and other people's small problems. Because this stuff is urgent, it appears important, but it's really not. Quadrant 3 is where The Yes-Man hangs out. He says yes to everything and everyone because he doesn't want to disappoint anyone. In so doing, he only disappoints himself. Avoid this quadrant at all costs.

Quadrant 4 is filled with time wasters and too much of a good thing, such as really long phone calls, endless Internet sessions, too much sleep, and mall marathons. Some of these activities are relaxing and necessary at first, but do them too much and they become a waste. This is the home of The Slacker. Don't waste your time here.

Just having a simple understanding of the Quadrants will help you immensely at school. See what it did for Sarah, a 16-year-old junior.

I was a very good student, but when tests came, I would do very poorly on them. I had no clue why I would bomb even though I knew the material being discussed. When I saw the Quadrants it made me realize I was definitely The Yes-Man. When I was supposed to be studying I would have interruptions that I thought were important, like a phone call. I was easily distracted. I would then cram the morning before the test to get as much information as possible in my head. I am learning to say no to people at times and saying yes to me. My teachers have taught me that it is OK to be a little selfish about my priorities.

HABIT 4 THINK WIN-WIN

For Habit 4, think of a high five.

The high five seems to have been around since the caveman and is a symbol of teamwork and the Win-Win spirit. Think Win-Win is an attitude toward life that believes everyone can win. It's not you, or me, it's both of us. Instead of being threatened by the successes of others, you're happy for them. Their success does not take away from you. Instead of stepping on other people (Win-Lose) or being the doormat for others to wipe their feet (Lose-Win), you're always thinking of ways for both sides to get what they want.

I remember reading a sermon from the Lake Street Church of Evanston that beautifully illustrates this point.

I was recently reminded of a story the late senator Paul Simon was fond of telling...Every time he told it, it choked him up and brought tears to his eyes. It is the story of a Special Olympics over which he officially presided. The time came for the footrace. All of the runners assembled at the starting line. Each one had a particular disability. The gun sounded and the racers sprinted.

About a third of the way through the course, one of the runners fell. The crowd gasped. But, amazingly, with utter spontaneity, the rest of the runners stopped in their tracks. They stopped and looked back at the one who had fallen. One by one they turned around and slowly made their way back to help the fallen runner. They pulled him to his feet and the race continued with everyone running arm in arm to the finish line. They all finished the race together. All of those runners could see themselves in the one who fell.

Although there is a place for healthy competition, like in sports and business, life is not a competition, especially when it comes to relationships. Think how silly it is to say, "So, who's winning in your relationship, you or your mom?" In relationships, if you're not both winning, in the end you'll both end up losing.

When it comes to making important decisions around choosing good friends, dating intelligently, and getting along with your parents, a Win-Win spirit is a must.

HABIT 5 SEEK FIRST TO UNDERSTAND, THEN TO BE UNDERSTOOD

For Habit 5, remember a big ear.

Most people don't listen very well and, as a result, one of the great frustrations in life is that we don't feel understood. No one seems to really understand our problems, our pain, our wishes, our unique situation.

Many Native Americans use a solution to this problem that's been around for centuries. It's called the Talking Stick. Whenever people meet together, the Talking Stick is there. Only the person holding the Talking Stick is permitted to speak. As long as you have the Talking Stick, you alone may speak, until you feel that everyone understands you. As soon as you feel understood, it's your duty to pass it on to someone else so that they too can feel understood. The Talking Stick, you see, ensures that everyone truly listens.

Wouldn't it be great to have the Talking Stick when you're trying to share your feelings with your parents? They wouldn't be allowed to speak until you felt completely understood. Imagine that!

The single most important communication skill you can ever learn is how to listen. Real listening doesn't mean you're just silent, it means that you're actively trying to understand another human being. Often we get into trouble because we jump to conclusions without understanding all the details, as this poem written by a teen named Logan illustrates.

The other day I saw my girl walking with some other man
They were walking and giggling and having a time
And I saw she was holding his hand!

I stood back and spied, my eyes filled with tears
As I watched this foul display
Some overly cheerful bicep with legs
Was taking my baby away!

As I spied over Dumpsters with feelings of hate
I saw them in a close embrace! Now I'm broken-hearted
'Cause before they parted, I saw her kiss his face.

That ended my garbage-can espionage
I thought I had seen quite enough
I decided to confront that devilish girl
Who I had once called my true love.

So I typed up an e-mail to that wicked female
And gave her a piece of my mind.
But I won't say what I said, in case there's kids present
But I will say my words were unkind.

I said it was the end, and right when I clicked send
I heard my telephone ring.
I picked up the receiver and couldn't believe her
It was my little ex...thing.

She said "Sorry babe that I haven't seen you all day
But my older brother's in town!
Did I ever tell you that he is a boxer
And one of the biggest around?!

"He'd like to meet you but he's quite protective
So behave whatever you do,
I'll just check my e-mail and then we'll come by
And...oh look! Here's an e-mail from you."

Healthy relationships with friends and parents are built on a foundation of good listening and withholding judgment. We'll take a closer look at how to better do that in the chapters ahead.

HABIT **6** SYNERGIZE

For Habit 6, visualize four interlocking arms.

Synergy is achieved when two or more people work together to create something better than any one could alone. It's not your way or my way but a better way, a higher way. Life is like four interlocking arms that form a circle. Each arm brings different strengths to the party and together they are stronger than any single arm alone. Builders know all about this. They know that one 2 x 4 beam can support 607 pounds, but two 2 x 4s nailed together can support not just 1,214 pounds (which is what you'd expect), but a whopping 4,878 pounds! So it is with us. We can do so much more together than we can alone.

Each of us is different, in background, race, and culture, in how we look, think, and talk, and on and on. And the key to synergy lies in appreciating these differences instead of being scared by them. A popular fable, "The Animal School," by George H. Reavis, illustrates why we should value differences and not lump everyone into the same mold.

Once upon a time, the animals...organized a school. They adopted an activity curriculum consisting of running, climbing, swimming, and flying...

The duck was excellent in swimming, better in fact than his instructor, and made excellent grades in flying, but he was very poor in running. Since he was low in running he had to stay after school and also drop swimming to practice running...

The rabbit started at the top of the class in running, but had a nervous breakdown because of so much makeup in swimming.

The squirrel was excellent in climbing until he developed frustrations in the flying class where his teacher made him start from the ground up instead of from the treetop down...

The eagle was a problem child and had to be disciplined severely. In climbing class he beat all the others to the top of the tree, but insisted on using his own way of getting there.

At the end of the year, an abnormal eel that could swim exceedingly well and also could run, climb, and fly a little had the highest average and was valedictorian.

Appreciate the fact that you may be an eagle, your friend may be a duck, your sister may be a rabbit, and your mom may be a squirrel. You all have different strengths and weaknesses and that's the beauty of it. Can you see how silly it is to compare an eagle with a squirrel and say, "Which one is better?" Likewise, can you see how nonsensical it is to compare yourself with someone at school and think, "I'm better than her," or "I'm not as good as he is"? No one is better or worse than anyone else, just different. You're okay; they're okay.

Valuing differences is one of the great secrets to a happy life. It's also a vital ingredient for learning to get along with your parents, as you'll soon discover.

HABIT 7 SHARPEN THE SAW

For Habit 7, picture a saw.

A lumberjack should never get too busy sawing to take time to sharpen his saw. Likewise, we should never get too busy living to take time to renew ourselves. We are made up of a heart, body, mind, and soul. Each needs time and attention.

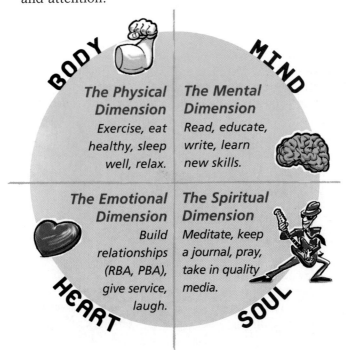

BODY

The Physical Dimension

Exercise, eat healthy, sleep well, relax.

MIND

The Mental Dimension

Read, educate, write, learn new skills.

The Emotional Dimension

Build relationships (RBA, PBA), give service, laugh.

HEART

The Spiritual Dimension

Meditate, keep a journal, pray, take in quality media.

SOUL

As English author Rumer Godden wrote, citing an Indian proverb:

"Everyone is a house with four rooms, a physical, a mental, an emotional, and a spiritual...unless we go into every room every day, even if only to keep it aired, we are not a complete person."

Chris, a teenage college student, put it this way:

In your teenage years, sometimes it is really hard to see the value and the benefit of sharpening the saw. But I know that sharpening the saw is important, so here's what I'm trying to do:

Social/emotional is kind of hard for me but one thing I have done to get to know people (because I'm not really outgoing) is to create a web page for my dorm floor. I've taken pictures of everybody and I learn a little bit about them. I think I've doubled the number of people I know on our floor as result of that.

Physically, I'm taking a health class—I run three times a week and I lift weights twice a week.

Mentally, college is great for sharpening the saw. We have some really great intellectual conversations. And we're always learning and changing. That's why you go to college.

And spiritually, that's something that needs to be developed a little bit. I know I need more balance.

Often, we feel guilty when we take time for ourselves because we're taught to think of others first. Don't allow yourself to feel this way. When it comes to sharpening your saw, it's okay to be a little selfish. I promise I won't tell.

WELL, PERHAPS YOU MIGHT CHOOSE ANOTHER TIME TO "SHARPEN THE SAW."

So there you have them in a nutshell: the 7 Habits of highly effective teens. They will be of great use to you as you make these six crucial decisions. I hope you never underestimate the power of habits in your life to make you or break you. Remember, "Bad habits are like a comfortable bed: easy to get into but hard to get out of." On the other hand, once they're in place, good habits are just as hard to break as bad ones.

A WORD ABOUT COVEY CLASSICS

I love movies. So does my family. As you continue reading the book, you'll notice that I can't get too far without bringing up a movie. My family's weird because we'll pick a few movies we like and then we'll watch them so many times that we can't talk to each other without quoting one-liners from them. People think we're psycho! We call these movies Covey Classics. Many of them really aren't that good. We just like them. Just for fun, I've listed all of them in the back of the book (page 324).

● ● ● COMING ATTRACTIONS ● ● ●

If you're curious to know what the 7 Secrets to getting good grades are, just keep reading. You'll find out soon enough.

BACK TO OUR CHART

On this page is the same chart you did before; however, this time I've divided up the box into nine equal squares. To find the numbers, just follow the pattern below. In other words, the first number is in box 1, the next number is in box 2, the next number is in box 3, the next number is in box 4, and so on up until box 9. Then go to box 1 again and repeat the same pattern.

1	2	3
4	5	6
7	8	9

Time yourself again for 1½ minutes and see how far you get this time. When you're finished, go back to page 16. Are you ready? On your mark, get set, go...

1 19 37 46 28 10	20 38 47 29 11 2	3 48 30 21 39 12
31 4 49 40 13 22	41 50 23 5 14 32	6 33 51 15 24 42
34 16 43 25 7 52	44 26 8 17 35 53	9 36 27 54 45 18

SCHOOL

Top 10
Things You Oughta Know About School

10. Don't watch TV while you're studying. Cammy Le, 17, Long Beach, California

9. Review your test papers after the tests. Jim Iantao, 18, Taipei, Taiwan

8. Work hard to get better knowledge even if your results are not the highest. Daniel Tilahun Mezegebu, 19, Addis Ababa, Ethiopia

7. Have an open mind about all points of view. Solongo, 16, Ulan Bator, Mongolia

6. Have smart friends. Janet, 17, Long Beach, California

5. If you have bad news from school, tell your parents the moment you enter the car. Otherwise, you are never going to tell them. Zeina, 15, Ramallah, Palestine

4. It's important to participate in school activities. Preyma Palansiamy, 17, Selangor, Malaysia

3. Do your work—get over it! There's no magic secret behind it. James Arnold, 17, Layton, Utah

2. Recognize that to start studying earlier is better. Azusa Uchiada, 17, Yokkaichi, Japan

1. Information is not equal to intelligence. Mario Godinez Parada, 19, Mexico City, Mexico

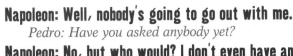

Napoleon: Well, nobody's going to go out with me.
Pedro: Have you asked anybody yet?

Napoleon: No, but who would? I don't even have any good skills.
Pedro: What do you mean?

Napoleon: You know, like nunchuck skills, bow hunting skills, computer hacking skills. Girls only want boyfriends who have great skills. — *Napoleon Dynamite*

There were three things I didn't like about high school—homework, homework, and homework. In that order. But there was one thing I *did* like—poetry. I had several friends that got into poetry, too. We'd write stupid poems and share them with each other to see who could come up with the dumbest of all.

My best candidate for the all-dumb list was written when I was about 16. It was New Year's Day. I'd been watching football games on TV with my brothers, David and Stephen. Lounging on the couch, we'd snarfed down a mountain of junk food—pizza, nachos, soda, and all other things unhealthy—and I had a whopping headache. Late in the day we dozed off. I later woke to a strange sensation. I looked and, to my horror, saw my calf stuck to Stephen's. We both were wearing shorts, you see, and our calves were kind of glued together by a thin film of sweat. Sick! I later captured the spirit of the moment in this poem:

I entered a few writing contests while in school and, based on my poem, I'll bet you're not surprised I never won a thing. But I did discover that I had a passion for language. And this discovery helped me decide what to study in college and what to do when I grew up.

This brings me to the first most important decision you'll ever make. What are you going to do about school, about your education? Why is this one of the 6 Most Important Decisions? It's simple. What you do about school during your teen years will probably determine how well you live the next fifty.

FAT AND WARM

Feeling as if I were dead,
Rolling thunder in my head.
Pizza, nachos, doughnuts too,
Bulging shirts, and smelly shoes.
Suddenly, sickly comes a storm,
Your leg touches mine...
It's fat and warm.

(By the way, on the previous page is a list of the top 10 things you oughta know about school. These are snippets of advice that I gathered from mostly older teens around the world. Each chapter has one. I thought you might enjoy them.)

Like all the other key decisions, it is a **fork in the road** decision.

You can take the high road—stay in school, do your best at it, and prepare for college and a career. Or you can take the low road—drop out of school, stay in but loaf, and fail to prepare. The choice is yours.

Since there are a bunch of important things to discuss in this chapter, I've split it into four sections.

The first section, **Sticking It Out,** is written to those of you who are thinking about dropping out of high school. Yes—I'm going to try to talk you out of it. In **Surviving and Thriving,** we'll talk about how to stay motivated, do well, and cope with all the stresses and everyday ups and downs that accompany school. **Off to College** will focus on how to prepare, get into, and pay for the college of your choice. Finally, in **Finding Your Voice,** we'll chat about what you want to be when you grow up.

SCHOOL CHECKUP!

Before going any further, take this 10-question checkup. It will help you figure out which path you're taking. So be very honest. Each of the chapters has a similar checkup.

CIRCLE YOUR CHOICE	NO WAY!				HECK YES!
1. I am planning on finishing high school.	1	2	3	4	5
2. I am planning on getting more education after high school.	1	2	3	4	5
3. I believe that a good education is essential to my future.	1	2	3	4	5
4. I am working hard at school.	1	2	3	4	5
5. I am getting good grades.	1	2	3	4	5
6. I am involved in extracurricular activities at school.	1	2	3	4	5
7. I am keeping up with my homework.	1	2	3	4	5
8. I am keeping my stress levels in check.	1	2	3	4	5
9. I am able to balance school with everything else I'm doing.	1	2	3	4	5
10. I spend time thinking about and exploring what I want to be when I grow up.	1	2	3	4	5

TOTAL

Each of the above questions is worth 5 points, for a total of 50 points. Add up your score and see how you're doing. Remember, this is not a test. It won't be graded. It's simply a self-evaluation, to help you assess the choices you're currently making. So, don't get all hung up about your score.

 You're on the high road. Keep it up!

 You're straddling the high and low roads. Move to higher ground!

 You're on the low road. Pay special attention to this chapter.

Sticking It Out————————————

Many years ago, the psychologist Walter Mischel conducted an experiment at a preschool on the Stanford University campus. He gathered a group of four-year-old kids around a table with an assortment of marshmallows in the middle. Mischel told them he had to leave the room for a few minutes. If they could wait until he got back, he would give them two marshmallows. If they couldn't wait, then they could have one marshmallow right then. One marshmallow right now, or two later. That was the deal. He then left the room.

- *A few of the kids couldn't resist and ate a marshmallow the second he left.*
- *Some lasted for a few minutes before they gave in.*
- *Others smelled their marshmallows.*
- *One kid even began licking his.*
- *A few kids were determined to resist the temptation and wait. So they covered their eyes, put their heads down, sang to themselves, played games, hid in the corner, or even tried to fall asleep.*

When Mischel returned, he gave those who held out their well-earned two marshmallows.

The researcher then followed the lives of each of these kids up through high school. Remarkably, those who had resisted eating the marshmallow had done far better in life than those who couldn't wait. They were better adjusted, more confident, more popular, and more dependable. They also did much better in school.

SEAN, DID YOU JUST STUFF THOSE MARSHMALLOWS IN YOUR MUSCLE CHEEKS?

I'M SAVING THEM FOR LATER.

So, what do marshmallows have to do with not dropping out of school? Lots, actually. Quitting school might be compared to eating the marshmallow now. That juicy marshmallow tastes really good. And dropping out of school may taste delicious at first too. For example, if you quit, you can immediately start making more money to buy things, like a car. You may be able to afford your own apartment. And you immediately get rid of the headache of homework and grades.

On the other hand, by dropping out now, you are sacrificing two marshmallows later. And that's a poor trade-off. The two marshmallows later show up down the road in the form of stronger skills, a better-paying job, a nicer car, more opportunities to help others, and a greater appreciation of everything around you.

Oh, sure, you've heard all the reasons for sticking it out and staying in school. But have you really thought about them carefully?

Do you realize that if you don't finish high school, the penalty will be low-paying work for the rest of your life?

Why? Because you won't have the skills you need to get a better-paying job.

A young teen named Yolanda said it well. "My mom has this little saying, 'Pay now and play later or play now and pay later.' What she means is if I pay now and do what I have to do in school, I will be a successful person; or I can play now and then pay for it later when I have a job maybe working at McDonald's flipping burgers."

Making $8 to $10 an hour may seem like good money right now, but it won't be enough. Trust me. Just compare it to how much more you can make if you finish high school, or even better, go on to college. Here's some salary information provided by the Bureau of Labor Statistics. Even though these figures will change from year to year, the differences always remain consistent.

How much money will you make?

$21,268 per year

$30,316 per year

$48,724 per year

Average high school dropout:	High school degree:	Four-year college degree:
$10.22 per hour	**$14.50** per hour	**$23.42** per hour

If you multiply these numbers over a lifetime of work (40 years), the difference is even more glaring.

LIFELONG EARNINGS

High School Dropout
$850,720

High School Graduate
$1,212,640

College Graduate
$1,948,960

In addition, if you drop out, kiss good-bye to ever having access to any of the great jobs below, all of which require at least a high school degree and usually some college or technical experience.

accountant	engineering technician	psychologist
administrative assistant	FBI agent	public policy analyst
architect	geologist	public relations director
automotive mechanic	graphic designer	real estate agent
commercial artist	hotel manager	registered nurse
computer analyst	insurance agent	scientist
computer technician	investment banker	social worker
dental hygienist	journalist	stockbroker
dentist	lawyer	surveyor
dietitian	management consultant	teacher
doctor	medical lab technician	university professor
economist	pharmacist	veterinarian
engineer	priest, rabbi, or minister	zoologist

BABES AND BABIES

If you drop out of high school, at first it may seem like you can make it. But as your needs increase, or if you decide to get married and have a family, you've got your work cut out for you. Teen writer Greg Byron put it this way.

"When you first leave home, you'll probably live cheap—and with roommates. But you'll get sick of roommates soon enough, and want the privacy of a better place to live, a newer car, vacations, and high tech toys. Then...you're in love...and then babies...A nice house and baby shoes, too.

Here's a table to show you how much you need if you live alone (single), or get married and have a kid or two (family):

MONTHLY BUDGET

EXPENSES	SINGLE	FAMILY
Housing (apartment or house)	$400.00	$900.00
Utilities (electricity, water, etc.)	$100.00	$300.00
Car, gas, maintenance	$350.00	$500.00
Food and household	$200.00	$900.00
Clothes and gifts	$150.00	$500.00
Insurance (life, car, health)	$350.00	$500.00
Entertainment	$100.00	$300.00
Savings and retirement	$100.00	$300.00
TOTAL MONTHLY BUDGET	**$1,750.00**	**$4,200.00**

"You don't make this kind of money working cash registers, or waiting tables—the kind of jobs high school kids can land. You need way better. To meet the household budget you see here, you need to make $15 an hour if you're single. If the babe and babies come, it takes a lot more cash. You'll want a decent place for them. You'll want to be a good provider. You promised. You just didn't know diapers cost more per day than baby food. Both parents must earn $18/hr each to support a family at this level. If one earns less, the other has to earn more to make up for it.

"If you both don't have jobs that pay well, you will live POOR. Being short of money gets really old. Really fast! Then ya bounce a couple checks and the bank service charge is $20 each. You argue over money and that was NEVER supposed to happen! You'll look at others who are doing better because they made better choices than you did about their own careers. You won't talk about that...but you'll FEEL it when you and your spouse see your friends have nicer houses, better cars. Who knew money would be that big a deal?"

Do some high school dropouts do well? A few do. But it's like playing the lottery. The odds are stacked against you. Why take the chance?

Here are the brutal facts:

- *Dropouts have a much harder time finding and keeping jobs: 50 percent of dropouts are unemployed.*
- *Dropouts are often labeled as people who don't complete things.*
- *Dropouts often just jump from job to job instead of building a career.*
- *Dropouts aren't even considered for most high-paying jobs, even if they're qualified.*
- *And, increasingly, in most countries, a high school degree is not enough. Says Vlad, a teen from Russia: "Today in Russia, you're almost nothing if you don't have a university degree. You won't find a job without it."*

I can just imagine the marketing poster now:

BREAKING THE CYCLE

Often the main reason teens drop out of school is that everyone else did. Their mom or dad dropped out. Their cousins did. Many of their friends did. Perhaps no one in their family had ever finished high school or gone on to college. So, why should they?

Sometimes we inherit bad habits or patterns that are passed down from generation to generation. For example, if your father is an alcoholic, the chances are good that *his* father was an alcoholic. The same pattern applies to child abuse, drug addiction, poverty, and dropping out of school. That's often why dysfunctional families keep repeating themselves in the next generation.

The good news is you have a choice. You have proactive muscles and you can flex them suckers. You can be the cycle breaker in your family. You can stop that bad habit from getting inside you and pass on good habits to your kids and to your nephews and nieces. *Wouldn't it be a great thing to be the first one in your family to go to college and to pass on that pattern to your children and grandchildren?*

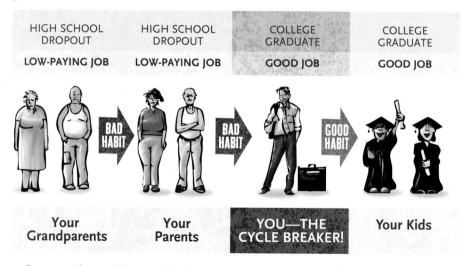

HIGH SCHOOL DROPOUT	HIGH SCHOOL DROPOUT	COLLEGE GRADUATE	COLLEGE GRADUATE
LOW-PAYING JOB	**LOW-PAYING JOB**	**GOOD JOB**	**GOOD JOB**
Your Grandparents	**Your Parents**	**YOU—THE CYCLE BREAKER!**	**Your Kids**

I remember talking with Sammi, who wanted to break the cycle she inherited. Sammi said:

I've been with friends that have dropped out of high school. One of them who I work with at McDonald's was held back three years. He was 20 years old and a junior. I looked at him and I just realized, I can't be like that. I can't be working at Wendy's or McDonald's for the rest of my life. I don't want to be like my father and my stepdad. I don't want to be looking back saying, 'Oh, I wish I would have done this. I wish I would have done that.'

Making the decision to stay in school may be the hardest thing you've ever done. You may have a difficult family life and virtually no support at home for succeeding in school. You may be full of self-doubt and fear about your ability to follow through with something. You may hate the very thought of going to school, even one more day. But, I promise you, you'll thank yourself forever if you stick it out. It won't be easy, but it will be worth it. Two marshmallows tomorrow always beat one today.

Surviving and Thriving

I'm going to list a word—you fill in the blank with the first word that comes to mind. Don't think too much; just write down or make a mental note of whatever pops in your head.

Teachers: _____

Grammar: _____

Homework: _____

Report Card: _____

Tests: _____

Lunch Lady: _____

I tried this with a group of teens and got answers like:

Teachers: **WARDENS**   Grammar: **HARD**

Homework: **DEATH**   Report Card: **JUDGMENT DAY**

Tests: **CRAM**   Lunch Lady: **JIGGLY ARMS**

What about you? When you think about school and academics, do you get positive vibes or get sick? It's different for everyone. But there's one thing all teens have in common: Everyone struggles in one way or another. While I was in school I hated the stress, standardized tests, and climbing ropes in gym.

There are lots of challenging things about school. The four challenges I hear about most are:

1 *"I'm stressed out."*

2 *"There's too much to do and not enough time."*

3 *"I just don't care."*

4 *"I'm just no good at school."*

The good news is there are remedies that really work. So, let's take a look at each.

Challenge 1: "I'M STRESSED OUT"

"What is it about school that most stresses you out?" I asked some teens. Here's what a few said:

❝ THE PRESSURE SOCIETY IN GENERAL PUTS ON US TO DO WELL, AND THE CONSEQUENCES OF NOT DOING WELL. ❞

"GRADES."

"Parent expectations."

"All the teachers give big stuff at one time. On Monday, I have four tests. They need to coordinate."

"Calculus is killing me."

"Competition."

"Lame teachers with monotone voices."

"It seems that everything from soccer practices to basketball games to homework overlaps and piles up. There is no escaping the endless work. One little break can get you thrown off for days. You don't do math homework one night and the next night you have twice as much."

The funny thing is, when you're done with school, the stress doesn't suddenly disappear. It only switches. Instead of feeling stressed out about school, you feel stressed out about bills, kids, work, and in-laws. Don't try to run away from stress. Learn how to deal with it. How? You sharpen the saw, regularly.

STRESSED?! WHAT MAKES YOU THINK I'M STRESSED, MOM?!

WELL, FOR ONE THING, SWEETIE, YOU JUST POURED YOURSELF A BOWL OF KITTY LITTER.

KITTY LITTER

Sharpen the Saw

"In case of an emergency, oxygen masks will fall from the ceiling. First, place the mask over your mouth. Then, place it over the mouth of the person or child next to you." So says the flight attendant on an airplane. I've often imagined the scene. There I am with my oxygen mask, breathing away to my heart's content, while the two-year-old next to me gasps for air. It seems so selfish.

The more you think about what the flight attendant is saying, the truer it gets. You can't do much to help someone else unless you're breathing yourself. That's why you should never feel selfish for taking time to renew the best thing you've got going for yourself—you. If you go too hard for too long and always put yourself last, you'll eventually burn out or become a stress-case and then what good are you? Never be too busy sawing to take time to sharpen your saw. Replenish the four parts that make you up: body (physical), heart (relationships), mind (mental), and soul (spiritual).

Take this little quiz to assess how well you're sharpening the saw.

Sharpen the Saw Checkup

CIRCLE YOUR CHOICE	NO WAY!				HECK YES!
BODY I eat pretty well, get enough sleep, don't stress too much, and get a lot of exercise. I keep myself in good shape.	1	2	3	4	5
HEART I make an effort to make friends and to be a good friend. I take time for important relationships. I get involved in things.	1	2	3	4	5
MIND I try hard in school. I feel like I'm learning new stuff all the time. I read a lot. I have hobbies.	1	2	3	4	5
SOUL I spend time serving others. I take time to think deeply about things. I renew myself spiritually in some way regularly (examples: writing in a journal, going for nature walks, praying, reading inspiring literature, playing a musical instrument).	1	2	3	4	5

So, is each part getting the attention it needs? If you gave yourself a 2 on Heart, maybe you need to spend more time with friends and family. If you gave yourself a 3 on Body, slow down a little and start taking care of yourself. Like the tires on a car, if one part of you is out of balance, the other three parts will wear unevenly. For example, it's hard to do well in school (mind) when you're exhausted (body). It also works the other way. If you're in tune with yourself and motivated (soul), it's so much easier to be a good friend (heart) and give your best at school (mind).

There are so many ways to reduce stress by sharpening the saw. Here's what some teens told me when I asked how they dealt with stress.

- *"I go running. It gives me a better perspective on my problems and helps me find solutions."*
- *"I allow myself one hour to feel sorry for myself and I cry."*
- *"I take a bath, read my journal, and sleep."*
- *"I play ball."*
- *"I lift weights to release the endorphins."*
- *"Helping others helps you forget about your own problems."*
- *"I just get out of the house."*

Walking Zombies

Let's go right to one of the biggest problem areas in the physical area—sleep. Research shows that sleep deprivation contributes to depression, lower grades, accidents, and emotional problems. Admit it, when you're tired, you blow things out of proportion. That little rude comment someone made about your haircut suddenly seems like an unforgivable offense. Or that upcoming history exam seems so huge it's more than you can bear. That's what happens when you're a walking zombie. You get overwhelmed and you start thinking wrong. Here are four sleep tips to consider:

1. GET WHAT YOU NEED. Most teens only get about seven or so hours of sleep a night. Some less. All the experts say that you need between 8.5 and 9.25 hours a day. Figure out how much sleep you need to be at your best and then, knowing when you need to get up, calculate when you need to go to bed. Remember, sleep is brain food.

2. GO TO BED EARLY. GET UP EARLY. I can't prove it, but I believe there's wisdom in the old saying, "Early to bed and early to rise keeps a man healthy, wealthy, and wise." Some health experts believe that every hour of sleep before midnight is worth two after. I know this works for me. There's something magical about going to bed early and getting up early.

3. BE SOMEWHAT CONSISTENT. For example, if you typically get to bed around 11:00 P.M. most weekdays, don't go to bed at 3:00 A.M. every Friday and Saturday night, then sleep in until noon. Weekend binge-sleeping can really mess you up when you try to get back into the groove of your normal schedule. You didn't hear me say that you shouldn't have some fun and stay up late on weekends. Just don't be so extreme. Keep your bedtimes within a range of a couple of hours.

4. RELAX BEFORE BED. Instead of gulping gargantuan amounts of caffeine before hitting the sack, try relaxing. Take a bath, write in your journal, read the comics. A few minutes of chill time before bed can make all the difference.

These tips are not rules, just guidelines. There'll be times you'll want to stay up late with your friends and times when you'll have to stay up to finish your homework. Or, maybe you have to work while going to school to help your family and you can't get as much sleep as you'd like. My point is: Do the best you can, use moderation, and be wise. If you're feeling depressed, confused, or stressed out, a steady stream of good night's rests may just be the cure you need.

Challenge 2: "THERE'S TOO MUCH TO DO AND NOT ENOUGH TIME!"

"I'm really busy," said one teenage guy. "I pretty much do everything. I'm in band and I'm on the badminton team and then there's driver's ed and I have two jobs and I teach a private lesson every week. I'm in five clubs here at school and I'm in a bunch of honors classes."

So much to do. So little time. How can I possibly do it all? You can do it all, or at least most of it, if you'll be more careful with your time. As Benjamin Franklin put it,

Wouldn't it be great if every day were a 25-hour day? Think about what you could do with an extra 7 hours per week. Well, you know what? I'll bet you you're wasting at least 7 to 20 hours each week and don't even realize it. To prove my point, track how much time you're wasting in four specific areas. Fill in the chart as we discuss each area.

TIME FINDER

ACTIVITY	HOURS SPENT HERE LAST WEEK	HOURS I COULD SAVE EACH WEEK
Watch Less TV		
Reduce Your Personal Time Waster (PTW) (My PTW:_____)		
Say *No* with a Smile (Less Important Activity:_____)		
Stop Procrastinating		
TOTAL HOURS		

Watch Less TV

TV by far is the biggest time waster. And it's what Slackers love to do for hours on end. A little TV is fine. Too much TV is a total waste, a Quadrant 4 activity that's neither urgent nor important (see the Time Quadrants on page 24). Did you know that the average U.S. teen watches 21 hours of TV per week? And then they complain that they don't have time for anything. Hmmmm...

> **TIME FINDER:** *Think back over the last 7 days. Add up how much time you spent watching TV or movies during that time, including weekends. Be honest, now. Record it in the Time Finder under "Hours Spent Here Last Week." Now, how much time do you think you could cut back without falling apart? Record it under "Hours I Could Save Each Week."*

Reduce Your Personal Time Waster (PTW)

We all do some Quadrant 4 Slacker activities to waste time regularly. I call them Personal Time Wasters, or PTWs. They're different for everyone. It may be spending too much time on the phone, text messaging, playing PlayStation or Xbox, shopping, putting on makeup, rearranging your room, or reading magazines. Hey, you need time to relax and kick back for sure. I'm not saying to get rid of your PTW, just cut back some. I know one 16-year-old, Michael-Sean, who spends two to three hours daily buying and selling shoes on eBay. I'm sure he could cut that time in half without freaking out.

> **TIME FINDER:** *Write down your PTW in the Time Finder. Now, think back over the last 7 days and record how much time you spent on it. Then record how much time you think you could cut back on your PTW without severe withdrawal pains.*

Say *No* with a Smile

Quadrant 3 is the devil, the home of The Yes-Man (see the Time Quadrants on page 24). In an effort to want to please everyone and not miss out on anything, you say *yes* to everything and overbook yourself. I'm all for getting involved in sports and clubs and other extracurricular stuff, but don't overdo

JOHNSON, MAYBE YOU'RE IN TOO MANY ACTIVITIES.

it. The first place to look is at your job. About two-thirds of U.S. high school students hold part-time jobs during the school year. Ask yourself: Do I really need to work while attending school? Of course, some kids have to work to help support their families. Fine. But many don't need to. The few extra bucks you earn for clothes or whatever is not worth it if it hurts your performance in school.

I like what author and teacher Tom Loveless says: "Some people argue that work teaches responsibility and how to function in the real world. A better way to learn responsibility is by taking the most difficult classes available and completing assignments promptly and efficiently. And, really, who is better prepared for the real world: someone skilled in math and science or in flipping hamburgers and making change at a cash register?"

Ask yourself, "Am I trying to do too much?" If you're involved in too many activities and your life feels out of control, drop the less important activities and focus on the few essential ones. Start saying no, and do it with a smile, as Elizabeth, from Hilliard Darby High School, learned to do.

Once I was asked to edit a senior class video. I knew nothing about editing videos. I eventually had to tell the person in charge that I wasn't gonna be able to do it. And it was really difficult for me, 'cause I didn't want to seem irresponsible. It's really come to the point where I have to learn to say no.

Simplify. Do a few things with excellence instead of many things with mediocrity.

> **TIME FINDER:** *Pick a lower-priority activity that you're regularly doing and record it in the Time Finder. Record how much time you spent on that activity over the last 7 days, including weekends. Now, record how much time you think you could save if you cut out or cut back on that activity.*

Stop Procrastinating

My brother and I shared a beat-up Honda Accord in high school. One day, I could tell that something was wrong with the brakes and that I should take the car in to get repaired. But I kept putting it off until the brakes started making scary sounds. Finally, I took it in, but by then the brakes were totally destroyed. It took several days and cost big bucks to repair them, about five times more than if I'd taken the car in earlier. All because I put off until tomorrow what I should have done today. Procrastination always costs more and takes more time in the end, whether it's putting off writing your term paper, delaying that apology you need to make, or waiting to apply for that summer job. Today I try to follow the slogan: "Whenever you have a job to do ask yourself two questions. If not now, when? If not by me, by whom?"

Do you have a habit of cramming? You know, do nothing for weeks, then cram all night before the test? Does it work? Maybe in the short term. Have you ever worked on a farm? Can you cram on a farm? You know, forget to plant in the spring, goof off all summer long, then show up in the fall to bring in the crop? I think not. Life, in the long run, is more like a farm than a school. You'll reap what you sow.

I confess. I was a professional procrastinator in high school. I'd put off studying, cram the night before the test, and do well. But I didn't retain much. I call it *academic bulimia.* Memorize and forget. Binge and purge. When I got into college and graduate school, I had to make up for years of cramming. In many ways, I never made up the lost ground and I deeply regret it.

There is a remedy for procrastination. It's called "Just do it." (Thanks, Nike!) Stay on top of your studies and don't let yourself fall behind. Get into Quadrant 2 (The Prioritizer) and develop the habit of planning.

I recommend using a planner of some type. Many schools give them to their students. If not, buy one. They don't cost much, and you can get one at almost any office-supply or discount store. Get one that has monthly calendars and space for weekly or daily note-taking. Or you may want to try an electronic version.

Bridgett, a 17-year-old junior from Joliet, Illinois, called her planner her "best friend."

My biggest challenge is just having enough time to do everything. So I use a planner. It is my best friend. It just helps me organize my thoughts. I'm a very forgetful person. But with a planner, you can write everything you need in it. And before you go home from school you just take one look at it and everything you need to do for the rest of the day is in there.

I didn't use a planner my freshman year. But at the beginning of my sophomore year I had a biology class from a teacher who was voted the hardest teacher for five years running. And I had to use a planner, because he assigns so much work. I mean a planner looks like it's stupid, like it's not gonna help you, but if you use it right, it really does.

Once you get your planner, write down everything: upcoming tests, due dates for papers, school breaks, holidays, games, birthdays, key family events, and so on. Writing things down will put your mind at peace because you won't have to remember everything. Then, at the start of each week, review what's coming up. Don't wait until the last moment to prepare for a test or write a paper. Chip away early on.

> **TIME FINDER:** *Over the past week, record how much time you think you spent making up for things that you procrastinated on earlier (examples: repairing a broken relationship you neglected, doing makeup work or extra-credit work because you got so far behind, fixing a piece of machinery that you didn't take care of, overcoming an illness that arose because you ran yourself into the ground). Now, record how much time you think you could save each week if you were to stop procrastinating.*

Now, add up the total in the "Hours I Could Save Each Week" column and see what you come up with. Did you reach 7 hours? 15 hours? More? Isn't that amazing? And you thought there wasn't enough time. Each of us has 168 hours each week to spend how we wish. Wrote Michael Altshuler, "The bad news is time flies. The good news is you're the pilot."

Challenge 3: "I JUST DON'T CARE"

Has anyone ever told you, "You're so lazy in school. If you only applied yourself, you could do so well"? If so, you're not alone. It's easy to fall behind, do poorly, or just not care.

If you aren't motivated and feel that school is being forced down your throat, think carefully about what you can and can't control about school. Obviously, there are lots of things you have no control over whatsoever. Surprisingly, however, there are lots of things you *can* control.

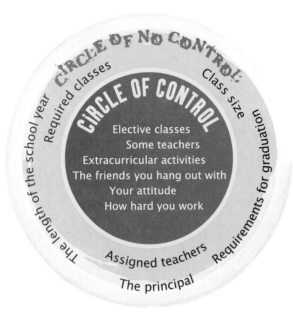

You don't have to love school, but please don't be a victim. Don't allow yourself the luxury of saying, "I just don't like school so I'm not going to try." Waaa! Instead, focus on what you can influence.

Your education is your responsibility, not your school's or your parents'. When you graduate from teenagehood, you'll want to know how to read, think, and talk well. You'll want to know a thing or two about history, countries, and cultures. You'll want to have read many of the classic books and know about many of the great men and women who came before you. That is what your education is all about. And it can be exciting! So stop letting your education happen to you. You happen to it. Here are some ways to turbo-charge your education.

- *Develop a hobby that you really love, such as photography, art, dance, or whatever gets your blood pumping.*
- *Sign up for an elective class you've always wanted to take.*
- *Get involved in fun and challenging extracurricular activities at school like a club or a sport.*
- *Apply for a summer job or internship in a field that excites you.*
- *Take a class from the teacher that everyone says is the best.*
- *Start your own business.*
- *Join an education track that suits you. Many schools offer education tracks that emphasize different things.*
- *Travel, at home or abroad.*

Just Outside Your Front Door

St. Augustine wrote: "The world is a book and those who stay at home read only a page." I couldn't agree more. Whether it be traveling to another continent or visiting a nearby monument, I can't think of anything as fun and educational as traveling. Here are just a few benefits, derived from Carol Carter's book *Majoring in the Rest of Your Life.*

1 *Traveling can jump-start a career that you'll love. You may have an interest or a passion for something and not know it until you broaden your experience.*

2 *Traveling can provide you a very specific, tangible skill: speaking a foreign language. In some fields, the more exotic the language, the more marketable the skill. Adding "I spent a summer in Romania" to your resume gives you an edge.*

3 *Traveling can boost your confidence and expand your comfort zone. After navigating a strange and foreign city, culture, and language, navigating the social scene back home will seem like a piece of cake.*

4 *Traveling can give you an appreciation for different cultures and people and bless you with a profound sense of gratitude for your own country and heritage.*

5 *Traveling is fun. Having fun while learning, imagine that! You'll get to see incredible sights you've only read about, like the Louvre in Paris, the Great Wall of China, or Times Square in New York City.*

By now you're probably saying to yourself, "Yeah, right. So how do I get started? Where will I get the money? And how in the world can I convince my parents to let me travel?" If you'd really like to travel, within or outside your own country, there are limitless resources, programs, and people willing to help. You don't have to spend a fortune. For starters:

- **Take advantage of your school's travel programs.** *Virtually every school has some. Just talk to a counselor, administrator, or someone else in the know. Often, you can get credit for foreign travel. While I was in high school, I went on a school-sponsored trip to Mexico, where I got to live with a Mexican family. One day I went jogging with my shirt off and I couldn't understand why all the Mexican kids were laughing at me. Finally, I realized they had never* *seen anyone with such white skin. Ouch! Anyway, I had an incredible experience and learned how to say "crazy" in Spanish.*

- **Join a volunteer organization.** *There are numerous organizations that are in desperate need of volunteers. You can travel to an impoverished area of the world and make a difference in someone's life while enriching your own. Dan, a 17-year-old neighbor of mine, has been involved with Operation Smile. Operation Smile is a group of doctors and volunteers who travel to various poor countries every year for several days to do thousands of quick surgeries on kids who have facial deformities, like cleft palates. These simple surgeries give these kids their lives back. "It's been the most meaningful part of my high school experience," Dan told me.*

- **Be a foreign exchange student.** *Sign up to live with a foreign family and fully immerse yourself in their culture.*

- **Travel with your parents on business trips.** *During the day, while your mom or dad works, you can take a city tour, visit the museums or zoos, or have lunch at local restaurants. At night, see the sights with them.*

To find out more about travel opportunities, simply do an online search, talk to a school counselor, visit the library, or talk to someone who's done it. Bridgett, a 17-year-old junior, got a real kick from her travels.

One day, I was talking to my mom. "Oh, I want to travel. It would be so much fun." She's like, "Well, maybe you can do that someday, like one of those foreign exchange things."

So, I researched online, found a bunch, and then went to talk with a counselor about 'em, to make sure they were legitimate. We found one called Youth For Understanding. So I looked into it and decided I wanted to go to Japan. But it was $5,000. So I applied for one of the Okinawa Peace Scholarships, and about three months later I found that I'd gotten one. It paid for almost the whole thing.

And I was off to Okinawa, the Hawaii of Japan. I was there six weeks and I didn't want to come home. My parents said no more six-week trips, but this year I'm going on a teacher-sponsored trip to Ireland!

It is a small world, after all, you know. (Hey, that sounds familiar.) So get out of the puny confines of your own head and start exploring this vast world waiting just outside your front door.

Challenge 4: "I'M JUST NO GOOD AT SCHOOL"

Maybe you're doing poorly in school. Or maybe you think that you just don't have what it takes. Keep your chin up, mate. Some of the greatest minds ever felt that way too. Did you know?

Albert Einstein, considered the most influential person of the 20th century, was four years old before he could speak and seven before he could read. His parents thought he was retarded. He spoke haltingly until age nine. He was advised by a teacher to drop out of grade school: "You'll never amount to anything, Einstein."

Isaac Newton, the scientist who invented modern-day physics, did poorly in math.

Patricia Polacco, a prolific children's author and illustrator, didn't learn to read until she was 14.

Henry Ford, who developed the famous Model-T car and started Ford Motor Company, barely made it through high school.

Lucille Ball, famous comedian and star of *I Love Lucy*, was once dismissed from drama school for being too quiet and shy.

Pablo Picasso, one of the great artists of all time, was pulled out of school at age 10 because he was doing so poorly. A tutor hired by Pablo's father gave up on Pablo.

Ludwig van Beethoven was one of the world's great composers. His music teacher once said of him, "As a composer, he is hopeless."

Wernher von Braun, the world-renowned mathematician, flunked ninth-grade algebra.

Agatha Christie, the world's best-known mystery writer and all-time bestselling author other than William Shakespeare of any genre, struggled to learn to read because of dyslexia.

Winston Churchill, famous English prime minister, failed the sixth grade.

In spite of their problems at school, these people made something of their lives and so can you. If school doesn't come easily for you it doesn't mean you're not smart. There are many types of intelligence. Yet school is based mostly on one kind of intelligence, known as IQ (intelligence quotient) or *mental intelligence.* IQ is our ability to analyze, reason, think abstractly, and use language.

IQ *EQ* SQ PQ

But there are other types of intelligence that are every bit as important. For example there's EQ, or *emotional intelligence.* People with high EQs have lots of intuition, can read social situations, and have an ability to get along with other people. School doesn't test for that. Then there's SQ, or *spiritual intelligence,* which represents our longing and capacity for vision, value, and meaning. It allows us to dream. School doesn't measure that either. Finally, there's PQ, or *physical intelligence.* Your body is naturally smart. You don't have to remind your heart to beat or your lungs to expand. Physical intelligence is also the ability to learn through bodily kinesthetic means, like physical sensations and touching.

> **HE HAS A VERY HIGH SQ!**

Your friend may be stronger in IQ and you may be stronger in EQ. One isn't better than the other. Just different. Be grateful for your unique gifts and talents, and don't let anyone ever lead you to believe you're not gifted in some way. And if you ever are teased, remember what Albert Einstein, who also got teased, said: "Great spirits will always encounter violent opposition from mediocre minds."

What If I Have a Learning Problem?

Perhaps you've been told that you have a learning disability, such as ADHD, ADD, dyslexia, or an inability to focus or concentrate. Here are a couple things you might try. First, visit a professional and find out if you really do have a problem, and, if so, what they recommend you do about it. Some kids take medication and find it useful. Others use alternative approaches such as diet, therapy, stress control, exercise, herbs, or a combination of many things. Still others may not have a problem at all, but only think they do.

Second, don't start thinking you're handicapped! You're totally capable of succeeding in school and life, no matter what you may have been diagnosed with. You'd be shocked to know that there are thousands of successful entrepreneurs, lawyers, doctors, teachers, musicians, actors and actresses, or whatever, who have been diagnosed with dyslexia, ADD, or some other kind of learning problem.

If learning is hard for you, think of it as a weakness you have to work with—just like an uncoordinated person has to learn to work with their weakness to become a good soccer player. True, you may have to work a little harder than others, but you can succeed and turn a weakness into a strength!

Greg Fox shared his experience.

A teacher whom I had never seen before touched my shoulder, and told me to follow her down the hall to a small room. She asked me questions about my life and took notes on everything I said. The next day we met in the same room and I began taking tests that would become a weekly routine throughout that year, and all the way through high school. A few other kids joined me in that small room also. We didn't know it at the time, but the school system had labeled us as L.D., or learning disabled.

As a learning disabled student, teachers treated me accordingly—disabled. They gave me answers to math problems, helped me finish my homework assignments, and allowed me to take untimed tests. They didn't expect much and so that was what they got back. By high school, I got used to the special treatment, and for the first time I found myself using my disability as a crutch that would let me ease my way out of assignments. I sold myself short.

During my senior year, I was placed in a class with several other learning disabled teenagers. The class was taught by a new teacher, Mr. Weisberg. A middle-aged man, Mr. Weisberg had given up his profession as a lawyer in order to help teenagers like me realize their true potential. He accomplished exactly what he set out to do. He didn't accept any of my excuses. For the first time in my life, I had to take ac-countability for my education, learning not to make excuses.

Like a recovering drug addict, I craved the crutch that had supported me for so many years. It was hard, but gradually Mr. Weisberg made me believe in myself as a human being with limitless potential. At first I hated him for not letting me be lazy, but together we broke down the label's invisible barriers.

I graduated from high school, and I am now receiving straight As as I prepare to earn a bachelor's degree in English. However, beyond the degree and the G.P.A., I have learned to believe in myself, and to take accountability for my future. I only regret those years that I confined myself to what others thought of me.

The truth is, we pretty much live up to what others think of us and what "we" think of ourselves. If you have a hard time learning, stick with it and don't sell yourself short. Fight the labels others may try to give you. And for heaven's sake, don't ever label yourself. Labels are short-sighted and don't take into account all the talent each of us was born with, as spoken about in this poem by the Persian poet Hafiz of Shiraz.

"There are so many gifts

still unopened from your birthday,
there are so many hand-crafted presents

that have been sent to you by God."

I remember meeting a bubbly girl named Amelia. She had just earned her degree from Weber State University in automotive technology, the only girl in her school to graduate in that major. She had done so well that several big companies offered her jobs, including Harley-Davidson.

Amelia had had every disadvantage growing up in Provo, Utah. She was one of five kids raised by her single mother, who worked multiple jobs to support the kids.

"My mom made it clear that she couldn't afford to pay for college and drummed into my head that a scholarship to college was my ticket to a better life."

During elementary school, however, Amelia didn't do well. It was especially hard for Amelia to read. Not until high school did she figure out what was wrong.

"One time I was reading aloud and I kept reading words wrong. That's when my mom was like, 'Why are you reading the words wrong?' And I said, 'I don't mean to. I have to read it two or three times to get it right.' It was then that my mom figured it out. After years of wondering why I hated to read and struggling in school, I was finally diagnosed with severe dyslexia. I didn't know why learning was so hard, and even my teachers and mom had no idea I had it."

Dyslexia, by the way, is where the letters you are reading get mixed up. For years, people with dyslexia were thought to be stupid, until Margaret Rawson discovered dyslexia and cleared the path for millions of kids who never knew what was going on in their heads. Below is how a sentence might appear to someone with dyslexia.

```
           h           w          w       "W              l k
 Onegay, Jo n anp Bop   n  froa  a k.    hatwo       ou i e
                      e t         l              ulpy
 t   o    a                      n'tk            r
  op  op y?, Boq  ske  John. "I do     ow, J     ed  ed,
   t          a    p                n     onh    li
           k                I            o        c
  hatwo lpyo  li e ot go?" It  in    mi ten  yw at   g a
 w      u    u                h  k   gh    j      hin
```

Trying to read this passage, you will experience the kind of difficulty
a dyslexic reader faces when deciphering normal typeface (Almeida).

from p.98, in: Capossele, T.L. (1998). *The Harcourt Brace Guide
to Peer Tutoring.* Orlando, FL: Harcourt Brace & Company.

Luckily, during high school and college, Amelia had some true friends who helped her deal with her dyslexia.

I was lucky to have a Second Mile college roommate, Abby. I had a very hard time reading even my own writing. Sometimes, I'd dictate my paper to Abby, who typed it up for me. She worked with me for hours. It would have been impossible to graduate without her. Often, when I'd get stressed out about my homework, my dyslexia would get really bad. In honors classes, I had to read five or six books per class, and Abby would read them all to me. She would finish her homework and then she would read me my homework until two in the morning.

Although Amelia's mom always wanted her to be a lawyer, she couldn't be more proud of her mechanical daughter. Through hard work and caring people, you too can thrive in the midst of serious educational challenges, just like Amelia.

7 SECRETS TO GETTING GOOD GRADES

I believe that everyone can get good grades if they want to, even if they have never done well before or if they struggle with learning. Of course, there's much more to school than getting good grades. In fact, you can get good grades and not learn a thing. But, in general, getting good grades is a sign that you've paid the price. What does *good grades* mean? It's different for everyone so you must decide for yourself. Here are 7 secrets on how to do it.

Secret 1: Believe you can

It all starts with your paradigm, what you think in your head. You've got to believe you can do it. A kid named Josh shared this.

All through high school I never got good grades. I was a good athlete but I just thought I could not get good grades. This really hurt my self-esteem. I took these same feelings into college. And guess what? I did not get good grades there either. I wanted to be a dentist but thought I could never get the grades I needed to get there.

One day when I was on the computer, an IQ test popped on my screen. I remember my parents telling me that I tested very high when I was in elementary school. Well, I did it, and the result astonished me. I scored a 140! I could not believe it. The computer gave me job descriptions of what it thought I would be good at. And, wouldn't you know, it listed dentistry. My way of thinking changed right then. My next semester of college I got all As and a B+. I wish I believed in myself in high school like I believe in myself now.

Don't ever start thinking you're dumb or "incapable of getting good grades." Everyone is capable, even those who have so-called learning disabilities, or have done poorly in the past, or may have no family support. It all starts with the belief in your head. (If you'd like to take an IQ test or something similar, visit the Help Desk in the back.)

Secret 2: Show up

"Eighty percent of success is showing up," said the great director Woody Allen. So many kids skip class and wonder why they get bad grades. If you show up to class, good things happen. You'll be there for that surprise quiz.

You'll be there when your teacher announces that extra-credit assignment. You'll be there when the teacher suggests how to prepare for the upcoming test.

Secret 3: Do extra-credit

Any time your teacher offers extra-credit, do it. Extra-credit assignments are usually pretty easy, but can get you a whole lot of points and help you prepare for tests. Surprisingly, most students don't take advantage of extra-credit. I remember taking a trigonometry class in high school and no matter how hard I studied, I could never do better than Bs or Cs on the test. But, by turning in all my assignments and doing every bit of extra-credit allowed, I got an A in the class. Ha!

Secret 4: Get on your teacher's good side

Say hello to your teachers. Be friendly. Show them respect. Change their perception of you by sitting in the front row. Don't get paranoid by thinking your teacher is out to get you. Ninety-nine percent of the time, they're not. If you didn't get your assignment done on time, don't be afraid to ask if you can hand it in late. Sometimes, they'll say yes.

Hey, teachers are just like you and me. If you're nice to them, they'll be nice to you and give you a break from time to time. My wife, Rebecca, was especially good at getting on her teachers' good sides while in high school.

As a junior at Madison High School, I took chemistry from a nerdy but brilliant teacher, Mr. Kramer. I was a total airhead in chemistry and didn't understand a thing. I'd get 30s and 40s on the tests. "Mr. Kramer," I'd plead. "Please help me. I'm flunking your class. But, I swear, I'm really trying." And then I'd start crying. I wasn't faking. I cried because I was flunking. So, I started going early in the mornings before class and he'd help me. I asked him if I could do any extra-credit and finished anything he offered. I'd stay after class. I ended up getting Bs in his classes. I think it was because he liked me and because I was trying so hard.

Now, you can call this kissing up, if you'd like. I'd call it smart.

Secret 5: Be strong in the red zone

The red zone is the final twenty yards of the football field before reaching the end zone. These are the hardest yards to come by. You can move the ball up and down the field all you want, but if you blow it in the red zone, you get no points.

So many kids work hard all semester long, then blow it during the final weeks because they get tired. In school, the red zone is those times when everything is on the line and you need to suck it up and get it done. It's that big test tomorrow that's worth more than all the assignments you've handed in so far combined. Or the final week of the term when you've got multiple tests to take and assignments to hand in. Or that big term paper that is due in three days and worth one-third of your grade. This is when you need to be strong. Often, the only difference between teens who get good grades and those who don't is that some are strong in the red zone and some aren't.

I'll never forget taking a final test in a college class. It was a three-hour test and worth half our grade. About halfway into it, a classmate stood up, handed in his test, and walked out. It was clear he was just tired and sick of it. I thought to myself, "You idiot. Why didn't you finish? You've been going to this class for four months. You've spent hundreds of hours doing homework. Yet, when half your grade was on the line, you couldn't endure 'til the end."

The moral of the story is, be strong when big points are at stake.

Secret 6: Gather your resources

While I was growing up, my dad would take our family waterskiing each summer. And whenever one of us kids would struggle getting up on skis, he'd yell out from the boat. "Keep trying, honey. You can do it. Alkaline your energies. Marshal your will. Gather your resources!" None of us ever knew what in the heck he was saying. But I've never forgotten those words. Although I've never figured out how to "alkaline my energies," I have figured out what he meant by "gather your resources."

When it comes to school, gather your resources means you get others involved in helping you get good grades, such as teachers, friends, cousins, grandparents, parents, counselors, mentors, and so on. Find someone who believes in you and cares about you and ask them for help in school. Most schools have excellent counselors who would love to help; many have awesome mentoring programs. Notice how Jennifer turned her grades around by getting someone who cared involved in her life.

When I was younger I always wanted to make straight As on a report card just to see what my parents would say or to see if they even cared. But I figured that there was no way for me to make straight As if my parents couldn't even make it through high school without quitting. My grades have never been a problem until this year. My usual As and Bs turned into Ds and Fs.

So, I went to someone who is a mother figure to me. We sat down and talked about my situation and she started making a list of what I needed to do. She expressed to me that I could do it. Just by her saying that put all kinds of strength and confidence in me because it seemed that she really cared about my grades and me.

I did exactly what she said and it worked because my grades came up really fast. I don't think I could have done it without her because I didn't want to let her down, which made me try even harder. When I told her how my grades had improved she told me she was proud of me, which made me feel like I was on top of the world.

Secret 7: Develop smart study habits

You're busy. You have school, friends, work, extracurricular activities, and other stuff to juggle. So, smart study habits are a must. Imagine two sisters, Janita and Maria. Janita is a sophomore in high school and is getting all As and Bs. Maria is a senior, and, although very bright, is getting Cs, Ds, and Fs. Let's investigate the study habits of each.

A Night in the Life of Janita

Janita plays soccer and has practice after school, so she gets home at about six. She eats dinner, relaxes a bit, and starts her homework at around 7:30. She goes to her mom's bedroom to study. Mom has a computer and a big desk, so Janita can lay out all her stuff. She makes sure that she has everything she needs (paper, pencils, books, fruit snacks) so she doesn't have to get up every five minutes.

Janita doesn't like homework, but she's learned that it's better to focus and do it fast than let it drag out. It usually takes her about an hour and a half

to get it done. During that time, Janita doesn't talk on the phone, watch TV, listen to tunes, instant message, or clip her toenails.

Janita studies with a plan. First, she works on everything that is due tomorrow. Then, she chips away at long-term projects, like reading 25 pages for a book report due next week. She knows when everything is due because she writes it on her calendar.

Janita uses a technique that helps her work faster and remember more. She scans the material first, then reads the material thoroughly, and finally drills herself on what she just read.

A Night in the Life of Maria

Maria also gets home around six most days. After dinner, she spends the next few hours on the phone, watching TV, and doing stuff in her room. She doesn't like having a set time to do her homework, but usually starts around nine or ten.

Maria likes to study in the kitchen area, where all the action is. She doesn't seem to mind the TV blaring in the background, the ringing phone, or the constant comings and goings of her brother and his friends.

Around eleven or so, when the action has died down, Maria is finally able to focus. But, since she hates even the thought of using a calendar, she can't always remember what assignments are due. So, she usually calls a friend or just guesses. Most of her time is spent cramming for whatever is due tomorrow; she can't imagine actually studying for a test that's several days away.

She has no particular method for studying, but just randomly jumps around from thing to thing. By about midnight, she's usually too tired to continue studying, so she goes to bed thinking: "I can't believe they give us so much homework."

The point is clear. To do well in school, you've got to have solid study skills (by the way, cheating is not a study skill and if you do it you will pay later). Here are the five we just saw.

Smart Study Habits

- **FEED YOUR HEAD.** *Remember, your brain is connected to your body. To work well, it needs food. So, if you're about to jump into your studies, but you're starving, grab a bite to eat.*

- **RIGHT PLACE.** *Find a good place that is quiet, and where you can spread out all your stuff, like a library or little-used room. Stay away from places where you have the habit of goofing off. Make sure you have everything you need—paper, pencils, scissors, stapler, snacks— so you don't have get up constantly.*

- **RIGHT TIME.** *Set aside a time every day when you'll do your homework. Avoid interruptions as best you can. If you have a hard time focusing, try the small-chunks approach. Do small chunks of work several times a day. For example, do fifteen minutes of homework. Then take a break and reward yourself. Then do fifteen minutes of homework again. Take a break. Repeat the process throughout the day.*

- **NOW AND LATER.** *Organize what you have to do. First, focus on the now, and do whatever is due tomorrow. Second, focus on the later, and chip away at big projects, papers, and upcoming tests.*

- **SCAN, READ, DRILL.** *Let's say you have one hour to study for an upcoming history test on chapter 9. Instead of just reading your textbook and class notes for one hour, try this method instead. (It is based upon numerous, proven retention methods that have been around for a long time.)*

  Scan. *(10 minutes) Scan chapter 9 and write down or make mental notes of the main headings, key points, key people, key words, key dates, review questions, and so on.*

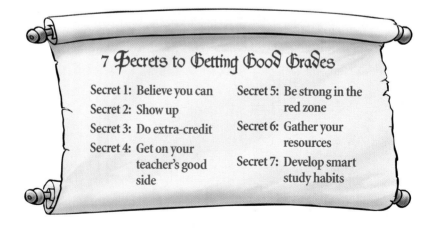

7 Secrets to Getting Good Grades

Secret 1: Believe you can

Secret 2: Show up

Secret 3: Do extra-credit

Secret 4: Get on your teacher's good side

Secret 5: Be strong in the red zone

Secret 6: Gather your resources

Secret 7: Develop smart study habits

Read. (30 minutes) Read chapter 9 and any notes you may have taken in class on chapter 9.

Drill. (20 minutes) Drill yourself by giving yourself a test. Answer chapter questions or make up and answer questions from your notes, vocabulary words, or possible questions from your teacher. Anticipate what your teacher is looking for and don't waste time on stuff you don't need to know. (For more information on study skills, please visit the Help Desk in the back.)

Off to College

As I was nearing high school graduation, I remember thinking, "The party's over. My friends are all scattering. I have to be responsible now and get a real job someday. I may even have to grow up. I'm so depressed."

That said, if I have to leave you with one piece of advice it would be: Get as much education as you can. Finish high school. Then, get a four-year college degree and more if you can. If that feels like too big a leap for you, at least get a two-year college degree. (In this chapter, I'm using the word "college" in a broad sense. I'm really talking about any education after high school, whether it be a technical degree, a military degree, a trade school, a community college, a distance learning program, or something else like it. They're all good.)

Does going to college really pay off? Absolutely! A college education offers three big benefits:

1. A college education will enrich your life!

I remember taking an English class in college on the short story. Our first assignment was to read two short stories and then discuss which one was better. After reading both, I wasn't sure. Over the next several months my professor taught me why one story was so much better than the other. One was rich in metaphor, symbolism, and character development. The other was entertaining but shallow. I couldn't see this at first. Yet, in a few months, my brain got reeducated and I could see the difference between good and bad writing and could appreciate literature at a whole new level.

So it goes with education. It gives us the ability to understand and appreciate all of life—music, art, science, people, nature, ourselves—at a whole new level.

Never forget: The primary purpose of going to college isn't to get a great job. The primary purpose of college is to build a strong mind, which leads to greater self-awareness, capability, fulfillment, and service opportunities, which, incidentally, should lead to a better job.

2. A college education will open doors!

Imagine reading about a great job on an Internet job site. It looks like something you'd love to do and you'd be good at. You're excited to apply and have an interview. But then you read, "This job requires a bachelor's degree." You're heartbroken. You may even be more qualified for the job than anyone else who applies, but it doesn't matter. They won't even consider you. More and more, jobs are being filled by people with college degrees. There are always some exceptions, but why take the chance?

3. With a college education, you'll make more money!

Now, there are many more important things than making money. And there is no shame in being poor. But, in general, more money means more opportunity, options, and chances to help others. And a few extra bucks never hurt anyone. Are you ready to be shocked? Just peek at the difference education makes in two different jobs. (This data is provided by the Employment Policy Foundation and again, although the numbers will change from year to year, the differences between them won't.)

Computer support specialists with no high school diploma earn just over $31,000 per year, which is among the better-paying jobs for someone with that level of education. However, workers with a high school diploma or a two-year degree earn salaries in the low-to-mid-$50,000 range. Computer support specialists with a four-year degree earn $74,000, while those with a master's degree earn $92,000. Some difference!

An electrician without a high school education has a median salary of about $32,000, which is a really high-paying job for a high school dropout. On the other hand, with more education, you could become an electrical and electronics engineer, and earn $57,000 with a two-year degree, $66,000 with a four-year degree, $76,000 with a master's degree, and $112,000 with a doctoral degree. Now, if that doesn't motivate you to stick with school, what will?

And if these numbers still don't convince you to get more education, just look at these babies, also provided by the Bureau of Labor Statistics.

HOW MUCH DO PEOPLE MAKE WHO HAVE:	EACH WEEK	OVER FORTY YEARS
No high school diploma	$ 409	850,720
High school diploma	$ 583	1,212,640
Two-year college degree	$ 699	1,453,920
Bachelor's degree	$ 937	1,948,960
Master's degree	$ 1,129	2,348,320
Professional or doctoral degree	$ 1,421	2,955,680

BEATING THE ODDS

Now, for many teens, especially those from poor homes, unsupportive homes, or developing countries, going to college may seem impossible. Even then, there are ways, if you want it badly enough. Just ask Andres Marroquin Gramajo.

Andres was born in Guatemala in a town near San Marcos. He was dirt poor. In Guatemala, less than 1 percent of the kids have access to a university education. Yet Andres always had this unusual desire to go to college.

He told me, "When I was eight years old, I knew that the only way to improve my possibilities and help my family was to do well in school. In elementary school, I was the first in my class. Not because I was smart, but because I worked harder than everyone."

Andres continued to work hard and excel. "My friends often went to play basketball, and I said 'no' a lot, so that I could study. I had no father and that was hard. But I replaced the lack of a father with success stories I learned about in books, movies, and on TV."

During his last year in high school, Andres set the goal to go to one of the best universities in Guatemala City. Everybody, even his teachers, told him: "Come on, Andres. That is an impossible dream. All of us had that dream, and look, we're all teaching and working here in San Marcos."

But Andres was focused. There was just one problem. He had no money. So Andres got proactive and creative. "I called up about 15 embassies in Guatemala and asked if they had any scholarships for college students. None of them did. I then found the name of the brother of the president of Guatemala in the phone book, and called and told him that I really wanted to go to college and needed a scholarship. He agreed to help me but then his brother left office and that put an end to that."

When none of these methods worked, Andres took the admissions exams to the three best universities in Guatemala City, hoping that if he did well, something good might happen.

One of the schools he applied to, Francisco Marroquin University (UFM), is the most prestigious and expensive university in Central America. An admissions officer, Mónica, recalls:

"I remember when we were checking the results of the admission exams from all the applicants. Andres scored a perfect 100 in the math exam and scored very high on the rest of the exams. We investigated but soon realized he would not be able to pay his way. We then interviewed him, as part of the admissions process. My team and I were so impressed with Andres that at the end of the interview we told him, 'Andres, you are accepted.'

"I remember him saying, 'Oh, thanks, now I can go back to my small village and tell everybody that I was accepted to this excellent university; but you must know that I can't afford it, so you can use my space to accept someone else. At least now, I am happy that I achieved my goal, even though I can't enroll.'

"'Don't worry, Andres. You will be the first one accepted into our new scholarship program, and it will pay for everything, your tuition, a place to live, books, and a generous amount for personal expenses. Congratulations!'

"Andres was overcome. And, for the next three minutes, he didn't say a word."

A few years later, Andres graduated from UFM with a degree in economics. He's now earning a doctorate degree in the United States.

Andres could have whined about all the obstacles he faced: "I'm poor," "It's too hard," "It's never been done." Instead he focused on the things he could control—his attitude, his initiative, and his goal.

CHOOSING THE RIGHT COLLEGE

What college is right for you? Only you can decide that. But here's what not to do when deciding. Don't go to a college just because a friend is going there. Don't choose a college because it has a reputation for being a party school. There are more important things to consider, like how hard it is to get into, how it ranks, where it's located, the physical campus, the cost of tuition, the living conditions, and what the school is known for. If, for example, you plan to get a degree in music, apply to a school that has a strong music program.

Choosing the right school is a big decision, so make sure you check out all your options. You may want to:

- *Attend a college fair.*
- *Talk with your parents.*
- *Talk with several people who are attending or have attended that school. Ask them what they like and don't like about it.*
- *Read college catalogs and visit the Web sites.*
- *Visit the campus. Nothing will give you a better feel than paying a visit to the campus. Walk the halls, attend a class or two, go to the library, stop at the dorms.*

- *Try a concurrent enrollment class, which is a college-level class offered to high school juniors and seniors. You can earn both high school and college credit and it gives you a chance to try out a college-level course.*

GETTING ADMITTED. YIKES!

So, how do you get admitted to the school of your choice? Although it's a little different at each college, they are all looking for the same basic things, including:

Desire: How badly do you want to get into this school? If you are truly enthusiastic, it will come through on your application and in your interview. You can't fake enthusiasm.

Standardized test scores: How well did you do on your SAT or ACT or other standardized tests?

Grades: What is your overall GPA? Did you take some hard classes?

Extracurricular activities: What other activities were you involved in, such as sports, clubs, drama, band, student government, church, or community?

Service: Have you volunteered for worthy causes?

Letters of recommendation: What do other people think of you? Choose people who know you well to write your letters; don't just go for the big names. Also, choose people you know will write you an *outstanding* letter, not just a *good* one. Don't take chances on this one.

Communication skills: How well can you express yourself in writing (based on your application essays) and verbally (based on possible interviews that some schools do)?

If your GPA or standardized test score is lower than you'd like, don't fret. You can still get into a great school if you are strong in other areas. The admission offices look at the whole package, not just one area. They also look for trends. For example, if you started off poorly in school but ended much more strongly, that will play in your favor.

If you're a late bloomer who did awfully in school but now sees the light and wants to go to college, don't think you can't make it. You can. Remember, a college is a business, and they want your money. They're always looking for new students. You may not get into the very best school or the school of your dreams, but there are many other good schools out there.

PREPARING FOR A STANDARDIZED TEST

There are only two things in life worse than taking a standardized test—parallel parking and eating liver. It didn't seem fair that my entire future depended upon how I did on a four-hour test. It made me feel better to think that Olympic sprinters only get 10 seconds to make or break their futures. At least I got four hours.

How can you prepare? It's simple. When you get into ninth grade, start picking challenging classes that stretch your mind and teach you how to think. There's no substitute for this.

Unlike other tests, you can't really cram for an SAT, ACT, or any other standardized test. So start practicing months before you take the real thing. There are numerous resources to help you. Just go to your favorite Internet search engine, like Google, and type, "Preparing for the SAT or ACT." Ten million entries will appear and you can choose from among them. Many are free.

A common mistake teens make in their preparation is that they practice in short chunks of time, an hour here and an hour there. Don't forget that these tests last for about four hours, and you need to condition your mind to focus for four straight hours. I recommend doing at least two full dress rehearsals of the exam. If the test runs from 8:00 A.M. to 12:00 P.M. on a Saturday morning, then practice doing a full test from 8:00 to 12:00 on a Saturday morning, at least twice. When you take the real one, there will be no surprises.

Keep in mind that you can usually take these tests as many times as you want. Knowing this may help you not freak out while taking it the first time. Oh, yeah, get a good night's rest and eat breakfast. That helps, too.

HOW WILL I EVER PAY FOR IT?

College is expensive. The good news is there are boatloads of scholarships and grant money available. In his book *How to Go to College Almost for Free,* Ben Kaplan shared how he did just that.

Reality has just bitten me—and bitten me hard. It happened one day during my junior year in high school, as I was leafing through glossy catalogs with dreams of wild collegiate adventures dancing in my head. Suddenly, I felt the reality of having to pay for my undergraduate education sink its ugly teeth.

What I hoped to do was enroll at a top university, but how would I ever pay the six-figure tab at the school of my choice?

One day at my high school's college and career center, however, I came across a stack of colorful applications for a nationwide scholarship program called the Discover Card Tribute Awards. As I held the application in my hands, my mind raced with questions. Were there a lot of scholarship programs like this one? Did a kid from a public high school in Eugene, Oregon, actually have a chance?

Despite my doubts, I decided to give the scholarship application a try. So I wrote a couple of short essays, diligently filled out the forms, and rounded up a few letters of recommendation.

A couple of months passed. Then I got a letter in the mail that changed my life: "Congratulations," it said. "You've just won a $2,500 scholarship." The story gets better. A few weeks later, I received a phone call notifying me that in addition to the first award on the state level, I had just won another $15,000 in the national portion of the scholarship contest! You should have seen my parents dancing around the house.

Then I made another life-altering discovery: Plenty of other corporations, associations, organizations, institutions, and community groups can't wait to give away college money. So I filled out more forms, crafted more essays, gathered more recommendation letters, and started expanding my involvement in school and community activities. Applying for these awards took a good bit of work, and I lost my share of scholarship contests. But by sticking to the process, I ended up reaping enormous rewards. By the time I headed off to college, I had applied for about three dozen merit scholarships, and amassed nearly $90,000 in scholarship winnings—funds that I could use at any school I desired. Thanks to these funds, virtually the entire cost of my college education was covered.

As Ben discovered, there's a ton of money out there from all kinds of organizations to help you get educated. Most scholarships come in two ways. First, need-based scholarships and grants, targeted to teens from low income families. Second, merit-based scholarships and grants, based on all sorts of talents, not just for getting high grades and test scores, though there are scholarships for that too.

To learn more, I recommend meeting with your high school's career counselor, talking with the financial aid department of the school you'd like

to attend, or buying Ben Kaplan's book. (For more information, visit the Help Desk in the back.)

Don't let a lack of money be the reason you don't go to college. I repeat, don't let a lack of money be the reason you don't go to college. If you need to take out student loans, and work while in school, do it. It will pay for itself many times over. There are only two things ever worth going into debt for: a home and an education.

Finding Your Voice

"So what do you want to be when you grow up?" I asked some little kids. They said:

- *"I want to be one of those guys in the brown truck who bring boxes to your house." —Nathan, 6*
- *"I want to be happy." —Mariah, 10*
- *"I want to be a harp teacher and a mom." —Beth, 11*
- *"I want to be a pizza man." —Mitchell, 8*
- *"I think it would be fun to be a nuclear scientist." —Peter, 11*
- *"I really, really, really, really, really want to be a computer tech guy." —Michael, 11*
- *"I want to be a photographer and travel everywhere, maybe even space." —Daysa, 10*
- *"I want to be an exotic vet." —Taylor, 10*

As a teen, if someone would have asked me that question I would have said, "I have no clue." I was still figuring out who I wanted to ask to the junior prom.

But as you near graduation from high school, it's time to *start thinking* about what you want to be when you grow up. I didn't say figure it out. I said, start thinking about it. Your ultimate goal should be to start building a career or profession, instead of settling for a series of jobs that don't lead anywhere.

The key is to find your voice. I'm not talking about vocal cords. I'm talking about finding your groove, your niche, what you were born to do.

Imagine four circles.

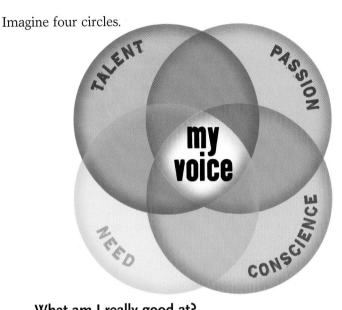

What am I really good at?

This is **t a l e n t .**

What do I love doing?

This is **p a s s i o n .**

What does the world need that I can get paid to do?

This is **n e e d .**

What do I feel I should do?

This is **c o n s c i e n c e .**

The place where these four circles overlap represents your voice. Think about them as you start plotting the college you want to attend, the jobs you take, the subject you major in, and so on. Ultimately, you'll want to build a career that taps your voice.

All four circles are important. For example, you may love music (passion) and even be good at it (talent), but you've also got to figure out a way to make a living from it (need). The chances of becoming a rock star are one in ten thousand, so don't bet on that. You could, however, earn a living by teaching music or writing music for TV commercials and films.

In like manner, you don't want to wind up in a career that pays well (need) but doesn't make you happy (passion) or tap into your gifts (talent).

Perhaps you feel, deep in your bones, that there is something special you should do with your life (conscience). For example, Ben Kaplan, who figured out how to go to college for free, is now building his career around helping other kids get grants and scholarships so that they too can go to college. This is Ben's special cause, driven by conscience.

I had a nice chat with Brinlee from California. By discovering her voice, she was able to turn her life around and is now on the path to building a career.

When I started high school in ninth grade, I was in the top program in the school. I wanted to be an overachiever at that point, but everything hit me all at once. I had family problems, and then my best friend betrayed me. I thought the whole world hated me.

So I turned to drugs and drinking and started hanging out with the wrong people, and partied a lot. I had a 1.1 GPA and things were just so bad. After months of this, I woke up one morning, doped on the drug I took the night before. I thought, "I can't do this for the rest of my life." That same day my cousin really laid it on strong. She's like, "Your mom's praying every day, and you're such a smart girl. What happened to you? I've been there, Brinlee, and you cannot waste your life away because you have so much going for yourself."

I stopped taking drugs all at once. I was addicted to alcohol, but after watching my dad, who was also an alcoholic, I decided I didn't want to be like him, and finally gave it up too.

My sophomore year came along, and I thought, "I have to change, I have to do things right." It was then I decided to join the school newspaper. In middle school, I loved writing short stories. I'd share them with my friends, and they'd be like, "Oh my gosh Brinlee, this is really good." And I'm like, "It's just a stupid story I wrote." And they're like,

"No, it's really good. I'm serious."

As a member of the journalism class, I started writing about five stories per issue. And the advisor of the paper said, "Wow, I'm amazed by you." Over the next several years I worked my tail off. Now, in my senior year, I am editor-in-chief of the school newspaper. I also work at a local newspaper. I want to be a publisher when I grow up.

It feels good to find something that you're good at, because it doesn't make you think about the negative stuff in your life. It keeps you busy, and you're having fun at the same time. Yesterday, when I was driving home, I was thinking, "Oh, my gosh. I'm so happy."

Brinlee is starting to find her voice. It may take much longer for you. Be patient. I didn't have a clear direction about what I wanted to do with my life until a few years after college. Here are a few items you might consider to help you find that voice of yours.

EXPLORE BROADLY

"Survey wide fields, but cultivate small ones," goes the saying. You won't know if you like something unless you try it. So, while in high school, take lots of different classes. There are such a wide variety of classes to choose from. Circle the ones that interest you.

aerobics	music independent study
astronomy	peer tutors
ballroom dance	photography
ceramics	Shakespeare
clothing	sign language
creative writing	sports entertainment marketing
film literature and history	study skills
foods	TV/video production
jewelry	weight training
journalism (school paper)	yearbook

There are also numerous clubs or teams you can join. Circle those that interest you.

academic challenge	jazz band
band	Key Club
cheerleading	language clubs
chess team	math league
choirs	mock trial
color guard/majorettes	Model UN
entrepreneurship	multicultural
fashion club	National Honor Society
forensics	peer mentoring program
fly-fishing	student council
Habitat for Humanity	theater society
health careers club	

Look around. Sometimes a single event can ignite something in you as it did in Justin.

One day my dad brought home a 3D architecture program, knowing that I have always loved designing things. He told me to install it and have some fun. That was only the beginning. In the seventh grade, my Algebra 1 teacher told the class that, for the final project, we would be designing a house. I was ecstatic. I got to work on it the next day, and finished it one week in advance. I got 99 percent on the assignment. This made me want to design more houses. One day I will be designing and building the tallest skyscraper in the world.

You'll also want to explore different jobs, when possible. Instead of applying for the same summer job each year, try doing something different. And, if you're really brave, try your hand at starting your own business and becoming a teen entrepreneur, also known as a *trep*. Here are just a couple of examples of treps featured in a magazine for small businesses called *The Costco Connection*.

```
Christopher Haas Enterprise
Christopher Haas
Temucula, California
```

Chris, age 17, always had a good basketball shot. Most of his classmates, however, didn't have the same skill. "I noticed a lot of kids didn't shoot well because they weren't holding the basketball correctly," says Chris. So, he went to his garage, dipped his hands in paint, and placed them on a basketball.

Little did he know he had stumbled on an act of genius: The handprint on the ball would show someone exactly how to hold a ball while shooting. Today, specialty sports stores from all over carry the Hands-On Basketball and the Hands-On Football. In fact, he has sold more than one million units of the Hands-On Basketball. It wasn't an immediate slam dunk, recalls Chris. "I was rejected by 12 companies over the course of a year and a half before one decided to take a chance on my product."

Today, Chris has earned enough money to pay full college tuition for himself and his brother and sister, who work with him in the family business.

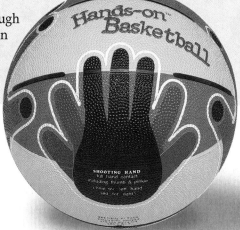

Photo used with permission of Sportime, LLC.

The Chocolate Farm
Elise and Evan Macmillan
Denver, Colorado

As a toddler, Elise, now 14, learned to make chocolate candies by her grandmother's side. A few years later, she made and sold some chocolate animals at a youth marketplace in Denver.

"We thought we'd just sell the chocolate for one day, but everyone really loved it," recalls Elise. "We sold out of everything, and people wanted to know how they could order more. We decided we might as well try to make some money out of this."

Elise combined her talent with that of her brother Evan, 16, a computer whiz. Elise began concocting chocolate recipes based on farm animals, such as Chocolate Cows, Sheep Munch, Chocolate Paws, and Pigs in Mud. Meanwhile, Evan designed an interactive Web site where people could e-mail recipe suggestions and other feedback. The orders began pouring in.

Today, www.chocolatefarm.com averages about 10,000 hits per day and has become a booming business. What are they doing with all that dough? Well, besides sponsoring a local scholarship, they are investing for college and putting money back into their business.

Photo by Jason McConathey

WATCH OUT FOR SERENDIPITY

Two of my favorite words are: plethora and serendipity. *Plethora* means "many," as in "Would you say I have a plethora of piñatas?" *Serendipity* means "happy accident." In other words, some unexpected event that turned out well. Often, serendipity can help us discover what we want to be when we grow up.

When I first tried out for the Provo High School freshman football team, I wanted to be a running back. But, seeing that we had no quarterback, Coach Drury made me play quarterback. "Quarterback? What a stupid position!" I thought. To make a long story short, I played quarterback in high school, and got a scholarship to play quarterback for a big college, where I took a class from a teacher who inspired me to major in English, which led me to write books, which in turn affected my whole career. Had I stuck with running back, I probably wouldn't have played football in college (I wasn't fast enough) and probably wouldn't have met that inspiring teacher and so many other things might not have happened. I'm so glad Coach Drury saw something in me that I didn't. Happy accident, wouldn't you say?

Be on the lookout for serendipity in the form of a lucky break, an accident, a turn of events, or a person who sees something in you that you don't see in yourself. So many times, the stumbling block you tripped over growing up becomes the building block of your future. I have a friend, John, who struggled immensely with self-esteem as a teen. Today, he has become a very successful author. Guess what? Most of his books are about how to cope with life as a teen. Sometimes we plan our careers, and sometimes we stumble upon them.

THINK DEEPLY

You'd be surprised at how many people end up in dead-end careers because they never really took the time to think about what they wanted to do. What should you think about? You should think about what you really like and hate doing, how much money you want to make, and what kind of lifestyle you want. If you like being your own boss, become an entrepreneur. If you don't enjoy moving and uprooting all the time, don't join the military.

My brother-in-law, Matt, did it right. He decided he wanted to be a doctor. He just wasn't sure which kind. So, during college and medical school he carefully studied various specialties. He talked with all kinds of doctors and examined their lives. What did they like and dislike about their jobs? What kinds of lifestyles did they lead? Although he was attracted to orthopedic surgery, the surgeons he knew led hectic lives and had long work schedules. So, he chose to be a family doctor instead, where he could make a good living, yet lead a more balanced life.

Perhaps most important, do something you love. I like how Maya Angelou explained it:

"You can only become **truly accomplished** at something you love. Don't make money your goal. Instead, pursue the things you **love** doing, and then do them so well that people can't take their eyes off you."

Although money isn't everything, it is a strong consideration and something you should be aware of. Study this chart to better understand your options:

SKILL LEVEL	$ PAY	EDUCATION REQUIRED	TYPES OF JOBS
Professional careers	Great money — upper-class lifestyle	High school (required) Bachelor's (usually required) Master's (usually required) Doctorate (often required)	CPA, advanced computer programmer, lawyer, architect, business executive, college professor, engineer, doctor, dentist, successful entrepreneur, banker
Skilled careers	Good money — middle-class lifestyle	High school (required) Bachelor's (usually required) Master's (sometimes required)	Computer programmer, police officer, lead mechanic, pilot, electrician, family farmer, financial analyst, real estate rep, schoolteacher, registered nurse
Semi-skilled careers	Fair money — lower-middle-class lifestyle	High school (usually required) Bachelor's (sometimes required)	Carpenter, auto mechanic, factory worker, store supervisor, truck driver, administrative assistant, insurance rep, car salesperson, enlisted soldier
Unskilled jobs	Poor money — lower-class lifestyle	High school (occasionally required)	Retail sales clerk, fast food worker, waitress, laborer, construction hand, custodian, lawn care worker, security guard, most part-time jobs

Let me be clear. How much a person makes and the kind of job they have has nothing to do with their worth. There is dignity in all hard work, whether in high-paying jobs like a doctor or low-paying jobs like a grocery store cashier. My point is: A good education gives you options. Most people in low-paying jobs are there not by choice but by default. They'd prefer a better-paying job but can't get one because they lack the skills.

THE VOICE FINDER

To help you further discover your voice, try the Voice-Finder* activity on the next couple of pages.

---

* For an online, printable version of the Voice Finder, go to www.6decisions.com.

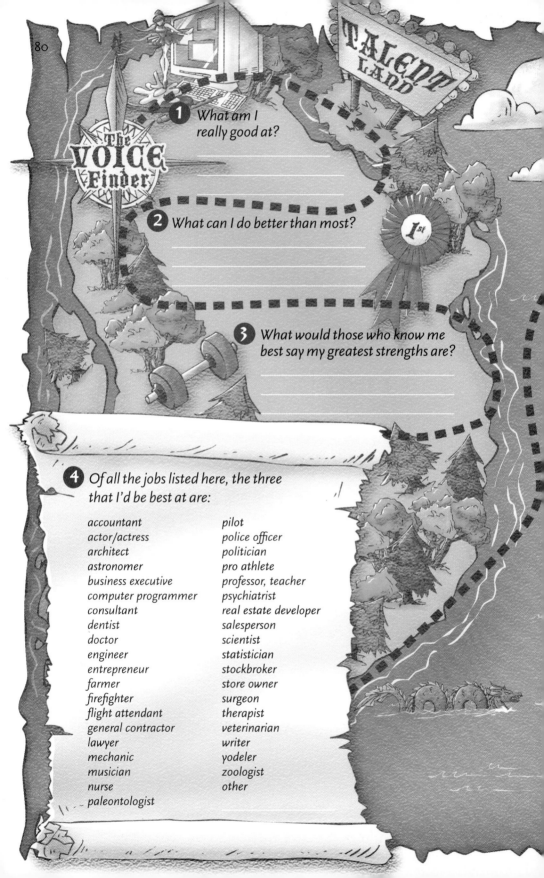

TALENT LAND

The VOICE Finder

1 What am I really good at?

_____

_____

_____

2 What can I do better than most?

_____

_____

_____

1st

3 What would those who know me best say my greatest strengths are?

_____

_____

_____

4 Of all the jobs listed here, the three that I'd be best at are:

accountant	pilot
actor/actress	police officer
architect	politician
astronomer	pro athlete
business executive	professor, teacher
computer programmer	psychiatrist
consultant	real estate developer
dentist	salesperson
doctor	scientist
engineer	statistician
entrepreneur	stockbroker
farmer	store owner
firefighter	surgeon
flight attendant	therapist
general contractor	veterinarian
lawyer	writer
mechanic	yodeler
musician	zoologist
nurse	other
paleontologist	

_____

_____

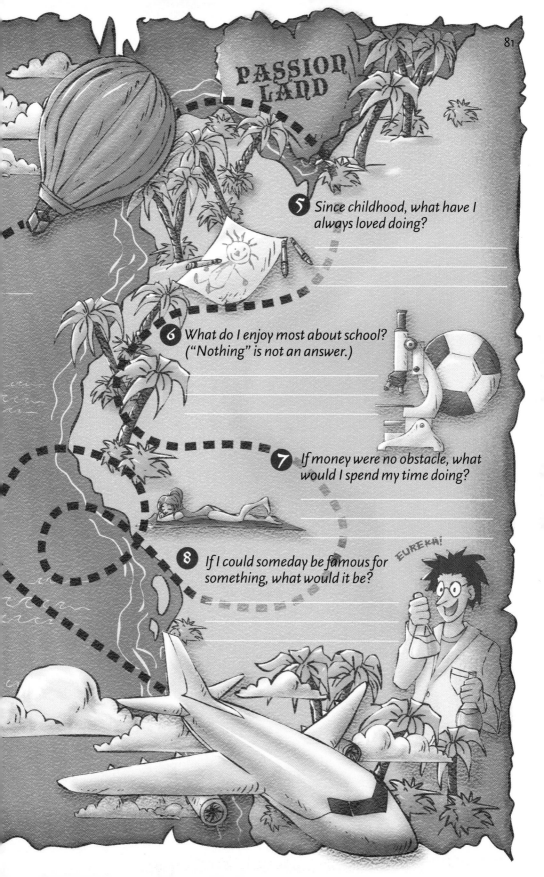

PASSION LAND

5 Since childhood, what have I always loved doing?

6 What do I enjoy most about school? ("Nothing" is not an answer.)

7 If money were no obstacle, what would I spend my time doing?

8 If I could someday be famous for something, what would it be?

EUREKA!

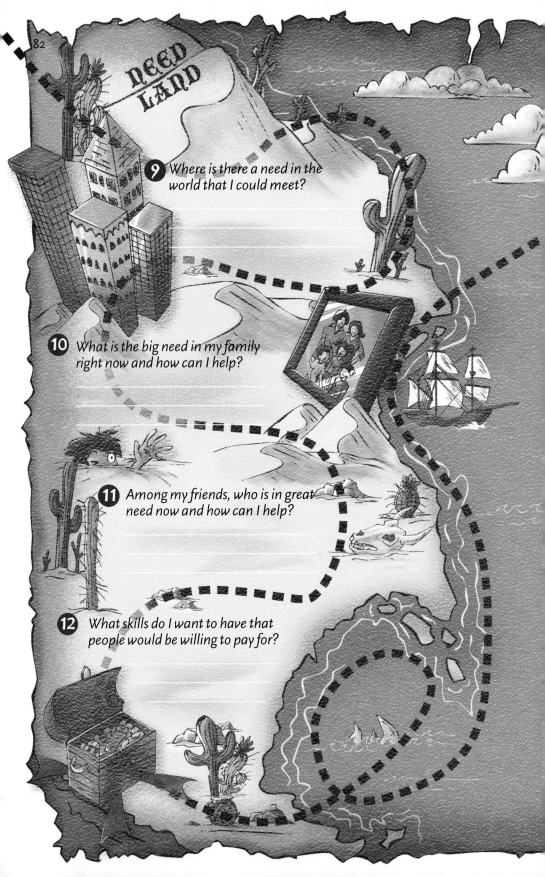

NEED LAND

9 Where is there a need in the world that I could meet?

10 What is the big need in my family right now and how can I help?

11 Among my friends, who is in great need now and how can I help?

12 What skills do I want to have that people would be willing to pay for?

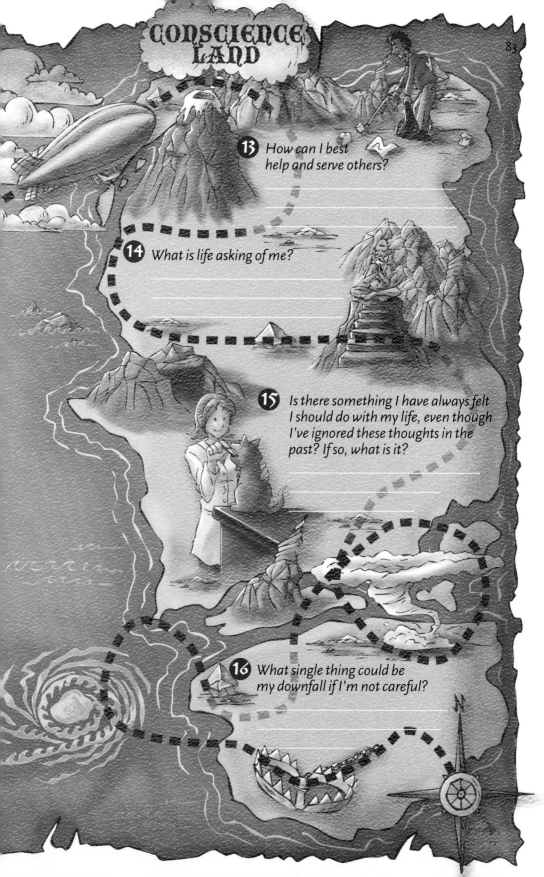

CONSCIENCE LAND

13 How can I best help and serve others?

_____
_____

14 What is life asking of me?

_____
_____
_____

15 Is there something I have always felt I should do with my life, even though I've ignored these thoughts in the past? If so, what is it?

_____
_____
_____

16 What single thing could be my downfall if I'm not careful?

_____
_____

Patience, My Dear

If you're still totally confused about what you want to be when you grow up, relax. There's no rush. You don't have to decide your profession, your major, or anything today. Just be on the lookout. Become aware of what really gets your juices flowing. Take note of what you're good at.

Once I was talking to some teens in Seoul, South Korea, about finding their voices and one girl asked: "What if what you *love to do* and what you feel you *should do* are different?" It was a good question. I said, "Conscience comes first, ahead of talent, passion, or need. Pay special attention to your intuition. It will come in the form of feelings, impressions, and ideas."

LUCKY COW — MARK PETT

YOUR LIFE'S WORK

When you were born, your life's work was born with you. In other words, I believe each of us has a purpose on this earth and a special something we need to do. I love how talk-show host Oprah Winfrey describes it.

> *Have the courage to follow your passion—and if you don't know what it is, realize that one reason for your existence on earth is to find it. It won't come to you through some special announcement or through a burning bush. Your life's work is to find your life's work—and then to exercise the discipline, tenacity, and hard work it takes to pursue it.*
>
> *How do you know whether you're on the right path, with the right person, or in the right job? The same way you know when you're not: You feel it. Each of us has a personal call to greatness—and because yours is as unique to you as your fingerprint, no one can tell you what it is.*
>
> *Pay attention to what makes you feel energized, connected, stimulated—what gives you your juice. Do what you love, give it back in the form of service, and you will do more than succeed. You will triumph.*

Today, Oprah is considered to be one of the most influential women in the world, but she didn't start that way. Oprah was born into poverty to a single mother. She was raised by her grandmother and experienced abuse and severe racial discrimination growing up. Through it all, however, she always felt she had something special to contribute to the world. And over many years, she slowly but surely found her voice—helping women lead happier, more fulfilling lives!

"Yeah, right," you might be saying. "I'm not Oprah." I agree. You're not Oprah, but you have unique qualities and gifts that no one else has. And surely there's something special you can do with your life that no one else can. There are so many ways to serve and make a contribution, at school, at work, or within the four walls of your own home.

Writing a mission statement can be a great way to express your voice. This one, written by a high school girl from Kuala Lumpur, Malaysia, expresses what she wants to be when she grows up and her educational plan for getting there.

MISSION STATEMENT

Accountant, lawyer, doctor, scientist

London

Oxford

Cambridge

Britain

Castle

Malaysian Hall

London Bridge

Big Ben

Trafalgar Square

Tower

Study hard

SUCCESS

THE PHEONMEANL PWEOR OF THE HMUAN MNID

Aoccdrnig to a rscheearch at Cmabrigde Uinervtisy, it deosn't mttaer in waht oredr the ltteers in a wrod are, the olny iprmoatnt tihng is taht the frist and lsat ltteer be in the rghit pclae. The rset can be a taotl mses and you can sitll raed it wouthit a porbelm. Tihs is bcuseae the huamn mnid deos not raed ervey lteter by istlef, but the wrod as a wlohe.

Isn't that amazing! And I awlyas thought slpeling was ipmorantt!

Your mind truly is a phenomenal thing. Don't waste it. Educate it. After all, what you do with that mass of gray material between your ears is one of the 6 most important decisions you'll ever make. I hope you'll choose the high road by staying in school, giving it your best effort (even when you don't feel like it), and preparing yourself for college and a great career centered on what you were born to do. If you've been trudging around on the lower road for years, take a detour to the higher road today. Sure, you may have some catching up to do, but better late than never.

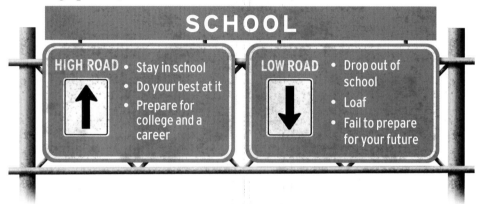

SCHOOL

HIGH ROAD
- Stay in school
- Do your best at it
- Prepare for college and a career

LOW ROAD
- Drop out of school
- Loaf
- Fail to prepare for your future

Alicia from Allen East High School put it this way: "Your education is like the safety net at the circus. Even if you fall in the middle of a stunt, it will be there to catch you." I couldn't agree more. With an education, you can lose your job and guess what? You'll find a new one. Job security doesn't mean having a stable job. Job security means having the ability to get a good job, anytime, anywhere, because you're employable, you know how to add value, and as Napoleon Dynamite put it, you have "great skills."

● ● ● COMING ATTRACTIONS ● ● ●

Do you have to deal with mean girls and bullies? Don't we all? Up ahead, see how others survived.

BABY STEPS

A Word About Baby Steps*

At the end of each chapter, I've included a list of 10 Baby Steps. Baby Steps are small, easy steps that you can do immediately to help you apply what you just read. Try them all, or just pick the ones that interest you. If you want to learn more about the origin of Baby Steps, check out the movie *What About Bob?*, starring Bill Murray. It's a riot!

1. If you're planning on dropping out of high school, prepare yourself for the future by repeating aloud each day: "I'm looking forward to low-paying jobs for the rest of my life."

2. List three benefits of finishing high school and going to college.

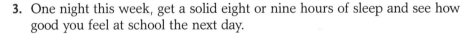

3. One night this week, get a solid eight or nine hours of sleep and see how good you feel at school the next day.

  4. Take the week-long **"Screen-Free Challenge."** Go for seven whole days without TV, movies, computer, video games, and so on, and see how much time you save. Using the computer for homework is allowed.

5. If you could visit any place in the world, where would it be? Brainstorm a quick list of ideas as to how you might get there someday.

   Ideas:

---

* To keep an online journal of your Baby Steps progress, go to www.6decisions.com.

6. If any one of your teachers ever offers extra-credit, do it!

7. Go out of your way to develop a good relationship with one of your teachers. **Say hello,** ask questions, be friendly, pay a compliment.

8. Develop your own homework routine and make it a priority. Set apart certain hours each day to study.

DAY	MY STUDY TIMES
MONDAY	
TUESDAY	
WEDNESDAY	
THURSDAY	
FRIDAY	
SATURDAY	
SUNDAY	

9. Think of someone you know who has a job you'd love to have some-day. Ask them if you could shadow them on the job for a day.

10. What topic would you really like to learn more about?

_____

How might you learn more?

Books, magazines to read: _____

_____

Web sites to explore: _____

_____

People to talk to: _____

_____

Classes to take: _____

_____

Places to visit: _____

_____

FRiENDS

So Fun...So Fickle

Top 10

Things You Oughta Know About Friends...

9. Don't be so intimidated by the cheerleaders and jocks.

— Kristin Peters, 17, Layton, Utah

10. Everyone appreciates a phone call or a card. I learned this when I was sick in hospital.

– John Greene, 19, Dublin, Ireland

8. It's okay to keep secrets between friends because everyone needs his or her own privacy, but deception is definitely not allowed.

–Jenny Fann, 16, Taipei, Taiwan

7. Have the courage to tell some friends that their paradigm which says to be evil is cool is wrong.

–Tsukasa Tsunoda, 15, Machida, Japan

6. Always remember your values and principles.

– Juana, 17, Long Beach, California

5. PROVIDE SUPPORT AND ENCOURAGEMENT TO YOUR FRIENDS.

–PREYMA PALANSIAMY, 17, SELANGOR, MALAYSIA

4. Everyone is unique so there is no point not being yourself. You are you, and no one should change that.

– Jane MacCallum, 15, Gullane, Scotland

3. FRIENDSHIPS ARE NOT GOTTEN IN ONE OR TWO DAYS.

–KARLA MANCILLA HINOJOSA, 18, MEXICO CITY, MEXICO

2. Sometimes arguing with friends is normal and necessary.

–Belen Llerena Muñiz, 15, Buenos Aires, Argentina

1. Association brings on assimilation. If you think your friends are stupid and crude, get new friends unless you want to be stupid and crude.

–Patrice Dean, 18, Vancouver, Washington

Don't walk in front of me, I may not follow.
Don't walk behind me, I may not lead.
Just walk beside me and be my friend.

— Albert Camus, author

In my entire life, I've only thrown one punch. It was when I punched a best friend.

I was in second grade playing a game of two-on-two football, and I began arguing with my friend, Clar, over the rules. Losing my cool, I pinned him down and punched him right in the eye. Shocked at what I had just done, I jumped up and dashed away as Clar screamed bloody murder.

Although Clar had a black eye for about two weeks, I was grateful that he forgave me and let me be his friend again, a friendship that has lasted to this very day.

There's nothing better than having a best friend, someone you can totally be yourself around. As one wise teen put it, "Friends are God's way of taking care of us." Then again, friends will sometimes turn on you, gossip about you, or get you so upset you want to punch them.

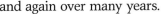

So, let's talk about **Friends,**
our next fork-in-the-road decision.

Who will you choose as your friends and what kind of friend will you be? You can choose the high road by choosing friends that build you up, being a true friend, and standing up to peer pressure. Or take the low road by choosing friends that bring you down, being a fair weather friend, and giving in to peer pressure. Like the school decision, the friend decision isn't one single decision. It's a series of decisions made again and again over many years.

FRIENDS CHECKUP*

Before diving in, take this quick checkup.

CIRCLE YOUR CHOICE	NO WAY!				HECK YES!
1. I have at least one or more true friends.	1	2	3	4	5
2. I make an effort to get to know new people and make new friends.	1	2	3	4	5
3. The friends I hang out with are a positive influence on me.	1	2	3	4	5
4. I'm inclusive of others and don't belong to an exclusive clique.	1	2	3	4	5
5. I don't judge other people before I get to know them.	1	2	3	4	5
6. I'm loyal to my friends and don't talk behind their backs.	1	2	3	4	5
7. I'm quick to forgive my friends when they make mistakes.	1	2	3	4	5
8. I'm a good listener and don't dominate discussions.	1	2	3	4	5
9. I'm kind to everyone, not just people I like.	1	2	3	4	5
10. I am able to resist peer pressure and be my own person.	1	2	3	4	5
TOTAL					

Add up your score to see how you're doing.

 40-50 **You're on the high road. Keep it up!**

 30-39 **You're straddling the high and low roads. Move to higher ground!**

 10-29 **You're on the low road. Pay special attention to this chapter.**

---

* To take this checkup or lots of other cool quizzes online, go to www.6decisions.com.

You're going to love this chapter. The first section, **Surviving the Everyday Ups and Downs of Friendships**, talks about fickle friends, mean girls, bullies, competition, and why we should never center our lives on friends. In **Making and Being a Friend**, we'll explore the essentials to making and being a good friend. Finally, **Peer Pressure** will look at how to resist negative peer pressure and build your own positive support system.

Surviving the Everyday Ups and Downs of Friendships

Sooner or later, friends show their TRUE COLORS, that is, what kind of friends they really are. Madison told me about how her best friend of three years turned on her to win the approval of an older guy.

HEY, YOU'RE NOT A BLONDE!

> One day, Bethany's friends discover her true colors

Our sophomore year, my best friend Shari was pursued by a senior football player named Mitch who had a really bad reputation. Football was very big at our school, and she saw Mitch as her ticket to popularity. Shari started acting like I was a goody-goody *and picked up Mitch's bad language and attitude. Since Shari and I had been close friends for years, I decided to write her a private letter and confided that Mitch was just using her and would bring her down.*

To my horror, Shari not only rejected what I wrote her, but she showed the letter to Mitch. Mitch became very angry, because I had attacked him personally. The next day, Mitch and a few of his huge football friends stood around my lunch table. In front of all my friends and the entire lunchroom, he went on a tirade, yelling and swearing, and calling me all sorts of horrible names.

The worst part of this public nightmare was that Shari stood behind him laughing. She had been my best friend for three years and had known him for less than a month. That hurt more than anything.

I did everything I could to keep from bursting out crying and ran home instead of going to class. I had only been in high school for a few weeks. I didn't think I could ever face people again.

My parents calmed me down and my dad called the vice principal, who warned Mitch to stay away from me. That just added fuel to the fire.

I went to school the next day and found that Mitch had written a nasty word on my locker. I was so embarrassed I had to miss class to wash it off.

Right then, I had to decide whether to let Mitch and Shari ruin my sopho-more year. My parents had taught me to take responsibility for my life no mat-ter what happened, so I decided to not let Mitch and Shari determine how I felt about myself. I took control and completely ignored Mitch and soon he lost interest.

Just as I suspected, after finding another cute sophomore to exploit, Mitch lost interest in Shari and moved on. But the damage remained. Now Shari had a bad reputation of being "easy," and no decent guy would ask her out. She also didn't have any close girlfriends because she had ignored them when she was involved with Mitch. Eventually she apologized for what happened between us. I forgave her and we were friendly to each other, but the trust was gone in our friendship and it was never the same again.

Does Madison's story sound familiar? Almost everyone I know has had an experience where a seemingly "good" friend shows their true colors and dumps them for someone they think is more popular. If this has ever hap-pened to you, take comfort in the fact that it's happened to lots of others, too. Contrast the fickleness of Shari in the above episode with the steadiness of Curtis Walker in this one.

When I was growing up it was a struggle to make friends. If I wasn't being ignored, I was being harassed. I always wished I was popular. The kids who did talk to me were the ones treated as outsiders, as I was, and most everyone thought we were weird.

As a sophomore, my athletic ability increased and I began to get some recogni-tion. I was playing on the football team for the first time in my life, and it seemed that my dream of being accepted was finally coming true.

On game day, the players wore their jerseys and hung around together. The day of our first game, a huge decision came my way at lunchtime. I had just loaded up my tray and saw the football players sitting together. Some of the guys I knew waved me over to their table.

Just as I started to walk over, I looked and saw my old friends sitting at their table. It was one of those moments that last forever. All at once it hit me. I knew who meant the most in my life. I made my way over to that humble table, to be with the guys who had always been there for me.

There were guys on the football team who treated me differently after that. I know that I missed out on a lot of activities with the popular kids at school. But in the end it was worth it because my character reached a milestone that day.

Wouldn't you love to have Curtis as a friend? Talk about true colors. In that moment of truth, he realized his old friends would always be there for him, even if his athletic skills were not. I hope that you and I will have the courage to be like Curtis.

Dealing with fickle or inconsistent friends seems to be a common challenge of friendships. Other common ups and downs include surviving the popularity game, enduring friends' little quirks, coping with gossip and bullies, and suffering through comparisons and competition.

Throughout this section, we'll talk about each of these ups and downs. I'll also drop a few survival tips as little reminders. Here's the first one.

 Choose steady friends who like you for who you are, not fickle ones who like you for what you have.

WHAT'S AT YOUR CENTER?

How can you possibly survive inconsistent friends? The key is not to make friends the center of your life. Your life center is whatever is most important to you. And whatever that is becomes your paradigm, or the pair of glasses through which you see the world.

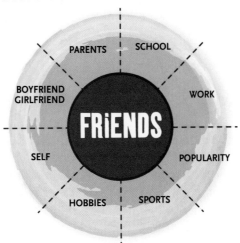

There are scores of possible life centers for teens, but the most common are girlfriends and boyfriends, sports, popularity, and, of course, friends. Making friends your life center may seem like a good idea, but it's not. Why? Because friends are imperfect, unstable, and human. They move. They change. And, sometimes, they turn on you. If you've centered your life on friends, it can topple you. Your emotional life will hinge on how many friends you have or how they've treated you lately. You'll surrender to peer pressure or allow friends to come between you and your mom and dad.

No one likes it when a friend gets possessive and wants you all to themselves. But that's what happens when you become friend centered. If you want to lose your friends, center your life on them. Teenager Paul Jones from Scotland put it like this:

"Always allow friends space and **don't cling** to them; they will always be there if they are worth keeping."

If friends don't make good centers, what does? Principles do. Yup, those time-tested natural laws that never go away, such as honesty, respect, and responsibility. Unlike friends, principles never fail. They don't gossip or turn on you. They don't get up and move. And here's the best part of all: Make principles your center and everything else will find its proper place, including friends. By putting principles first, you'll actually make more friends and become a better friend. Ironic, isn't it? How so? Because your security won't come from outside you. It will come from within. You'll be steady, and everyone likes to hang around steady people.

 Make as many friends as you can, but never center your life on them.

IT'S ALL ABOUT POPULAR!

When you hear the word *popular,* what comes to mind? Do you crave it, or does even the thought of it make you want to throw up? Well, like most things, popularity has a good and a bad side.

On the dark side, the word *popular* is linked to stuck-up, snotty, bratty people who think they're better than everyone else. You know, it's those good-lookin' kids who say the right things and wear the right clothes. Even though they think everyone adores them, they're hated by many. So, in reality, they're really only popular among themselves. Popularity has become their life center. It reminds me of the musical *Wicked*, where Glinda, the conceited witch, tries to coach her new friend Elphaba on how to become popular like she is.

"POPULAR!

You're gonna be popular!
    I'll teach you the proper ploys
when you talk to boys
            Little ways to flirt and flounce
I'll show you what shoes to wear
        How to fix your hair
    Everything that really counts
                To be popular"

There's also a positive side. We all know people who are well liked and respected because they're genuinely decent people. They're friendly to everyone. They're not stuck-up. And they've often worked hard to excel at something. My friend Duane was one of these guys. He was voted "most preferred" by all the girls in my high school. He was a great athlete, but he was also nice to everyone. He was popular, in every good sense of the word. Let me be clear: Popularity is not a bad thing; it only turns bad when people start thinking they're better than someone else.

So, what if you're a good person but aren't popular? Don't worry about it. Don't center your life on popularity or try to become popular for popularity's sake. It doesn't work that way. Instead, just be your best self. If you put your focus there, good things will happen. Then, if popularity comes, fine. If not, fine. After all, popularity is secondary, not primary, to greatness. It's based on the external stuff that the world says makes a person great: fame and fortune, beauty and biceps. There's nothing wrong with this stuff. It's just that, ultimately, it's really not that important or lasting.

Primary greatness, on the other hand, is not what you see on the outside, but what lies within. Primary greatness is your character—who you really are. This is lasting.

What's more, the whole idea of popularity seems to be fading. It used to be that the only definition of coolness was being the athlete or the cheerleader. No longer. Thanks to an explosion of extracurricular activities, it's no longer so clear who's in and who's out. There are lots of ways to be cool.

LUCKY COW   MARK PETT

Stop trying to be popular. Just be yourself, be nice to everyone, and good things will follow.

QUEEN BEES, WANNABES, AND GAMMA GIRLS

In a classic *Newsweek* article, Susannah Meadows analyzes *Queen Bees & Wannabes*, a book by Rosalind Wiseman that takes a look at popularity and fitting in. Wiseman writes about three groups of high school girls she's studied. She calls them the *Alphas,* the *Betas,* and a group not always highlighted, the *Gammas.* (By the way, Alpha, Beta, and Gamma are simply the names for the first three letters of the Greek alphabet.)

The Alphas are the Queen Bees, the ones to whom popularity means everything. The Queen Bees protect their clique at all costs and will boot out anyone who tries to threaten their reign. The Betas are known as the Wannabes. They will do whatever it takes to get in good with the Queen Bees.

The Queen Bees and Wannabes are so caught up in the lure of popularity and staying there, they don't realize that another group has one up on them. Wiseman calls them the Gamma Girls—kids who may not be known as the most popular, but they're definitely not losers. Quite the opposite. They're girls who are comfortable in their own skins. They're not mean. They like their parents. They're smart.

And they think popularity is overrated.

The article highlighted girls from Valhalla High School in California who "don't long to be invited to parties; they're too busy writing an opinion

column in the school paper or surfing and horseback riding." Gamma Girl Reyna Cooke put it this way: "In order to fit in, I would have to wear certain clothes, have a certain girlie attitude, go to parties, smoke pot and drink beer. It's kind of degrading." Instead, Gamma Girls are involved in a variety of school, church, and social activities, and play competitive sports.

Gammas were often picked on or made fun of before and because of it have developed independence and self-confidence. They have strong values, enjoy being with their families, and have decided to wait until marriage to have sex. Alphas and Betas look out! The Gammas are here to stay. (Sorry, guys. But this survival tip is more of a girl thing.)

If you're tired of playing the Queen Bee and Wannabe game, be a Gamma Girl.

QUIRKS, FAULTS, AND FOIBLES

Just like you, your friends are trying to figure out who they are and what the purpose of life is. They change their minds, have ups and downs, and make mistakes. Sometimes they even talk behind your back without really meaning any harm. Or they get a little jealous. Although you shouldn't hang with friends who are regularly mean or act like jerks all the time, you should be tolerant of your friends' everyday weaknesses and not overreact to the little mistakes they make.

Forgive their little quirks, faults, foibles, and inconsistencies just as you hope they forgive yours.

Kevin shared this story.

One day before baseball practice, I set my drink down on the bleachers and went to the bathroom. When I got back, I took a big drink of my soda. Everyone started laughing hysterically. I found out that someone had spit in my drink. But instead of blowing up in front of everyone, I pushed the "pause" button in my mind. I had just read the 7 Habits and so I rehearsed in my mind making proactive vs. reactive decisions.

After some time passed, I went up to the guy who spit in my drink and asked, "Why did you do that?" We talked it out, he apologized, and I forgave him because he was my friend. I went home that night feeling good about myself because I made the decision of talking it out, and I maintained our friendship. I realized sometimes with friends there are normal ups and downs, and the best thing to do is not to over-react, but to forgive and forget.

Kevin followed the proverb that says,

"A **fool** uttereth all his **mind:** but a **wise** man **keepeth** it in 'til afterward."

There's a time to forgive our friends when they blow it. There's also a time when you need to draw the line, as Kristine found out:

A few times, my friend Cindi played some mean tricks on me. Once, she and her friend Monique took my swimsuit, underwear, and shorts and hid them from me. All I had to wear was a long T-shirt and I had to walk about a mile to get home. Other times Cindi would take me to parties up the canyon where there were beer kegs, even though she knew I didn't drink, and would refuse to take me home. Of course I would get grounded. Then she would call, apologize, and promise to never do it again, and it'd start all over.

It looks like Kristine needs to change friends. So should you if you've got a friend who's continually using you or bringing you down. But there's a big difference between that and hyperventilating over small hiccups. As Richard Carlson writes, "Don't sweat the small stuff."

Be quick to forgive your friends all their little faults, just as you hope they'll forgive you yours.

MEAN GIRLS, GOSSIPS, AND BULLIES

Boys bully by threatening or pushing someone up against a locker. Girls bully in more subtle ways through backbiting, gossip, exclusion, name calling, rumors, and ever-shifting friendships, all carefully designed to inflict pain on targeted victims. That's why the term *mean girls* was invented.

Gossiping is especially nasty. Lacey's mom thought Lacey ought to give homeschooling a try, so she pulled her out of the public middle school she was attending. It wasn't much later that one of Lacey's classmates started spreading rumors that Lacey was kicked out of school because she did something horrible. This rumor spread like wildfire. When she heard about the rumor, Lacey was devastated. Indeed, sticks and stones can break your bones but words can tear right through you. We should treat each other's reputations with great care.

If you are being gossiped about, there are a couple of things you can do.

First, you may want to confront it. Instead of gossiping about the person who is gossiping about you, go directly to them and say something like: "I've heard that you've been talking about me behind my back. I'd really appreciate it if you'd stop doing it. I'm really not that bad a person when you get to know me." It takes guts, but it will often shut them up, especially if you say it when you're in control of your emotions. Be careful, however. Some people are so mean that confronting them might make the problem worse.

Second, live above it. Sometimes the best thing to do is just ignore it and move on.

Kaitlyn shared how she dealt with backbiting.

"I am drum major in my school's marching band and I'm only a junior. A lot of the seniors are extremely mad! I heard a lot of talking about me behind my back, but I decided not to lash back at them. Though they still talk about me, at least I was nice to them."

Maybe you're reading this and thinking, "Wait a minute, I'm the very thing you're talking about. I'm the mean person, the bully." If so, please start being nice. So many people are hurting. One mother told me that her daughter was picked on so badly during high school that she is still dealing with it today. And she graduated over ten years ago! Besides, "What do we live for if it is not to make life less difficult to each other?" wrote George Eliot.

One of my favorite comedies is a classic called *A Christmas Story*. It's about an insecure kid named Ralphie who has to deal with a bully named Scott Farkus. Ralphie is persecuted by Farkus (is that the ugliest name you've ever heard?) for years until one day Ralphie loses it, knocks down Farkus, and beats the crud out of him. I don't ever recommend *violence* as a way of solving problems, but *self-defense* does have a time and place.

See how Brandon Beckham dealt with a Farkus of his very own.

As I started attending junior high, I was intimidated, bullied, and physically hurt. I was a small kid, and fighting wasn't part of my character. My mother counseled me to always turn the other cheek. My father told me not to go looking for fights, but to defend myself if needed.

One day in gym class, I was sitting with a friend and all the other students waiting for the teacher. I made brief eye contact with a student sitting at the other end of the group.

Immediately, he reacted and yelled out profanities at me. What the #$+% are you looking at? I just said nothing and looked away. He came over to me. Yelling more profanities, he threatened me and asked me to get up and fight. I got up, but turned the other way and kept walking. By now, every person was up as well, trying to persuade us to fight. I just kept walking. He followed, shouting out racial slurs and belittling me. I thought maybe the teacher would be out by now, but there was no sign of him. He began pushing me and telling me to turn around so he could hit me. After ten minutes of this, I felt it was a matter of self-defense. As he followed me, I began to slow down to where he got close enough to my reach. I cocked my elbow and swung it back right at his nose. It was abrupt and hard. He fell back on the ground, stunned. Blood ran down from his nose and into his hands. He looked at me with amazement. I ran at him. His buddies pulled me off. With adrenaline going through me, I ripped out of my shirt and escaped, unwounded.

Why did this experience change me? It made me realize that I was completely able to defend myself, if needed. I became a more confident person and other kids respected me for standing up to a bully. I chose not to take the abuse anymore.

FRIENDSHIP SURVIVAL TIP #6 — **If people are gossiping about you or you're being bullied, confront the bully or find a way to live above it.**

CRABS AND COMPETITION

Crabs are funny creatures. If you put a few in a bucket, none will ever get out because as soon as one starts to make headway, the others will pull it back down. Do you ever feel this way? As soon as someone gets ahead everyone else gets jealous and starts pulling them down?

It's so natural to look around and compare your clothes, your looks, your abilities with others'. It's so natural to want to compete, to win, to get ahead. It's so natural to feel jealous when your friends succeed. But natural isn't always good. In fact, competing with your friends is downright dangerous. Don't get me wrong. Competition is good in things like sports and business. But it has no place in friendships.

The cure for getting out of the rat race of competing and comparing is to practice Habit 4: Think Win-Win. It's a frame of mind that says "Life is not a competition. I want to win and I want you to win. There's enough success to go around."

Lora wrote me about the magic that happens when you let go of the need to compete.

Dear Sean:

It's really hard trying to break the habits I've formed along the path of my life (16 whole years). One of the major things is that I've stopped trying to compete with this girl at school. She is very bumptious (sorry, I just learned this vocab word and think it is too cool! Bumptious means rude, forward, and pushy) and also interested in the same things I am so we've been pushed together a lot. In the past, I have let my dislike of her poison my enjoyment of certain things like the school play and speech tournaments.

Well, I am getting so much better at this! I have forgiven her and moved on. Today, I wrote in my journal a note to myself telling me to remember, life is NOT a competition. And you know what? I feel SO MUCH BETTER! I feel like I have this huge burden off my back.

Thinking Win-Win doesn't mean that you cave in and let your friends walk all over you. That's called Lose-Win and it's not a healthy choice either. See if you can relate to this comment told by Sonya, a 16-year-old honor-roll student.

I am a peacemaker with my family and friends. I always thought it was the easiest way out. I find myself not saying anything because I don't want to hurt anybody's feelings. I never want to start an argument and find myself tearing myself down. I am a doormat. Everyone takes advantage of me. Everyone might be happy, but if I am not happy with myself, I will soon just burst.

When it comes to friendships, stop competing or comparing and start thinking Win-Win.

HOW COME YOU DON'T KICK WITH US NO MORE?

My best friend in elementary school was a guy named Paul. We were inseparable. We played on the same tennis, basketball, baseball, swimming, and football teams. We slept over at each other's homes. We were the best of friends.

When we got into high school, we went our separate ways. Paul didn't abandon me and I didn't abandon him, we just developed different interests. Paul went into basketball and I went into football. We started hanging out with different friends. We always felt a close bond—we just didn't do much together anymore.

YOU'VE CHANGED, MARSHA.

Be open to the fact that you and your friends change, and that's okay. Your best friend this year may not be your best friend next year, especially when you move from one school level to another, like from middle to high school. There's a big difference between abandoning your friends and developing new friends because your interests have changed. So don't get upset if you naturally start drifting apart because your interests take you in different directions.

Remember, you and your friends may change and pursue different interests and that's okay.

There are 101 everyday ups and downs in friendships. We've only touched on a few. But no matter how challenging friendships can be, we all need friends. They are the "bacon bits in the salad bowl of life." As someone told me, "Friends in your life are like the pillars on your porch. Sometimes they hold you up, and sometimes they lean on you. Sometimes it's just enough to know they're standing by."

Making and Being a Friend

I asked a few teens to define a true friend. Here's what they said.
A true friend:

"Takes someone as they are and leaves them improved." — Tyler

"Has the same standards you have." — Jay

"Knows when to listen and when to talk." — Elise

"Isn't overbearing." — Jarrett

"Will stick up for others." — Charles

"Is someone who doesn't put you down or make you feel stupid." — Natalie

"Knows you don't have just one friend." — Metta

For some, making friends is a piece of cake. For others, it's like pulling teeth. "I'm a loner at school," Jose told me. "I just want to have someone to talk to and tell them about how my day has been and stuff like that. I guess my whole problem at school is not having self-confidence. I always feel 'less' than other people. I just can't help it."

One high school girl wrote how hard it was to deal with being called "Shamu" by some kids at school because of her weight (how mean can you be?). She said, "It hurt that people never took the time to get to know me, they just saw me as the fat chick who was really loud and obnoxious."

Believe me, *everyone* is trying to find their place, feel accepted, and fit in.

If you're anxious to make and keep good friends and be a good friend yourself, read on. I'll introduce you to seven essentials as to how to do it.

BE SLOW TO JUDGE

I'm convinced we cut ourselves off from all kinds of friends because we are too quick to judge.

At Hilliard Darby High School in Ohio, teacher Susan Warline initiated a Mix It Up Day to promote tolerance and help students step out of their cliques and meet new faces. During lunch on this day, she encouraged students to chat with people they'd never talked to before.

One student had come from Somalia to escape civil war and poverty in her country. At lunch, she boldly asked one of the jocks of the school, "Why do you call us 'Smelly Somalians?'"

He immediately shot right back, "Well, why are you here anyway? Why don't you just go back to your own country?"

She was silent for a few seconds. Then, in a soft voice, she told him how she saw her whole family get shot right in front of her, except for one brother and a few cousins who escaped. She told him how Somalia was controlled by warlords and how grateful she and her surviving family members were to live in a free country.

You can imagine how stupid he felt. What a paradigm shift! Before they talked, all he knew was that she looked different, and he resented her. Now that he knew the full picture, he saw everything differently. As the saying goes, "Keep your words soft and sweet, just in case you have to eat them!"

This same teacher found that out of the 582 teens surveyed in her school, 88 percent believed they were judged solely by their physical appearance.

Furthermore, a majority felt they were judged on whether they were athletic or not and on the language they spoke. How would you like to be judged by those factors alone without anyone getting to know the real you?

I guess high school hasn't changed that much since I was there. Labels are still everywhere.

Stephanie from Warren Central High put it this way. "It is way too often that you judge others, out of pure habit. Everyone, including myself, automatically makes a judgment of that random person you just passed in the mall, or at school, or anywhere without even realizing what you have just done."

Such was the case with Anna when she changed schools. "I didn't know anyone at first. After I did make friends, they told me that I had come across as stuck-up. I couldn't believe it. The truth was I kept to myself because I was so shy."

Go outside your comfort zone and get to know new people. There's always more to a person than you think. Strangers are just friends waiting to happen.

YOU MAKE THE EFFORT

I know a girl who's always complaining that her friends make no effort to include her. However, when I watch her interact with her friends, I realize that she makes no effort to include them, either.

If you want to make friends, be proactive and make the effort first. Don't just wait for friends to come to you. "Man must wait long time with open mouth for roast duck to fly in," goes the Chinese saying. *You* need to take the first step and *you* need to persevere, if at first you don't succeed.

See if Angela's story sounds familiar.

I know all too well what it feels like not to belong to a group of friends. My first year of high school was a lonely time. I was not very self-confident or outgoing and desperately wanted to make friends.

There was a large youth group at my church. The first time I went to an activity, I walked in alone and spent all of my time and energy trying to look like I was talking to someone. I told my mom I didn't want to go back. But she asked, "How will you ever make friends, if you aren't there?"

I wanted so desperately to belong to a group of friends that I went back alone, week after week with no success.

One night we sang a song by Michael Smith called "Friends." I was paying close attention to the words of that song and my eyes filled up with tears. Inside I was feeling so alone and worthless. Why didn't any of these girls want to be my friend?

At times your social life may consist of tending your sister's kids Friday nights and watching the Disney Channel! It won't always be like this. Keep trying and don't shut yourself off by feeling sorry for yourself. I love motivational speaker Og Mandino's words:

"Always have faith that conditions will change.

Though your heart be heavy and your body bruised and your purse empty, and there is no one to comfort you—hold on. Just as you know the sun will rise, so also believe that your period of misfortune must end. It was always so. *It will always be.*"

For Angela, her misfortunes did come to an end. She later wrote, "A few weeks later, I started going to a different youth group and eventually found a wonderful group of friends. I have some wonderful memories from the rest of my high school years; I just had a rough time starting out."

BUILD THE RBA

The amount of trust you have in a relationship is like a checking account at a bank. I call it the Relationship Bank Account or RBA. If you make lots of small deposits with your friends by being thoughtful, loyal, and other such things, you'll develop high trust, or a high RBA. If you make lots of withdrawals, by being rude, disloyal, and the like, you'll deplete your RBA.

IT'S YOUR RELATIONSHIP BANK ACCOUNT STATEMENT, AND YOU'RE REALLY OVERDRAWN.

Pretend you have an RBA balance of $500 with your friend Allie. On Monday, when you see her new haircut, you blurt out in front of everyone, "Allie. Your hair! I'm so sorry!" Nice work. You just took a $200 withdrawal from your RBA with Allie. Your balance is down to $300.

On Wednesday, in an attempt to be funny, you ask her in front of her boyfriend if her hemorrhoids are still painful. He doesn't think it's funny and Allie turns bright red. Again, you made another $200 withdrawal and you're down to $100 in your RBA. If you keep it up, you'll actually go in the hole. You begin to feel a strain on your normally close relationship.

So, you look for chances to make deposits. On Friday, you get your chance. At one in the morning, after the dance, Allie calls. After a few minutes of chitchat, she opens up and talks until two o'clock A.M. about how her boyfriend spent the night flirting with another girl. Although you're exhausted and have to get up early for practice, you make a genuine effort to listen.

In the end, you both agree that maybe she should start dating other guys. She hangs up feeling a huge weight lifted off her shoulders and grateful to have a friend she can talk to.

Bingo! You just made an enormous deposit of $500, bringing your balance up to $600. Your relationship can now withstand the normal, small withdrawals that we all make from time to time (sometimes on purpose, sometimes by accident).

Can you begin to see how to build friendships?

Here is a list of five key deposits you can make to build a friendship. With each deposit, there is a counter-withdrawal.

DEPOSITS	WITHDRAWALS
+ Do small acts of kindness	- Do little mean things
+ Say you're sorry	- Be too proud to apologize
+ Be loyal	- Gossip and talk behind people's backs
+ Keep promises	- Break promises
+ Listen a lot	- Talk too much

The deposit that wins the most brownie points with friends is to listen. This is Habit 5: Seek First to Understand, Then to Be Understood. You see, everyone wants to be understood; it's the greatest need of the heart and the foundation of all good communication. Never forget that we each have two ears and one mouth—use them accordingly.

Everyone hears what you say.
Friends listen to what you say.
Good friends listen to what you don't say.

MAKE YOURSELF MORE LIKABLE

You can't make people like you, but you can always make yourself more likable. How? By becoming aware of your weaknesses and trying to improve those you can do something about.

I like how author John Bytheway writes about it.

In driver's education classes, students are constantly warned about "blind spots"—places where other cars may be hiding that you can't see, even with your rearview mirrors! It might be a good idea for each of us to find an adult we trust and ask for help in identifying our personal "blind spots." Simply ask, "If you ever notice anything that I'm doing that might make it harder for me to make friends, would you please tell me about it?" It might take some humility, but it might also help you see some things that will help you.

One time, I remember my dad sitting me down and letting me know about one of my blind spots. He told me that I had the habit of leaving messes everywhere, or *temporizing*, as he called it. If I ate a snack in the kitchen, for example, I'd leave a big trail of evidence behind. He warned me that it was a pattern I needed to change or it could carry over into other areas. It only hurt a little, but I was glad to learn about a blind spot I never knew I had.

If you're struggling to make friends or even if you have a lot of friends, it may be helpful to take an honest look at yourself to see if you're someone *you'd* like to be around. From time to time, ask yourself the following questions and make adjustments if needed.

- *Have you been told that you're obnoxious, too loud, inappropriate, or just won't shut up?*

- *Do you ask people about their lives, or is it always about you? Can those around you barely get a word in?*

- *Could you practice better hygiene, bathe more often, use deodorant, or wash your hair and clothes more frequently?*

- *Do you dress appropriately? Are your clothes too skimpy, too outdated, too bizarre? Do you wear too much makeup? Or could you use a little?*

- *Do you think you're better than everyone else? Or, are you always putting yourself down by talking about what a loser you are and how everyone hates you?*

- *Do you take yourself way too seriously or do you always have to be funny and make everything a joke?*

When it comes to making yourself more likable, focus on things you can control, not on the things you can't. You can't control your height, your features, or your general body type. But you can control your personal hygiene, how fit you are, your mannerisms, your dress, and the way you carry yourself. Theologian Reinhold Niehbuhr summed it up well.

"God grant me the serenity to accept the things I cannot change, the courage to change the things I can, and the wisdom to know the difference."

BE INCLUSIVE

Do you remember Angela's story about struggling to make friends? Well, when she entered college, the tables were turned when someone tried to break into her newly formed group.

When I went to college I met Leslie, who became my lifetime friend, even to this day. Finally, I had a close girlfriend I could tell my secrets to and share clothes with. We also made friends with two great guys who were fun and looked out for us like brothers. The four of us became inseparable.

There was another girl, named Alyssa, who really wanted to be a part of our group. I'm not sure why I was so against it. I think I was fearful that she would come in and take my place.

One day in the cafeteria, the four of us sat down at a table. Alyssa found us and asked if she could sit with us. Feeling pressured, I said "yes," but I had mixed feelings about it.

Alyssa pulled up a chair at the end of the table and was made to feel different and uncomfortable just by her position at the table. Throughout the meal we basically ignored her, and talked and laughed to each other about things only the four of us knew about.

Later, Alyssa found me and said she had made a mistake trying to sit with us. She said that we had made it clear that we didn't want her around. After she left I felt like crying. I couldn't believe I had made another person feel so bad. And the worst thing was, I knew how she felt and I still did it. She was desperately lonely. Yet I had not been secure enough to share my friendship with her for fear of losing what I had.

Right then I made a commitment to myself that I would never make another person feel like they didn't belong again. Since that day, whenever I see someone who looks uncomfortable in their surroundings, I go out of my way to introduce myself and do what I can to make them feel at ease.

You may be enjoying the security of a close-knit group of friends right now without realizing there are people on the outside wanting in. Even the kids who seem to have everything often feel insecure. Katie is a good example.

I remember the faces in the stands and the sounds of the band playing as I walked down the field. It was the homecoming football game and I had been nominated for homecoming queen. When they announced me as the winner, I have never felt such a mixture of happiness and loneliness.

The next night was the homecoming dance but I didn't have a date. What was wrong with me? How could people vote for me and yet not one guy wanted to take me to the dance?

I remember almost resenting the crown as it was placed on my head and spent a miserable night at the homecoming dance. I left early and went to my friend Lindsey's house, feeling sorry for myself. However, when I arrived, I was welcomed with such warm smiles and friendly faces I couldn't help but smile myself. We had so much fun that night, just the girls, that it changed the whole feeling about one of the worst nights of my life.

Emily Dickinson wrote:

"They might not need me, but they might,
I'll let my head be just in sight.
A smile as small as mine, might be
Precisely their necessity."

Katie's friends may never know that their smiles were precisely the necessity that saved Katie from a depressing night.

Be inclusive when it comes to friends. Open your heart and let others in.

TREAT UNKINDNESS WITH KINDNESS

How often do you hear, "Why should I be nice to him when he's so rude to me?" It's easy to be nice to people who are nice to you. Anyone can do that. The real challenge is being nice to the mean, treating unkindness with kindness. But it works wonders.

In Romania, a girl named Iulia was new at her school and received a lot of attention because of it. This made some of the more popular girls jealous, so they sabotaged her. They began gossiping about Iulia and spreading ugly rumors. They purposely excluded her from their activities and made sure she knew that she wasn't welcome in their group.

This made Iulia's life so miserable that she wondered if she should transfer to another school. But one girl, Catalina, tried to be a friend to Iulia. Iulia had an upcoming birthday party and Catalina encouraged her to invite the very girls who were bad-mouthing her.

At first Iulia rejected this idea but, after thinking about it, she decided to show them kindness. The girls were stunned when they received an invitation inviting them to Iulia's big birthday bash. They not only came to the party but brought flowers and gifts to apologize for what they'd done. The

very girls who set out to ruin her reputation ended up loving her as a friend once they gave her a chance.

Abraham Lincoln was often criticized for trying to make friends with his enemies instead of trying to get rid of them. He replied, "Isn't that what I'm doing when I make an enemy a friend?"

LIFT OTHERS

I know of a boy named Kyle who had grown up part of a great neighborhood group of friends. He later got mixed up with a rowdy group of kids his senior year and became too cool to hang out with his old buddies. One time, these new friends gave him a dangerous combination of drugs and dropped him off at home to suffer through a terrible trip that almost killed him.

After Kyle completed a drug rehab program, his parents asked his old friends if they'd include him in their circle again. Instead of excluding him, they welcomed him back.

At first it was uncomfortable to have him around because he dressed like a thug and constantly bragged about what he'd tried. None of these neighborhood boys were into drugs and they wanted no part of that lifestyle. But they were patient and kept inviting him to basketball games and church youth activities. Little by little he changed his ways and dress to match theirs. Soon they found common interests again in sports and rock climbing, and spent time just hanging out at each other's houses.

A year later, thanks to his friends who rallied around him and with a lot of hard work and commitment, Kyle totally turned his life around. He even inspired his old friends to face and overcome their own challenges because they realized they were minor compared to his.

Kyle had two different groups of friends. One group tore him down and brought out the worst in him. The other built him up and brought out the best. **What kind of friends do you have? The ultimate test is: Are you a better person when you're around them?**

In sports, every now and then you come across a unique athlete who can lift the play of those around them. Michael Jordan, considered the greatest basketball player of all time, had that kind of influence. Everyone played better when he was on the court. Those are the kind of friends you want.

That's also the kind of friend you want to be—someone who lifts the play of everyone around you. So occasionally, ask yourself: Are my friends making better decisions when I'm around?

I read about students at Murray High School who elected Shellie Eyre their homecoming queen. Shellie, a 17-year-old senior, was born with Down syndrome. Her first attendant, April Perschon, also had physical and mental disabilities resulting from a brain hemorrhage suffered when she was just 10 years old. When Shellie and her attendants were crowned, the gym erupted into a standing ovation.

When the cheering had stopped, the school's vice principal said, "Tonight the students voted on inner beauty." Parents, teachers, and students openly wept. Said one student, "I'm so happy, I cried. I think Murray High is so awesome to do this." Now that's a great example of a large group of friends lifting the play of everyone!

Poet John Greenleaf Whittier put it nicely:

"Thee lift me and I'll lift thee and we'll both ascend together."

Peer Pressure

"How high are we?" I shouted at the boat below.

"About 70 feet," they yelled back. "Let's see ya jump."

"I don't know about this," I hollered. "It looks pretty high up here."

Here I was at Lake Powell, cliff jumping with my friends. We started at about 30 feet but kept challenging each other to go higher and higher. The pressure was intense. No one wanted to be a wimp.

"C'mon! Jump!"

Gathering all my courage, I leaped forward.

On the way down I kept thinking, "I'm such an idiot!"

I SHOULD HAVE TALKED TO MY PARENTS ABOUT THIS...

When I hit, the water felt like concrete and my whole body shook violently. I clawed to the surface and gasped for air. I quickly checked and was relieved to find that all my body parts were still intact. Whew!

Peer pressure makes you do stupid things, things you wouldn't normally do

when you're alone or thinking more clearly. In peer pressure situations, it's almost as if you leave your brain at the door.

I remember reading about a 14-year-old boy from New York City who was dared by his friends to ride on top of a subway train and go "surfing." Not wanting to disappoint, this kid climbed on top and was struck by an overhead beam that knocked him onto the opposing track where he was run over and killed by an oncoming train. Who knows what he could have made of his life?

What is peer pressure, exactly? It's when you feel pressured by people in your age group to act a certain way. Positive peer pressure is when your friends expect good things from you. Negative peer pressure is when your friends persuade you to conform or do something you don't want to do, like skip school, shoplift, have sex, do drugs, lie, vandalize, swear, dress a certain way, gossip, bully, and on and on.

You give in because you want to be accepted. You want to please. You don't want to draw attention to yourself. You just want to be like everyone else.

Mette, from Denmark, told how she felt pressured to pick on someone:

Once, in high school, I went to a party with some boys from my class. At some point, a boy arrives who suffers from a disorder causing his body to retain a lot of water, so he is quite fat. The boys decide that we should draw straws for who is to go up to the boy, pat his behind and ask him why he has breasts. We draw straws, and I lose. Then I do something I have since regretted a thousand times. I feel so pressured because they would think me a lousy sport if I didn't do it. I walk up to the boy, say it, and hurry to the washroom. The boys thought I was so cool, but I felt so bad. I have never gotten around to apologizing to the boy, and since then I haven't had the nerve to look him in the eye. The boys still laugh about it and slap me on the back and I feel a twinge of conscience every time. Because I have been mobbed myself, I was surprised that I could even think of making someone else unhappy.

On our own, we'd never think of doing something so mean. But, in a group setting, when the pressure's on, we check our brains at the door and do stupid things. As Professor Dumbledore told Harry Potter:

"It takes a great deal of courage to stand up to your enemies, but a great deal more to stand up to your friends."

To stand up to your friends, you need a defense mechanism of some kind. I call it the Peer Pressure Shield. The three vital pieces are preparation, a strong support system, and showing courage in the moment.

PREPARATION

You know that yucky feeling you get when you're about to take a test and you're not prepared? On the other hand, doesn't it feel great when you are?

I'm convinced we often give in to peer pressure because we are simply not prepared and haven't thought through what to do in tough situations. Here are a few high pressure situations you should think through right now.

TOUGH SITUATION	WHAT I WILL DO ABOUT IT
The group starts making fun of someone.	
I feel pressured to lie, cheat, or steal.	
I'm offered drugs.	
A boyfriend or girlfriend starts pressuring me to get more physical than I would like.	
Other:	

Getting clear on your goals and winning the Daily Private Victory are two other ways to prepare.

Get Clear on Your Goals

It's so much easier to say no to peer pressure if you're clear on your goals. Once I was talking to some students and asked if anyone would volunteer to share their goals. A high school sophomore named Kameron came up to the front.

I was expecting him to rattle off a few goals he hadn't really thought about, as usually happens. Instead, he pulled out his wallet, took out a laminated card, and read his goals to the group.

- *Get and maintain a 3.7 GPA.*

- *Get BFS (bigger, faster, stronger). By senior year, weigh 200 pounds, run a 4.6 forty, bench press 200 pounds eight times.*

- *Be one of 22 starters on the varsity football team by senior year. Contribute to winning the state championship.*

- *Be a good brother and example to my three little brothers.*

Everyone was impressed and thinking, "Wow! Maybe I should get some real goals, too." With specific goals like that, can you see how much easier it will be for Kameron to resist negative peer pressure? Can you see how much easier it will be for him to study hard in school, stay in good shape, and treat his brothers with respect, despite outside pressures to do otherwise?

Begin with the end in mind and get clear about what you want. If you haven't done so, write down a few goals or develop a personal mission statement. Laney Oswald says that her simple mission statement helps her live true to her values and say no to things she doesn't want to do.

My Mission Statement

» **BE HONEST.**   » **TRY YOUR HARDEST.**

» **DO WHAT'S RIGHT.**   » **GIVE EVERYTHING YOUR ALL.**

» **BE KIND TO EVERYONE.**   » **HAVE FUN.**

» **AND ALWAYS REMEMBER WHO YOU ARE AND WHAT YOU STAND FOR.**

Win the Daily Private Victory

You can win the public challenges you face each day long before they hit you, in the privacy of your own room. Just try this simple 20-minute, three-step routine each morning or evening. I call it the Daily Private Victory.

- *Get in touch with yourself through writing in your journal, reading inspiring literature, praying, meditating, or doing whatever inspires you and increases your self-awareness.*

- *Review your goals, ambitions, or mission statement.*

- *Visualize the challenges you will face in the upcoming day. Decide now how you will handle them.*

I do it most mornings and it takes me about 20 minutes. It grounds me so I can resist peer pressure (adults have it too) and prepares me for a successful day. When the challenges come, I've already won.

A STRONG SUPPORT SYSTEM

After preparation, the next step in shielding yourself from peer pressure is building a strong support system. Surround yourself with friends, family members, and trusted adults who inspire you to be your best. Set goals with each other, and hold each other accountable. Get involved in extracurricular activities as well. They make great support structures. If you're playing on a sports team or acting in a school play, you won't have time to get into trouble. Trouble usually happens when you've got nothing to do.

See how these five boys from Memphis, Tennessee, built their own positive support system.

When Ahmaad, Derron, Victor, Tyrone, and Tyjuan were in junior high, they looked around and saw that most kids they knew were not succeeding and often got into trouble with the law. Others used drugs and alcohol and worked late-night shifts in low-paying jobs with little chance for a better future because they had dropped out of school. They realized they were headed down the same path.

They often talked about wanting more from life and asked themselves questions like: What makes a champion or a drug dealer? What does it take to get a good job? They decided they wanted to break away from the racial stereotype and succeed. Instead of working night shifts, they wanted to be the guys behind the desks wearing suits and ties approving people for loans or working in other respectable businesses.

During a get-together one day, these five friends made a pact with one another. First, they agreed to get good enough grades to go to college. Second, they agreed not to use drugs. Third, they agreed they would not drink alcohol. Victor had seen abuse in his family because of drinking and wanted none of it.

The results of this pact on these boys' lives was extraordinary.

As a freshman, Ahmaad made the varsity football team and received a lot of attention from the seniors, who invited him to hang out. Worried that Ahmaad might adopt the bad habits of these much older boys, Ahmaad's four close friends came to him and said, "*We're* your boys, Ahmaad. You don't have any business hanging out with seniors."

At first, Ahmaad was angry at them for butting into his life, because he was flattered by all the attention the seniors gave him. But he knew his friends were right, and from then on, he stuck with them.

Once, he traveled to St. Louis for a game with some older boys who brought a stripper to their room without telling him. Ahmaad immediately jumped up and said, "I'm outta here." The boys were mad and threw him down on the bed. Ahmaad got into a big fight before he was able to get out.

Ahmaad continued to excel in football and received a scholarship to play for the University of Alabama. He was one of five finalists for the coveted Doak Walker Award given to the best running back in the nation until he blew out his knee. Most people thought he'd never play again, but through hard work and lots of rehab Ahmaad finally was drafted by the NFL. He is now working in a law firm.

Derron and Tyjuan also became great athletes and stars on their high school's basketball team. They both received scholarships to Fisk University, where they were roommates. Derron was playing well until his mother was diagnosed with cancer. He immediately quit the team and flew back to take care of her and his younger brother. Before his mother died, he promised her that he would finish college and raise his 14-year-old brother, both of which he accomplished. He has no regrets about his decision.

Tyjuan graduated from college and teaches children with special needs and coaches high school basketball now. He and Derron have remained very close friends and often vacation together.

Victor did well in high school, graduated from college, and became a teacher in California, where he is now helping kids from all walks of life to succeed in the midst of challenges.

Tyrone was also a very successful athlete and currently plays in the NFL. Although he has yet to finish college, he is committed to completing his degree.

Against great odds, all five of these friends created great lives for themselves, and all but one of them has graduated from college. They are professionals and wear suits and ties when they feel like it. Looking back on their experiences together, Ahmaad said:

"Friends are extremely important, especially if you agree on certain values and you're accountable to each other. We talk openly all the time. Sometimes we don't always feel the same about everything, but we help each other make good choices, even if they're not popular choices. We all want to help each other succeed. It's our support system. We're kind of a check and balance on each other."

American poet Edwin Markham wrote:

"THERE IS A DESTINY WHICH MAKES US BROTHERS, NONE GOES ON HIS WAY ALONE. All that we send into the lives of others, COMES BACK INTO OUR OWN."

The Gang Thang

All too often, teens who don't have a strong support system join a gang. It is a kind of support system, after all. Just not the kind you want. Once you're in a gang, the peer pressure is immense. A Tongan named Haloti Moala told me what life is like in a gang.

Haloti grew up in Tonga, one of nine children. His parents knew that if they wanted their kids to have a future they had to get out of Tonga, where there was little opportunity for education and high unemployment. After saving money for nine years trapping fish, Haloti's father moved his family to California, where he believed his dreams for his kids could come true.

Haloti recalls: "I remember running hard after the bus to take me to my English class and crying bitterly after missing it. I knew, even at age six, that learning the language and getting an education was vital to my success in my new home."

Haloti's family lived in Lennox, the ghetto of Englewood. The streets and schools were rough and it wasn't long before Haloti joined a gang.

Looking back, I realized my gang activity consumed me down to the clothes I wore, who I hung out with, the illegal activities I pursued, and what I valued every day. We didn't care about anyone but ourselves, and spent our time stealing, fighting, and causing trouble. My parents had no idea what we were doing because they were too busy working. I used to think they didn't support me in anything, but now I realize they were supporting me in the only way they knew how.

Although Haloti didn't use drugs, as an eighth grader he began selling them to make money and stay in the gang. That's when everything changed.

I was doing a drug deal with a friend when some guys drove up and started yelling about some bad drugs I had sold them earlier. Without warning, someone in the car shot my friend and they drove away. I watched my best friend bleed and die right in the road.

I couldn't believe what had just happened. The closest person in the world to me had just died. If the bullet had veered an inch or two it would have been me. I knew it was only a matter of time before I would end up dead.

By the time the police came they put it down as a drive-by shooting. I knew better. It was the drugs, the gangs, and one bad choice after another that killed my friend. From then on, I didn't try to stay away from drugs and gangs; I stopped cold turkey. I realized you are who you hang out with, and I didn't want a part of any of the stealing, lying, and violent lifestyle anymore.

About this same time, Haloti moved in with his sister and his brother-in-law, who became mentors for Haloti and channeled him toward school and sports. They became his new support system. "Although I stopped hanging out with gang members, it took a while to get the gang mentality out of me, and I still got in fights."

After graduating from high school, Haloti went to the University of Utah, where he played football, earned a college degree, and met his wife. Two decades later, Haloti is raising kids of his own and fulfilling his parents' dream. Unfortunately, a few of Haloti's brothers never escaped the gang life and are still in and out of prisons.

"I was fortunate," says Haloti. "The day my friend died I woke up and got out of a life that would have destroyed me."

If you're thinking about joining a gang, think again. If you're in a gang, get out, while you still can. Follow your gut. If it's telling you things aren't right with your group of friends, stop hanging out with them! You're better off having no support system at all than having the wrong kind.

This poem, written by teenager Jonathon Maldonado, exposes the brutal reality of gang life.

"Ten bald headed guys standing on the street corner
Smoke rising, eyes red, closed, seeing all in slow motion.
Throwing a party, bustin' a keg, confused, going nuts
Yelling, having a blast screaming, 'A que poner los borachos!'
Kick back at Isauul's canton, no school, but partying
With chicas, 'Que estan my chulas!'
Cruising on the dark highway, sneaking out with blue spray cans
Ready to landmark.
All this—all my homeboys will cause chaos.
Looks cool now. Later, a ticket to jail."

Here are four red flags that suggest that you may need a new group of friends.

1. *You have to change your clothes, language, friends, or standards in order to keep your friends.*

2. *You're doing stuff you don't feel good about, like stealing, fighting, or doing drugs.*

3. *You feel like you're being used.*

4. *Your life feels out of control.*

COURAGE IN THE MOMENT

No matter how well you prepare or how strong your support system is, you will face tough moments of peer pressure that you can never predict. You won't even have time to think, but must show courage in the moment.

Kourtney, a sophomore, was walking home from Skyline High School and came across a big group of kids standing in the middle of the road. As she got closer, she recognized a younger boy in her neighborhood named John. He looked terrified as he was being taunted by several older boys and being shoved back and forth among them. Forgetting that she was younger than the boys, and a girl at that, Kourtney pushed through the crowd and confronted the bullies.

"Hey, what are you doing to John?" she demanded. "What a bunch of sissies you are! What is it, ten to one? Leave him alone, and get out of here! Go on! I mean it!"

Surprisingly, after a few moments of silence, and with a few choice words spoken under their breath, the bullies slowly backed off. After about a minute they all left, one by one. John, who was visibly relieved, muttered "thanks" and quickly ran home.

John called Kourtney that night and told her he didn't know what he would have done if she hadn't stepped in. With emotion in his voice he said, "I didn't know you even knew my name."

Looking back, Kourtney confessed, "I don't know what I would have done if they had refused to leave. But it just wasn't right. They knew it too, and I called them on it."

In our tough moments, I hope we too can show courage like Kourtney.

BE A FRIEND ANYWAY

We've talked a lot about friends; how to choose them, how to make them, and how to be one. I encourage you to choose the high road. Choose friends who lift you, be a true friend yourself, and stand up to peer pressure. Be careful not to center your life on your friends. If you don't have enough friends, just follow the essentials of making good friends, and as surely as night follows day, they will come.

FRIENDS

HIGH ROAD
• Choose friends who build you up
• Be a true friend
• Stand up to peer pressure

LOW ROAD
• Choose friends who bring you down
• Be a fickle friend
• Give in to peer pressure

If you've made lots of bad friend decisions in the past, don't beat yourself up over it. Learn from it. You can make better decisions starting now.

One of the most amazing people of our time was Mother Teresa, a small, frail woman who devoted her life to helping the poor and the sick in impoverished countries. Her influence, beginning in the slums of Calcutta, India, now extends around the world. She owned no possessions, had no titles, and sought no fame. Yet she became an inspiration to millions. On a wall in her home in Calcutta was this beautiful poem, a version of "The Paradoxical Commandments" by Kent Keith. I like to think of it as rules to live by when it comes to friends.

People are often unreasonable, illogical, and self-centered.
LOVE THEM ANYWAY.

If you do good, people will accuse you of selfish ulterior motives.
DO GOOD ANYWAY.

If you are successful, you will win false friends and true enemies.
SUCCEED ANYWAY.

The good you do today will be forgotten tomorrow.
DO GOOD ANYWAY.

Honesty and frankness make you vulnerable.
BE HONEST AND FRANK ANYWAY.

What you spend years building may be destroyed overnight.
BUILD ANYWAY.

People really need help but may attack you if you help them.
HELP PEOPLE ANYWAY.

Give the world the best you have and you'll get kicked in the teeth.
GIVE THE WORLD THE BEST YOU HAVE ANYWAY.

● ● ● COMING ATTRACTIONS ● ● ●

Coming up, learn about the mysterious phoenix.
You'll never look at a bird the same way again.

BABY STEPS*

1. Be nice to everyone for one whole day. No bullying, gossiping, ignoring, excluding, hitting, scoffing, criticizing, sneering, sulking, snickering, or backbiting allowed. Sign your name and date only after you do it perfectly.

   Signature _____

   Date _____

2. In the center of the diagram, write down your life center. Consider the following possible centers: friends, school, popularity, work, fun, sports, hobbies, enemies, heroes, self, boyfriend, girlfriend, parents, faith, or something else. Consider the impact of that center on your life.

3. Write down a deposit you can make into one of your friends' RBA.

   Friend: _____

   Deposit I can make:_____

4. What are the top three things you could change that would make you a more likable friend?

   _____

   _____

   _____

   _____

* To keep an online journal of your Baby Steps progress, go to www.6decisions.com.

5. Is there someone who's been trying to break into your group of friends? If so, open your heart and let them in.

   Person trying to break in: _____

   What I can do to open my heart: _____

6. Memorize the quote by George Eliot, "**What do we live for if it is not to make life less difficult to each other?**"

7. Think of a friend who may have offended you recently. Sometime this week, shock them by treating unkindness with kindness.

8. If there's someone you constantly find yourself competing with or comparing yourself to, tap your heels together three times while repeating aloud: *"I will stop competing with and comparing myself to _____ "*

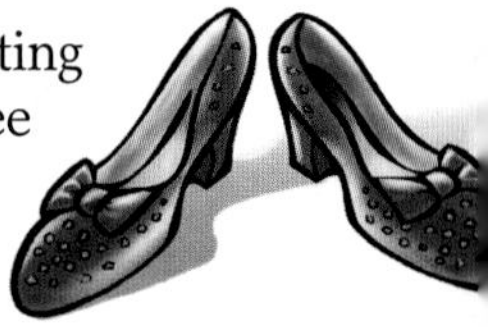

9. Do you have a friend or group of friends who are bringing you down? If so, figure out how you can exit the relationship or group.

   My exit plan: _____

   _____

10. Make a list of five things you would be willing to stand up and fight for in the face of peer pressure:

    _____

    _____

    _____

    _____

    _____

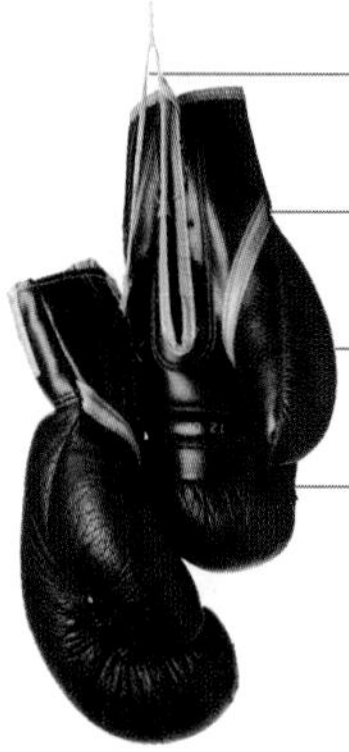

DECISION
3

PARENTS

HOW EMBARRASSING!

Top 10
Things You Oughta Know About Parents . . .

10. Recognize how hard child raising is.

Yuichiro Watanabe, 18, Tokyo, Japan

9. Seek your parents' advice and ask their opinions on hard things.

Preyma Palansiamy, 17, Selangor, Malaysia

8. Blood really is thicker than water – your family will always be there.

Aimee Peyton, 17, Tacoma, Washington

7. The less you push your parents for something, the better your chances are for getting what you want.

Naomi Davidson, 18, Layton, Utah

6. You'll be respected only when you respect them.

Arúnbold, 17, Khentíí, Mongolia

5. Nothing good comes from fighting with your parents and being against them.

Ai Babba, 19, Tokyo, Japan

4. Help around the house.

Ellen Jaynes, 15, Rexburg, Idaho

3. Do not underestimate their ideas and advice.

Daniel Tilahun Mezegebu, 19, Addis Ababa, Ethiopia

2. Do your homework, buy them flowers, and save money.

Joy Wu, 15, Singapore

1. Your parents don't always have a reason.

Mario Goninez Parada, 19, Mexico City

When I was a boy of fourteen, my father was
so ignorant I could hardly stand to have the old man around.
But when I got to be twenty-one, I was astonished at how
much he had learned in seven years.

— Mark Twain, author

During my first year of college, I began playing quarterback for our junior varsity team. The previous week, my team had just come off a big win. I threw lots of touchdown passes, and people were nice to me after the game.

The next week we played one of the best teams in the nation at our home field. Of course, I wanted to play well in front of my home crowd. Plus, my dad flew back from somewhere just to watch me play. I didn't think he would make it, but there he was, just before the whistle blew.

I had the worst game of my life. Their star defensive lineman repeatedly slammed me into the turf. I remember thinking, Could things get any worse? And they did. I made lots of stupid mistakes, threw a bunch of interceptions, and got physically beat up. We lost by about 30 points.

After the game, I was embarrassed and wanted to hide. You know how it goes after you lose badly and play poorly? In the locker room, everybody avoids you in case you're contagious. I showered and dressed in silence. When I came out, my dad was waiting for me. He took me in his arms, hugged me, looked me right in the eyes, and said, "That's the best game I've ever seen you play. Not because you won or had great stats, but because you were tougher than nails today. You were getting killed out there and you kept getting up. I've never been so proud of you."

I was shocked. I'd just played the worst game of my life and he had never been so proud? I didn't think that anyone could say anything to make me feel better, but he did. Instead of reminding me of all my mistakes, he focused on the one thing I did well: I kept getting back up. His affirming words sort of put everything into perspective. The world wasn't coming to an end. Life would go on.

I was lucky to have a great dad growing up. A great mom, too. Even though they embarrassed me a lot, they also really cared. And although I was convinced they came from another planet at times, mostly they were pretty cool. Just ask my friends.

I hope you're as lucky. I hope you have a great mom, or a great dad, or both. If you're not living with your own mom or dad, I hope you're being raised by a great uncle, grandmother, stepdad, or whatever. The good news is, even though they have problems and don't look as hot as they once did, most moms and dads really love their kids and would do anything for them.

This brings us to our third fork-in-the-road decision: **parents.**

What are you going to do about your relationship with your parents? Why is this one of the most important decisions you'll ever make? Because, like it or not, your parents are going to be a part of your life for a very long time. Ten years from now, your friends won't be around. You think they will be but they won't. You'll go your separate ways. Not so with your parents.

You'll probably live with one or both of them until you're 18 or 19, and then, depending upon the nature of your relationship, they will either be a great source of support or a real pain in the rear for the next several decades. They'll be around for all kinds of things, like graduations and marriages, births and deaths, ups and downs. Can you begin to see why your relationship with Mom and Dad is so huge?

Throughout this chapter, I use the word *parents* only for convenience. I realize there are all kinds of families. You may be being raised by your mom and your dad, just your mom, just your dad, an aunt or uncle, your mom and a stepdad, a grandmother, a guardian, a couple of aliens, or whatever. So, whenever you see the word *parents*, or *mom*, or *dad*, substitute the right word for your own situation. It doesn't take blood to be family, it only takes love.

So, what road will it be? You can choose the high road by building good relationships, working through problems, and showing love and respect. Or, you can take the low road by giving up on relationships, fighting or sulking each time you have a disagreement, and showing no respect.

PARENTS CHECKUP!

Before moving on, try this quick checkup to see where you stand on this parent thing.

CIRCLE YOUR CHOICE	NO WAY!				HECK YES!
1. I have a good relationship with my parents.	1	2	3	4	5
2. I show my parents respect.	1	2	3	4	5
3. My parents trust me.	1	2	3	4	5
4. I frequently help out my parents without being asked.	1	2	3	4	5
5. I know a lot about my parents, such as their likes, dislikes, dreams, values, and what makes them tick.	1	2	3	4	5
6. My parents know a lot about me, such as my likes, dislikes, dreams, values, and what makes me tick.	1	2	3	4	5
7. My parents and I communicate well with one another.	1	2	3	4	5
8. We are pretty good at solving problems or conflicts.	1	2	3	4	5
9. If and when we do fight or argue, my parents and I make up pretty quickly.	1	2	3	4	5
10. I can honestly say that I love my parents.	1	2	3	4	5
TOTAL					

Add up your score and see how you think you're doing.

 40-50 **You're on the high road. Keep it up!**

 30-39 **You're straddling the high and low roads. Move to higher ground!**

 10-29 **You're on the low road. Pay special attention to this chapter.**

This chapter is divided into four sections. The first section is called **The Relationship Bank Account.** Like the RBA for your friends, this is a nifty way to build better relationships with Mom and Dad. In **You're So Annoying,** we'll discuss how to cope with those things your parents do that annoy and upset you. **Closing the Gap** will explore ways to close the communication gap with your parents, even though they seem to speak Martian and you speak something human. I realize that some of you may have parents who are not coping with life, addicted to drugs, or abusive. That is a totally different type of situation, which needs special treatment. The last section, **When You Have to Raise Your Parents,** is written especially for teens with these challenges.

The Relationship Bank Account

Growing up, what pushed my mom's hot button was when I'd forget to take out the garbage. Too often, on Friday mornings, I'd hear Mom screaming: "Sean, get your rear end out of bed! I can hear the garbage truck coming and you forgot the garbage—again!" Eventually, she resorted to posting reminder notes on everything—the door, the fridge, the vanity, my pillow. "SEAN. DO THE GARBAGE OR DIE!"

I also learned ways to get on Mom's good side. Mom just loved it when I'd get good grades. She'd stick my report card up on the walls for all her friends to see and would brag, brag, brag. She also loved it when I'd help do the dishes or carry the groceries in. That's how I made up for all those missed garbage runs and kept our relationship in the plus column.

In the previous chapter on friends, we spoke about the Relationship Bank Account (RBA), which represents the amount of trust you have in a relationship. When it comes to your parents, how's your RBA? If $1,000 represents a strong relationship with your parents, how much do you have deposited? Is there really $1,000 in the bank or is it more like $500? Perhaps you're down around $0 or are overdrawn at -$1,000. Whatever your situation, the formula is the same: You build a relationship a deposit at a time.

Here are five deposits that seem to work well with parents. Of course, with every deposit, there's an opposing withdrawal.

DEPOSITS	WITHDRAWALS
✦ Understand what's important to them	– Assume you know
✦ Tell the truth	– Lie and cover up
✦ Sense the need and do it	– Wait until you're told
✦ Remember the little things	– Forget the little things
✦ Open up	– Close yourself off
✦ Use the most important words	– Avoid the most important words

UNDERSTAND WHAT'S IMPORTANT TO THEM

Never assume that a deposit for you is also a deposit for your parents. When you're with your friends, you might consider it a deposit if your parents leave you alone. However, when your parents are with their friends, they might consider it a deposit if you were to hang around and talk. You see, your parents use a different kind of cash than you do. I asked several parents the question: "What is the biggest deposit your teen could make into your RBA?" Listen carefully to what they said.

- *"Reading a book."*
- *"Keeping his room clean enough so that I can at least open the door to it."*
- *"The biggest deposit my daughter could make would be to be kind to her brothers and sisters."*
- *"I went into my daughter's room to say hi to her friends and to chat a minute. When I was leaving, she and her friends said, 'Stay and talk to us.' What a deposit that was!"*
- *"Our daughter attended a meeting where students were encouraged to forgive their parents for all the mistakes they had made. She told me that she felt I couldn't have done anything better. Wow!"*
- *"Doing their chores every day without being asked."*
- *"Doing anything without being asked."*

This is good stuff, and you could score a lot of points with Mom and Dad by trying out some of these cash deposits.

TELL THE TRUTH

Nothing destroys trust faster with your parents than lying. It's a huge withdrawal, and it takes months or even years to earn trust back. As one teen put it, "Be honest. Although the truth may be hard, it's ten times harder for your parents to find out that you lied."

Here's the thing—they're going to find out eventually. Parents have this amazing lie-detecting capability and they can sniff out cover-ups. So, be straight up with them because honesty never goes out of style.

Janna's story is a good illustration.

When I was 13 years old, I met Alfonso, who was 17. We thought we were in love. My parents, on the other hand, didn't want me to date until I was 16, especially an older guy. That's when the fights began.

One Friday night, I really wanted to be with Alfonso, so I made up a lie that I was going to a girl-friend's house and went to see him. It only took my parents about an hour to figure this out and I was busted. I was never to speak to Alfonso again and I was grounded for two weeks with no phone privileges. I was so mad!

This cycle of sneaking around and my parents catching me went on for years. It was hard because I loved my parents and all I wanted was for them to just realize that he wasn't a bad guy and to let me be with him. Alfonso and I stayed together, even though my relationship with my parents was horrible. They didn't trust me and I didn't even want to look at them.

When I turned 16, I was so happy because I could date Alfonso whenever I wanted. We dated for about six months. Then I realized that I was missing out on so much and just wanted to be a teenager. He was older and in college and I was not ready for that yet. I decided I needed to break up with Alfonso and apologize to my parents.

The situation was not easy to fix. I had lied to them for so long that they had zero trust in me. I felt like I was walking on eggshells. I knew that it was going to take time. I did everything that I could possibly do. I cleaned the house, took care of my sisters, and most of all told the truth about everything.

Eventually they decided that I was sincere and they began to open up to me again. I knew that they always loved me, but I needed to show that love in return. I now know that they knew a little bit more about life than I did.

SENSE THE NEED AND DO IT

Do the dishes need to be done? Does your little sister need a ride home? Does your mom need a break? If so, don't wait to be asked—sense the need and do it.

"My parents have never really expected a lot out of me," said 13-year-old Ryan. "I mean, I do my homework and some things at home, but that's about it. Once when my mom was really tired after dinner, I offered to clean up the kitchen for her. She almost died. It made me really happy to see her relax a little."

If you have a younger brother or sister, one of the greatest needs of parents is for you to be friends with your sibling(s) and help raise them. I remember when my younger brother Joshua was starting high school and how worried my dad was about him. He'd gone to a different middle school and hardly knew anyone. He was skinny and awkward. I sensed the need and I tried to be there for Joshua. I even helped coach his freshman football team. I'll never forget how grateful my dad was for my efforts. Ka-ching!

I was talking to a 16-year-old named Destin, and, when I asked him about his mom, his eyes lit up. "My mom? I would turn the world for my mom. I love her. Sometimes we bump heads. But we make up."

He told me his mom had just divorced and was overwhelmed. He was really worried about her. He figured the best thing he could do was to help her out with his 7-year-old brother and 9-year-old sister.

"Right now," said Destin, "I'm basically what you could call the man of the house. I try to help keep everything level, so Mom isn't stressed or upset all the time. After school, I pick up my sister and brother and I take them home, make sure they do their homework, eat, then have time to play and do stuff like that. If she needs me I'll run errands or just basically do anything I can for her."

REMEMBER THE LITTLE THINGS

When it comes to relationships, the little things are the big things. What are the little things? A kind word. A warm smile. A thank-you note. Gabby told me this story:

Although my relationship with my mom isn't horrible, it still had damage. I decided I should write my mom a letter and tell her how much she truly meant to me. I slipped the note in her car and went on with my day. I can't say I gave it much more thought. To my surprise, when I got home my mom was waiting at the door and gave me a hug. She told me that was the best gift she had ever received from me—just a simple thanks and recognition for all she does.

This reminds me of the time I gave my mom a special gift for Mother's Day. Instead of buying her the usual bottle of perfume that she'd always pretend to appreciate ("Oh, Sean. Perfume...again! How splendid!"), I wrote a poem about what a great mom she was called *A Boy and His Mother*. She told me it was the best gift I'd ever given her and even hung it on her "wall of fame."

OPEN UP

Does this sound familiar? If so, you're normal. Sometimes you just don't feel like talking, especially when it feels like an interrogation. However, to everything there is a season—a time to clam up and a time to open up. The fact is, you'll never get close to your parents unless you share what's going on in that head of yours.

Teens often find it hard to say, "Mom, Dad, what do you think I should do?" But it's smart because your parents may not always be cool, but they're usually wise. You know more about fashion and trends but they know more about love and happiness. They're especially good at helping you cope with betrayals, resolve boyfriend and girlfriend dramas, and feel better when you've had a horrible day.

I once had an old friend of the family tell me: "Sean, if you will talk to your parents about all your important decisions, you will never make a major mistake." His advice was so unusual that I've never forgotten it and tried to follow it.

But what if you want to open up to your parents but you're afraid of the outcome? You're scared they might get angry or disappointed, and say things like "You did what?!" or "What a stupid idea!" Here's a method that works almost every time. Start by saying something like, "Mom, I really want to talk to you about something but I'm afraid you'll get mad if I tell you."

"Oh, no, I won't get mad," your mom might say.

"Yes, you will. You always get mad and then I regret saying anything."

"I swear, honey. I won't jump down your throat. Just tell me what's going on." By this point, her curiosity will be so strong she'll be dying to know what's up.

"Well, OK. But you've got to promise to listen and not get upset."

This approach will prepare them for what you're about to say. As a result, they'll probably listen better and be more careful about their response.

USE THE MOST IMPORTANT WORDS

When it comes to getting along with your parents, the single most important word is **please.** The two most important words are **thank you.** The three most important words are **I love you.** The four most important words are **How can I help?** There is power and magic in each.

Saying **please** is polite and shows respect. The same goes for **thank you.** Nothing perturbs parents more than ingratitude. So look for ways to say **thank you,** whenever you can.

"Thanks, Mom. Dinner was yummy."

"Dad, thanks a lot for letting me use the car last night. I had a great time."

I love you is the next most important phrase. In some homes, hugs and *sure love ya*s are passed around freely. In others, it's not so warm and fuzzy. In fact, it's downright cold. If that's your lot, try being a cycle breaker and starting a new trend in your home, where you express love and affection in one way or another. It only takes one person to get started. Here's how Sherwin did it.

My dad—he's really cool. It's just that he has a really short temper, so like I'm afraid sometimes. When I was small my dad would always yell at me and it was hurting my soul. But, inside, I wouldn't blame him. I always thought it was me.

I was watching a show where the dad dies and the kid never got to say "I love you." So, I was like, what if I never tell my dad I love him and the last thing I say to him is, "Yeah, I'll put the lasagna in the oven." Since then, every day I give my dad a hug. It's my way of saying, "I love you."

The first time I gave my dad a hug I was surprised he didn't find it weird. I told him that I never wanted to say good-bye. No matter what happened I wanted us to be on each other's good side. He felt the same way. He made it perfectly clear that I could always turn to him if I needed him. I love him. Even though at times I might hate his guts, I hug him every day. No questions asked. Our relationship has really gotten better.

As James Taylor sings,

"Shower the people you love with love. Show them the way that you feel."

How can I help? is the next most important phrase. Caution: Make sure your parents are sitting down when you try this out on them because it might give 'em a stroke.

"Mom, I know you're totally stressed right now. How can I help?"

"Oh, no! Look at the garage. It looks like a tornado hit it," says your dad.

"How can I help, Dad?" you say back.

After all that's been said about building the RBA with your parents, if I had to narrow it down to one thing it would be: *Always keep your room clean.* For some strange reason, they really like that. You can even make a boatload of mistakes and be forgiven as long as your room is clean. It also helps if your brother or sister has a really messy room, because it gives you an advantage.

You're So Annoying

As we all know, parents can be annoying. Specifically, these are five of the top complaints:

>> MY PARENTS ARE ALWAYS COMPARING ME.

>> MY PARENTS ARE NEVER SATISFIED.

>> MY PARENTS ARE EMBARRASSING.

>> MY PARENTS ARE OVERPROTECTIVE.

>> MY PARENTS ARE ALWAYS FIGHTING.

With each complaint, you have a choice to make. You can let it drive you insane and lash out. Or, you can find ways to deal with it.

If you're struggling with what your parents are like, remember to focus on your circle of control. Don't waste your energy on things you can't control, like your parents' weaknesses or their annoying habits. Instead, focus on what you can control, like your attitude and your reactions to what they do. You can't make choices for your parents. You can only make choices for yourself.

MY PARENTS ARE ALWAYS COMPARING ME

"Why can't you be more like your brother?" Ouch!

"Why don't you get involved in extracurricular things, like your friend Tayva? Now, she has her act together." Ouch!

Sondra told me how she always felt put down by her father whenever he compared her to others.

When I was small, my dad was really nice and stuff, but not anymore. I have two little brothers and an older sister. Me and my sister are just 11 months apart. My dad compares me with my sister a lot. My sister is really smart. He always tells me, "You're not capable enough." He tells me I'm not university material. But it's fine. I mean, I'm kind of used to it.

Just recently, we were at my aunt's house and they were talking about who looks like who. My dad said, "Yeah, Sondra looks like me, but her brain doesn't look like mine, but her sister's does." My dad has a big forehead and so does my sister, and he said, "People with big foreheads are smart; that's why Sondra doesn't have a big forehead." I was feeling really bad about myself. I wanted to have the relationship that he had with my sister.

I'll bet you a thousand bucks that this father really loves Sondra and is unaware of how badly he's hurting her feelings. It's hard not to compare yourself to that girl with the perfect hair or that guy with the 4.0 GPA. And, just as you struggle, so do your parents. It's a human tendency. For some strange reason and with the best of intentions, parents think that comparing you to someone else will motivate you. As every teen knows, it does the opposite.

Sometimes they won't come right out and compare you but they'll do it in subtle ways: As McKayla put it: "My mom says things about my friends being feminine which implies I'm not."

If you're being compared a lot, consider this. First, try not to take it too personally. Just remember how it feels and make a resolution not to do it to your kids.

Second, you may want to make them aware of how you feel. The next time your mom or dad compares you to a sibling, a friend, or a Greek god, say something like, "Mom. Dad. You know what? It really hurts when you compare me to so and so. I'm different from so and so and I'd appreciate it if you wouldn't talk that way anymore."

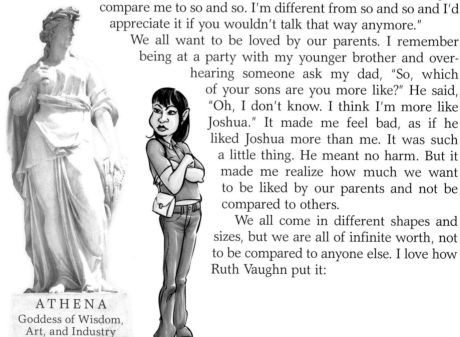

We all want to be loved by our parents. I remember being at a party with my younger brother and overhearing someone ask my dad, "So, which of your sons are you more like?" He said, "Oh, I don't know. I think I'm more like Joshua." It made me feel bad, as if he liked Joshua more than me. It was such a little thing. He meant no harm. But it made me realize how much we want to be liked by our parents and not be compared to others.

We all come in different shapes and sizes, but we are all of infinite worth, not to be compared to anyone else. I love how Ruth Vaughn put it:

ATHENA
Goddess of Wisdom,
Art, and Industry

"YOU ARE A
once-in-a-lifetime,
NEVER-BEFORE-ON-EARTH,
NEVER-TO-BE-AGAIN,
personality.

Understand the importance of that."

MY PARENTS ARE NEVER SATISFIED

Sarina told me:

Me and my dad don't see eye to eye. He thinks that I could do better in school even though I pulled six As and two Cs. All he could say to me was, "Get your grades and your attendance up." Which really, really made me mad.

This is a classic challenge I call the never-satisfied syndrome. Your parents constantly rag on you. You can't seem to do anything right. You want them to be proud of you, but you can't seem to satisfy them.

If this is how you feel, don't start thinking that your parents don't love you. Like the comparing thing, they often don't realize what they're doing and they do mean well. Maybe this is the way they were raised. When you become a parent, it's not like you get a user's manual on how to be an awesome parent.

One thing you can try is to point out all the good stuff you are doing. For example, Sarina might say: "Yeah, I can always do better, Dad. But you have to admit that getting six As last term is pretty good and it's a lot better than last year."

MY PARENTS ARE EMBARRASSING

I don't know how it is with you, but my parents embarrassed me so badly when I was young that I don't get embarrassed anymore. I'm immune.

I was born in Ireland, where my family lived for a few years, and my mom picked up on some Irish traditions. When we moved back to the States, on each St. Patrick's Day she'd show up at my elementary school with her big hair and a big box of shamrock cookies. She'd then sing a medley of Irish folk songs like "When Irish Eyes Are Smiling" in her operatic voice. My teachers and classmates always got a big kick out of it. I'd be hiding under my desk—dying.

Even more embarrassing was Dad. We'd go to movies together, and when he got tired he'd wad up his coat for a pillow and take a nap in the aisle. One time he took me and my siblings to a Broadway play in New York, mysteriously disappeared during the middle of the play, and showed up thirty minutes later with sacks of Chinese food.

My dad is an author, and people would often say to me, *"Are you Stephen R. Covey's son?"*

"Uh, yeah."

"Wow! What's it like to have such a famous father?"

"Uh, I dunno."

"Would you please tell your dad that his books have changed my life?"

"Ummm. OK. Whatever," I'd say.

But I'd be thinking: "Do you realize that my dad goes jogging in black knee-high dress socks?"

YOOHOO...SON! YOU FORGOT YOUR ATHLETIC SUPPORTER!

When I turned nineteen, I finally read one of Dad's books to see why everyone was so enthralled with him and was amazed at how much he had grown.

So, maybe your mom and dad embarrass you like mine did. Or maybe they're out of touch when it comes to fashion and music. So what! They're usually very much in touch when it comes to important things, like how to bounce back after you just got dumped.

In case you hadn't noticed, they do have quite a bit more experience than you do. As Anya, a student from Florida put it, "They have experienced so much: They're my number-one resource to the real world." Author Wayne Rice uses a little mathematical equation to make this point, as shown below.

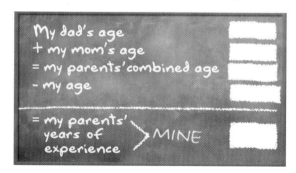

My dad's age
+ my mom's age
= my parents' combined age
- my age

= my parents' years of experience > MINE

They're probably smarter than you think. It's like this sign I once read, "Oh, to be only half as wonderful as my child thought I was, and only half as stupid as my teenager thinks I am."

MY PARENTS ARE OVERPROTECTIVE

Jake always felt his parents were overprotective.

Growing up, I was not allowed to watch the Power Rangers *TV show because it was too violent. When I was nine, I came home from school a few weeks after my birthday and went into my parents' room and absentmindedly opened a chest at the foot of their bed. The first thing that caught my eye was a green Power Ranger action figure, still half covered with wrapping paper and a tag that read*

To: Jake

From: Steve

I couldn't believe it. My own parents had swiped my present! So I confronted them about it. After a short argument, they conceded that they should have told me about it. I asked if I could have it now since I found it. They still refused to let me play with my own Power Ranger action figure.

Maybe your parents aren't swiping your presents like Jake's did. But do you ever feel they're too controlling?

Check each statement below that is true about your parents.

- ☐ **They always have to know exactly where I've been and whom I've been with.**
- ☐ **They have set a strict curfew for me.**
- ☐ **They always rescue me when I get into trouble.**
- ☐ **They are judgmental about the friends I hang out with.**
- ☐ **They are very selective about whom I date.**
- ☐ **If I mess up, they put additional restrictions on me.**
- ☐ **They are nosy and don't respect my privacy.**
- ☐ **They are overly strict and have too many rules.**

If you checked many of these, there are two different conclusions you might draw. Your parents don't trust you or they care about you a bunch. In most cases, so-called overprotective parents simply care a lot and show it through lots of rules and wanting to know everything. So don't get too hung up about parental rules. After all, if you had to choose, don't you think you'd rather have parents that seem to care too much than parents who don't seem to care at all?

If you're fully worthy of your parents' trust and you think they're still ridiculously strict, what can you do? Unfortunately, I don't have a good answer except to say: remain worthy of their trust. Keep telling the truth. And be careful not to become so preoccupied with their strictness that it makes you want to rebel.

In high school I had a good friend Randy who had a very strict mother. His mom always seemed to have some reason for not letting Randy do stuff with the guys, like going camping or to a concert. At first, Randy didn't seem to mind. After a while, he let it drive him crazy. When he finally got out on his own, he rebelled for several years just to get back at his mom. He finally settled down, but it was a sad few years for Randy and I believe he regretted his choices.

One of the big challenge areas is curfews. Your parents like them—you don't. Like 'em or not, most teens have curfews, even if they won't admit it. As all teens know, curfews were invented to ruin your life. In reality, your parents are worried about drugs, drunk drivers, and psychos who roam the night. It sounds ridiculous, but it's the truth. A curfew, however, can work to your advantage as well. If you ever have to get out of an uncomfortable situation, blame it on your curfew. "Sorry, but I've gotta leave. It's that stupid curfew of mine."

"Friday night you stayed out until almost 9:00, yesterday you had cola instead of milk and this morning you forgot to floss. Your father and I are afraid you're getting too wild."

© 1999 Randy Glasbergen.   www.glasbergen.com

The good news is: Curfews can usually be negotiated a little. Here are three techniques you may want to try.

1. **I'll scratch your back if you scratch mine.** Sometimes parents will bend the rules a little if you do something big for them. "Mom, if I clean the basement, will you let me stay out late this Friday?"

2. **The Reservoir.** Show that you are responsible by obeying your curfew with exactness for a period and building a reservoir of trust. "Mom, if I religiously follow my curfew all summer, could we push it back an hour later starting next fall?"

3. **The Big Event.** If you have something big coming up, let your parents know well in advance. Often they'll be willing to make exceptions. "Mom, next Saturday, Laura's having a party for semester break. Would it be OK if I stayed out late that night?"

MY PARENTS ARE ALWAYS FIGHTING

What's it like in your home? Peaceful or a war zone? As one teen put it, "My parents fight a lot and have a lot of arguments. They usually make up but it scares me."

When you add a little alcohol to the mix, it can really spark things, as April shared. "My father drinks. He drinks a lot. When we're sitting together at the table for dinner he kind of starts with my older brother. My mom tries to stop them, and at that moment, my family just falls apart."

The fighting and yelling can get so bad that you can hardly stand to be home, as these lyrics from "Stay Together for the Kids" from the group blink-182 illustrate.

"Their **anger** hurts my ears
Been running strong for seven years

Rather than fix the problems,
they **never** solve them
It makes no sense at all
I see them every day
We get along, so why can't they?

If this is what he wants
and this is what she wants

then why is there so much **PAIN?**"

In such situations, the only thing you can control is you. You can't change your parents, but you can choose not to yell, scream, and fight back. You can be pleasant. You can be a peacemaker. And that's a start.

Danette faced just such a challenge.

My parents didn't get along so well. When I was fifteen, my parents had been picking at each other as usual and I went off to bed. The next thing I remember was being awakened by the sound of my mother yelling something about "Don't you leave without saying good-bye to the kids."

I was completely shocked as my father entered the room to tell me that he loved me. I sat straight up and asked what was going on. I still remember the panic that gripped my heart. He told me good-bye and all I could say was "Wait!" I was thinking there had to be something I could do to fix this.

"Can we just talk about this?" I asked.

Their bedroom was right across the hall and the three of us went in there and sat down. I remember reminding them of the commitments they had made, how much I loved and needed them both, and asked them to pray together. I prayed aloud for us all. My parents were both in tears when I finished. My dad stood up and told me thank you and that he loved me and left.

I cried most of the night and was in a daze the next day at school. But, when I came home, my dad was back. He explained that he just needed some time and space to think.

I think my mom did, too. I had reminded them both of why they were together and learned, once again, that I can't make choices for anyone but myself.

This story had a happy ending but all endings aren't so happy. The point is, Danette was a positive influence and a peacemaker in her own home. She focused on what she could do something about.

Dealing with Divorce

All that fighting can sometimes lead to divorce. It's sad to say, but about every other marriage ends in divorce. My parents are still together, so I can't say, "I know how you feel." I don't. But Lindsey does. Lindsey struggled with her parents' divorce but has since adjusted well. I asked her what advice she'd give to other teens.

I'd start by saying, it's not your fault. When my parents got divorced they made it a point to let me know it didn't have anything to do with me.

At first it's really hard because you feel like you'll never be able to adjust to life without both parents being at the same house. After a while, though, it becomes sort of natural and you'll even find that there are ups to the situation. For example, you'll most likely get twice the Christmas gifts and birthday presents, even though you don't get to enjoy holidays with both parents.

The divorce made me feel like something was missing. I didn't realize it was the divorce that was causing that feeling. I was frustrated, mad, and sad for a long time, but I eventually got used to the idea. I realized that I wouldn't want them to be together if they weren't happy. I felt alone because I didn't think other people understood what I was going through. Then I realized that all of my three siblings did! So we started talking and it made it a lot easier for all of us.

At first, I was really mad at my big brother who chose to live with my dad. I regret holding that against him because now we are practically best friends. All in all just try to make the best of it and take it one day at a time.

Dr. Ken Cheyne also offered this advice on what teens can do to make divorce easier:

Be fair. Most teens say it's important that parents don't try to get them to take sides.

Keep in touch. It can be a good idea to keep in touch with a parent you see less often because of distance. Even a quick e-mail just to say, "I'm thinking of you" helps ease the feelings of missing each other.

Live your life. Sometimes during a divorce, parents may be so caught up in their own changes it can feel like your life is on hold. When things are changing at home, it can really help to keep some things, such as school activities and friends, the same. Take care of yourself too, by eating right and getting regular exercise—two great stress busters.

Let others support you. If you're feeling down or upset, let your friends and family members support you. These feelings usually pass. If they don't, and if you're feeling depressed or stressed out, or if it's hard for you to concentrate on your normal activities, let a counselor or therapist help you. There are therapists who specialize in teens who are dealing with divorce. Your parents, school counselor, or doctor can help you find one. Also, it can really help to talk with other people your age who are going through a similar experience.

THE PHOENIX

You may have heard the myth of the Phoenix. After a life of one thousand years, it lies down on the funeral pyre and burns to ashes. From the ashes, a new bird arises that lives for another thousand years. The point is, sometimes new life is born out of the ashes of a setback, like the divorce of your parents. For example, your parents may be happier living apart. Coping well with a divorce can help you build strength, compassion, and maturity. You may develop closer bonds with a brother or sister because you have to count on each other more.
Bethany wrote:

The day before my senior year in high school, everything changed. I came home from work to discover that my dad had left my mom and me. The note read "That's the way it goes. Bye."

At first, I felt okay with the situation. Not having my dad in the house was almost a blessing, because I didn't have to hear him say mean and nasty things about my mom. However, we soon discovered that the bills were at least a month behind. My mom could only work three days a week because of a broken ankle. I had to change jobs, but, even then, I wasn't making nearly enough money.

My whole senior year was spent crying and trying not to spend my money so I could help with bills. At first, Mom had a really hard time accepting help from me. She wouldn't tell me how far behind she was. I was young and naïve, and didn't realize how much we were in debt.

I applied and was accepted to college. After two months, I had to come home to help my mom with the bills. I remember so many times I would just burst into tears because it was so unfair. I was supposed to be at school having fun and getting my degree, but instead I was working a full-time job to help support myself and my mom.

I finally realized that I couldn't let the bad things that had happened ruin my life. I had to prove that I was strong enough to make something of my life.

That was four years ago. Since then, I purchased my own house where I now live with my mom. I work a full-time job as a supervisor at an office-supply store, and I also run my own business. I'm in a loving relationship with the man of my dreams. There's not one thing I would change if given the chance. I believe, that in some strange way, I owe it all to the hard times I faced when my dad abandoned us.

Closing the Gap

"Haven't you heard of knocking?" Natasha complains as her mom enters her bedroom.

"You need to clean up your room, Natasha. This is ridiculous."

"I'll get to it later, Mom. I'm busy right now."

"No, you'll do it now."

"This is my room, Mom. I'll clean it up. Just give me a few minutes. And don't barge into my room anymore without knocking."

"This is my house. So don't start telling me what I can or can't do in my own house."

"If you can hear me, give me a sign."

"Yeah, but this is my room, and I need my privacy."

"You're not getting any privacy until your room's clean. So let's get movin'."

"Ucht, Mom. **Please** just get out."

Do you ever feel like you and your parents speak different languages? Well, you do. Sort of. You see, while you worry about what your friends are going to say about your new haircut, they worry about how they're going to pay the bills. You and your parents see life through a different pair of glasses. You say one thing and your parents hear something else. Or vice versa.

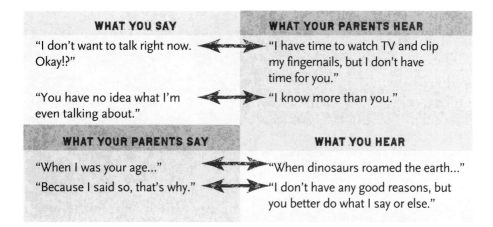

WHAT YOU SAY	WHAT YOUR PARENTS HEAR
"I don't want to talk right now. Okay!?"	"I have time to watch TV and clip my fingernails, but I don't have time for you."
"You have no idea what I'm even talking about."	"I know more than you."

WHAT YOUR PARENTS SAY	WHAT YOU HEAR
"When I was your age..."	"When dinosaurs roamed the earth..."
"Because I said so, that's why."	"I don't have any good reasons, but you better do what I say or else."

To understand what I'm talking about, try this little experiment. Turn to page 150 and look at the picture for just one second. Then, without looking at it yourself (no peeking, now), hand this book to someone near you, preferably one of your parents, and have them turn to page 159 and look at the picture on that page for one second.

Now, together, both of you look at the picture on page 163 and describe what you see. Is that a picture of a young woman or a saxophone player? Most likely, you will see a saxophone player and the other person will see a woman. Keep talking until you both see both images. You may want to look at the pictures on page 150 and 159 to understand how you were conditioned to see what you saw.

Think about it. If a one-second experience can make you see this picture differently, don't you think years of experiences can influence you and your parents to see the world differently? When you communicate with your parents, they see a young woman and you see a saxophone player, and both of you are right. There are always two sides to the story. This is called a *communication gap*.

GETTING TO KNOW YOU

One great way to overcome the communication gap is to get to know each other better. You may spend a bunch of time with one or both of your parents, but just how well do you know them?

Grab a pen and try to answer these fifteen questions about your parents. You can answer them about your mom only, your dad only, or both. When you're done, hand your parents this book and see if they can answer the fifteen questions about you on page 149. Then, when you're all finished, get together and talk about your answers. I'll bet there's a bunch you never knew.

How Well Do You Know YOUR MOM/DAD?

1. What color are your mom's/dad's eyes? _____

2. What is your mom's/dad's favorite thing to do? _____
_____

3. What would your mom/dad consider to be the nicest thing you could do for her/him? _____
_____

4. If your mom/dad had all the time and money in the world, what would they spend their time doing? _____
_____

5. What are your mom's/dad's views on marriage? _____
_____

6. What is your mom's/dad's greatest unfulfilled dream? _____
_____

7. What was your mom's/dad's first full-time job? _____

8. Who is your mom's/dad's closest friend? _____

9. How did your parents first meet? _____
_____

10. What is your mom's/dad's favorite kind of music? _____

11. What is your mom's/dad's favorite TV show? _____

12. Who did your mom/dad vote for in the last election? _____

13. Does your mom/dad gas up the car when the tank is half-empty or wait until it is nearly empty? _____

14. Where is your mom's/dad's favorite vacation spot? _____
_____

15. What would your mom/dad rather do: watch a good TV show, go out to the movies, go to dinner with some friends, or read a book? _____
_____

How Well Do You Know YOUR TEEN?

1. What is your teen's favorite subject in school? _____

2. What would your teen consider to be the nicest thing you could do for them? _____

3. What would your teen like to become when they grow up? _____

4. What is your teen's favorite kind of music? _____

5. What is your teen's hot button, the thing that really makes them mad?

_____

6. What is your teen's favorite Internet site? _____

7. What is the one thing your teen wishes they could change about him- or herself? _____

8. What would your teen really like to talk about with you, but is afraid to?

_____

9. What pet would your teen prefer to have: a dog, a cat, a hamster, a horse, a bird, a turtle, a snake, no pet at all, or all of the above? _____

10. Who is your teen's best friend? _____

11. If your teen could travel anywhere in the world, where would they go?

_____

12. What would your teen rather do: go to a movie with friends, read a good book, play games on the computer, or play their favorite sport? _____

13. Does your teen have a boyfriend or girlfriend right now? If so, who is it?

_____

14. What has been one of the high points of your teen's life so far?

_____

15. What was your teen's favorite vacation ever? _____

_____

So, how well do you know your parents and how well do they know you? If either of you got 11 or more of the 15 questions right, not bad! If you got between 6 and 10 right, you ought to hang out together a little more. If you got 5 or fewer right, you should start communicating. It's called *talking*. It's always helpful to see life through the eyes of another. It reminds me of Jack Handy's deep thought:

> **❝** Before you criticize someone,
> you should walk a mile in their shoes.
> Then, if you do, you're a mile away — and
> you've got their shoes. **❞**

ALL IT TAKES IS ONE

Do you ever feel that you have the same conversation again and again with your mom or dad? Or that you can predict the outcome of almost every conversation?

"Marc, don't you think you've had enough soda for one day?"

"C'mon, Dad. It's not going to kill me."

"Well, it's not going to make you healthy either."

"I don't tell you what you can drink, so why are you always telling me what I can or can't drink?"

"I'm not telling you what you can do, I'm only saying..."

"Yeah, yeah. I know. I've heard it all before."

If you and your parents have a communication gap, even one the size of the Grand Canyon, have hope. You can change the outcome of almost every conversation if just one of you is willing to take a different approach. You may be thinking, "Yeah, but you don't know my dad. He's never going to change. He's impossible." Well, maybe he *is* impossible and maybe he *won't* ever change. But you can. You can start to communicate in a better, smarter way. Here are three time-tested skills that are foundational to all good communication.

Skill #1: Think Win-Win

Are you always thinking about what's in it for you, without thinking about what's in it for them? As Mariel put it, "Ever since I entered my teenage years, I have had trouble communicating with my parents. When I wanted something I would tell them what I wanted and how it was going to be. I never really cared about what they wanted."

Well, you've got to care about what they want, too. This is called *Think Win-Win,* the 4th habit of highly effective teens.

The ironic thing is that if you care about what they want, you'll get a lot more of what you want. The opposite of thinking Win-Win is thinking Win-Lose, or only thinking of yourself. You see conversations as a competition, and you're out to win. It sounds something like this.

Reggie comes home from school. He's tired, so he turns on the TV and plops on the coach as his mom hurriedly enters the room.

"Reggie, honey. I don't think you have time to watch TV. I really need your help right now."

"I'm tired, Mom. I just want to watch for a few minutes."

"Sorry. But we don't have time for that today. The Guercios are coming over tonight and I need your help cleaning the house, right now. It's a wreck."

"The Guercios? Why do they always have to come over? I can't stand them. Yuck."

"You don't have to like my friends, but I at least want you to be polite and say hello."

"Fine. But I'm not helping you clean the house."

Reggie, by only thinking of himself, just blew it. He won and his mom lost, at least in the short term. But the problem with Win-Lose is it will come back to bite you. Two days from now, when Reggie wants permission to use the car, his mom might think, Why should I let you take the car when you refused to help me the other day?

HELLO.

With only a smidgeon of effort, and a little Win-Win thinking, Reggie could have turned the whole thing around. Let's try it again.

"Reggie, honey. I don't think you have time to watch TV. I really need your help right now."

"I'm tired, Mom. I just want to watch for a few minutes."

"Sorry, but we don't have time for that today. The Guercios are coming over tonight and I need your help cleaning the house, right now. It's a wreck."

"Well...Okay. I'll help you clean for a few minutes. But I don't want to spend all night with your friends. I'll just say hello, and that's all."

"That's fine. Thanks so much for helping me clean up. You have no idea how busy I am right now."

By sacrificing a little bit of what he wanted now, Reggie just made a big deposit into his mom's RBA. He will probably get more of what *he* wants later.

When you and your parents don't see eye to eye or when you really want to persuade them to see your point of view, trying using a T chart. You can do it in your head or you can write it down. On one side, list what the Win is for you. On the other side, list what you think the Win is for them. In the case of Reggie and his mom, it might look like this.

WHAT'S A WIN FOR YOU?	WHAT'S A WIN FOR THEM?
I'm tired and want to watch TV	Mom desperately needs help cleaning right now
I don't want to hang out with Mom's friends all night	Mom wants me to make a little effort with her friends

Try out these Think Win-Win phrases and watch the magic it creates:

- *How do you see it?*
- *What would make this a win for you?*
- *I think the important things for you are...*
- *What's your side of the story?*

Skill #2: Seek First to Understand, Then to Be Understood

This is the 5th habit of highly effective teens. It simply means listen first, then talk. Our tendency is to talk first, then pretend to listen.

Tyrone is 16 and has a curfew of midnight. Tonight, he is going out with some of his friends to play pool, and wants to stay out later. He approaches his dad.

"I'm sorry, Tyrone. But we've talked about this before. You know your curfew. I want you home at twelve tonight and that's final."

"But, Dad. You're so unfair. All of my friends have much later curfews than I do. Their parents let them do what they want. Steve doesn't even have a curfew."

"I don't really care what kind of curfews your friends have. In our family, we have our own rules."

"Why are you always trying to control my life? I'm sick of it," Tyrone says with an attitude.

"If you keep talking that way, son, I'll never let you stay out later."

"I don't see why you're making such a big deal out of this. Jeez, it's not like I'm ten years old anymore. I'm outta here."

Notice what happened here. Since no one was listening, no real communication was going on. Tyrone's dad is clearly a little high-strung. But Tyrone, by making no attempt to understand, didn't help his cause.

So, how do you listen? You act like a mirror. What does a mirror do? It reflects. It doesn't argue or fight back. Mirroring is simply this: *Repeat in your own words what the other person is saying and feeling.* It's almost mimicking as a parrot would, but unlike a parrot, your goal isn't to mock the other person, your goal is to really understand them.

For example, your mom says to you, "I really don't like you hanging out with Kara Johnson. I don't like what she does to you. You always act so bratty after being with her."

Your typical response might be: "Well, too bad. I like being with her."

A mirroring response would be: "So, you think Kara is a bad influence on me."

Your dad says, "I think it's a huge mistake to quit soccer. You've been playing since you were eight and you're going to throw all that away."

Your typical response might be: "It's none of your business."

A mirroring response would be: "I can see you're really worried about me quitting."

Our tendency is to prepare our next comment while the other person is talking, and, as a result, we don't really listen. When you listen sincerely, you'll find that there is usually a deeper issue than what appears on the surface. It's like peeling an onion. You may have to peel back several layers before uncovering the real issue.

Let's return to Tyrone, but this time let's pretend Tyrone tries to understand his dad.

"I'm sorry, Tyrone. But we've talked about this before. You know your curfew. I want you home at twelve tonight and that's final."

MOM, DAD...I'M GLAD WE HAD THIS TIME TOGETHER...I TOTALLY SEE YOUR POINT OF VIEW!

"You take this curfew stuff pretty seriously."

"You bet I do. Kids get into so much trouble late at night. That's when all the accidents happen. You read the papers. Nothing good happens after midnight. I just want you to be safe."

"So, it's a safety issue for you, huh?"

"That's it exactly. I know you probably think that I'm too strict, but I'm doing it for your own good. You've got a lot going for you, son, and I don't want you to mess up. That's all."

Tyrone nods and remains silent.

"Listen, Ty. Just come home on time tonight, then we can talk about this more some other time. Maybe we can push your curfew back a little or make some exceptions. My goal isn't to ruin all your fun, I just want you to be safe. Know what I mean?"

Compare this conversation with the previous one. What a difference! And all it took was a couple of mirroring responses by Tyrone. For the first time, Dad feels understood. In addition, Tyrone better understands his dad. He realizes that his dad isn't such a jerk—he simply wants Tyrone to be safe. Although Tyrone may not get exactly what he wants right now, he's on his way to having more flexibility on his curfew later.

When trying to understand someone, sometimes the best thing you can do is just be silent, as Tyrone did. You're not ignoring them, you're just absorbing what they're saying, and it gives them a chance to fully express themselves without being cut off.

Below is the traditional Chinese character for listening. Notice that listening involves more than just your ears; it also requires your eyes and heart.

EARS — EYES — HEART

Here are some great Seek First to Understand phrases to use:

- *"So, you're saying that..."*
- *"As I get it, you feel..."*
- *"If I understand you correctly, you think..."*
- *"You feel _____ about _____."*

Skill #3: Synergize

Do you ever hit roadblocks with your parents? You see things one way and your parents see it another. You want more independence and they want more control. You want a credit card and they don't think you're ready. It seems as though it's either your way or their way.

In truth, there is almost always a third option, a new and better way. You just have to be mature enough to talk it through. I call this *Synergize,* Habit 6 of The 7 Habits.

I know a teen named Nikki who really wanted a dog. Her mom, on the other hand, would rather die than have a dog. She was a germ freak and couldn't stand the thought of an animal spreading disease throughout her house. "Do you want a dog or do you want a mother?" she'd often say.

They argued about it for months.

"Why won't you let me get a dog? All my friends have dogs and their parents don't even care. What's the big deal?" Nikki would cry.

"There's no way we're getting a dog. It's like taking care of another child. And I'll end up having to take care of it. We're not getting a dog, and that's final," her mom would shout.

Finally, seeing she was getting nowhere, Nikki stayed up late one night and wrote out a proposal to her mom. She carefully thought through her mom's concerns and wrote up a contract of all the things she would do to address them if her mom would let her get a dog. She then placed the letter on her mom's pillow.

Nikki's mom was so taken aback by the letter she actually opened her mind to the idea of getting a dog. Nikki and her mom then spent several weeks researching dogs together on the Internet. Nikki wanted an affectionate and loyal dog. Mom wanted a small dog that didn't bite, shed, bark,

Dear Mom, if you will let me get a dog, here's what I promise to do:

1. I will practice piano five times a week.
2. I will try harder to be nicer to my brothers and sisters.
3. I will be more helpful when we clean up and stuff like that.
4. I will be nicer to my mummy and daddy.
5. I will be more organized in my life and keep my bedroom and bathroom clean.
6. I will be happier in life.
7. I will try harder to eat better and exercise more.
8. When the school year starts I'll do my homework and try my hardest to get good grades.
9. I will read more books.
10. I will try harder to not get in fits and obey you and not talk back.
11. I will take good care of my dog.

or even poo. They both genuinely listened to each other for the first time, knowing that if they couldn't agree on the kind of dog, there would be no dog.

On her fourteenth birthday, a dog owner from another state showed up at Nikki's door with a little white Maltese, the cutest, fluffiest dog you've ever seen.

When you and your parents disagree on something, instead of fighting, take the mature approach and synergize. Talk it through. Try to find a solution that works for both of you. There are always good options if you'll talk openly. Here's a simple five-step process to help you get there.

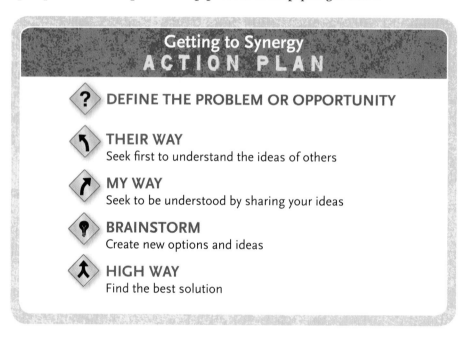

Getting to Synergy
ACTION PLAN

? DEFINE THE PROBLEM OR OPPORTUNITY

↰ THEIR WAY
Seek first to understand the ideas of others

↱ MY WAY
Seek to be understood by sharing your ideas

💡 BRAINSTORM
Create new options and ideas

⤢ HIGH WAY
Find the best solution

As you probably noticed, *Think Win-Win* and *Seek First to Understand* are built right into this action plan. These three skills all work together.

Pretend you and your mom are in an ongoing argument over school. She is constantly badgering you to do your homework and get better grades. You, on the other hand, are tired of her nonstop nagging. Most of your conversations sound something like this.

"Honey, I think you'd better turn off that TV and start your homework."

"Lighten up, Mom. I'll do it later. I swear."

"There is no later. There is only now."

"I'd really appreciate it if you'd get off my back. If you haven't noticed, your nagging doesn't help."

"I wouldn't have to talk about your homework if you'd actually do it. But you don't. It's like you don't even care."

"Yeah, I know. I'm such a loser. Just go away."

This kind of conversation is way too typical. And it's lazy. Fighting and arguing is simply lazy. But, you just learned about the Getting to Synergy Action Plan recently. And you're stoked about trying it out. After all, what do you have to lose?

So, late one night, when your mom is in one of her good moods, you approach her.

Define the Problem or Opportunity

"Mom, can I talk to you about something?"

"Sure, honey. What's on your mind?"

"Well, I just wanted to talk about school. I'm sick of always fighting about it."

"Yeah, me too."

Their Way (seek first to understand the ideas of others)

"Can you help me understand why you're always on my back? I mean, how do you see the whole thing, Mom?"

"I'm sorry that it feels like I'm harassing you. I don't mean it that way. I'm just worried about your grades. You could do so much better if you only tried a little harder."

"You don't think I'm giving it my best?"

"No, I don't. Sometimes I feel like you couldn't care less about school. I feel like if I didn't constantly remind you to do your homework, you wouldn't do a thing. It's really important to get into a good college and you need the grades to do it."

"So, what you're saying is you feel like I really don't care much about school and it's important to you that I get into a good college. Does that pretty much sum it up?"

"Yeah. That's kind of the way I see it."

Your Way (seek to be understood by sharing your ideas)

"Would you mind if I told you how I feel?"

"No problem. It sounds as though I need to hear it."

"I really do care about school, Mom. Probably not as much as you do, but I do care. I just like to do my homework on my own terms. Not when you tell me I have to. So it really bothers me when you get all over me about it."

"What do you mean?"

"Well, your constant nagging about my homework doesn't motivate me—just the opposite. It makes me not want to do it and makes me feel like a loser, like you don't think I'm capable of doing anything."

"Really?"

"Yeah, I think I'd do a lot better if you'd stop ripping on me and just be there if I need help."

Brainstorm (create new options and ideas)

"So, what do you think we should do?" says Mom.

"For starters, I'd really like it if you stopped nagging me all the time."

"I don't like the nagging either, darling. But it seems like it's the only way to get you to do your homework."

"What would I need to do to keep you from doing it?"

"Well, you'd need to prove to me that you're staying on top of things. That's all."

"Mom, did you know that you can go online anytime and look at my grades and assignments for any class?"

"No, I didn't."

"Yeah, you can. I just need to give you my password. So, what if we tried this? You go online whenever you want to check how I'm doing. If I'm not turning my stuff in or doing bad, you can nag all you want. But, if I'm on top of things, you leave me alone."

High Way (find the best solution)

"That'd be fine. But you need to show me how to get to that Web site."

"No problem, Mom. So what do you think? Does this sound like a good idea? Do we have a deal?"

"Sounds good to me, dear."

It's not always this easy. But sometimes it is. There are always solutions to disagreements if you'll talk it through with your parents. It takes patience. It takes effort. But it works. In review, the three gap-closing communication skills are:

- *Think Win-Win—always think about what the win is not only for you, but also for your parents.*

- *Seek First to Understand, Then to Be Understood—take the time to really understand your parents' point of view before opening your mouth. Repeat what they're saying and feeling in your own words.*

- *Synergize—talk through your differences. Try to see their point of view first. Then share your point of view. Finally, explore all your options and pick the best one. It's that simple.*

Armed with these skills, you may now consider yourself a dangerous communicator.

DISARMING YOUR PARENTS IN ONE LINE OR LESS

Often, parents say things that really push your buttons, like, "Because I said so. That's why!" or "You'll do what I say or else..." In a sense, they have picked up their sword and publicly challenged you to a duel. The worst thing you can do at this point is to pick up your own sword and engage in battle. You'll never win one of these. Instead, disarm them by doing one of three things.

1 *Apologize.*

2 *Bite your tongue and say nothing.*

3 *Seek first to understand by repeating in your own words what they are saying and feeling.*

By not picking up your own sword, it will cause them to drop theirs. And it usually only takes one line to disarm them. Just watch.

Scene 1: You and your mom are arguing about your choice of clothing. The conversation starts heating up as you start getting upset with your mom.

Your mom says, "I can't believe what you're saying. I'm your mother. How dare you talk to me that way?"

Now, if you want to engage in battle you might say: "I'll talk to you any way I want to."

But if you're smart and want to disarm your mom, you'll say: "Sorry, Mom. I shouldn't have said that."

Scene 2: You've been complaining to your dad about how unfair it is that you have to do all the hard chores, while your little sister gets all the easy ones.

Your dad, visibly frustrated, sighs, "I've already explained how I feel about it. I don't want to hear one more peep out of you. And I mean it. Do you understand?"

If you want to start World War III you could say: "Peep."

If you want to disarm your dad, you could try biting your tongue and just being silent.

Scene 3: You and your dad have been talking about a new guy you've started dating whom your dad doesn't like.

Your dad says, "Honey, I don't have a good feeling about that guy. I really don't think you should be going out with him. I feel really strongly about this."

Saying, "It's really none of your business, Dad," might be the first thing that comes to your mind, which will really boil his blood.

However, you could also disarm him, and then go on to have a real conversation by reflecting understanding. "Dad, I can tell you're really concerned about him."

TWO CLASSIC BLUNDERS

There are two classic blunders teens often make that tick off parents and destroy trust. Avoid them. They're not worth it. You may feel good for a moment by taking that jab at your parents, but you'll pay for it later. The two blunders are *getting in the last word* and *telling your parents you hate them.*

The Last Word

Marshall is running late for work as a bagger at the grocery store. Mom has just come out of his messy room and has fire in her eyes.

"Marshall. Get downstairs right now and clean your room. I'm not asking you again."

"C'mon, Mom, my room is clean."

"Clean? You call that clean? There are clothes thrown all over the floor. Your bed's unmade. And garbage is strewn everywhere. I can't believe I'm raising a slob."

"Mom, I'm going to be late to work. I'll do it when I get back. I swear."

"No, you won't. Your work will just have to wait while you clean your room."

"You're not serious? I can't believe you."

"You better believe me, 'cuz I mean business."

Marshall dashes downstairs to his room. As he passes his mom he says under his breath: "Jerk!"

"What did you just call me?"

Marshall just had to get the last word in. He couldn't help himself. And by so doing, he started a nuclear war. Parents have bionic ears, you see, and they hear all those nasty little words you say under your breath, like "jerk," "idiot," "you're so out of it," "you don't know anything," and a few other words I can't publish. After the conversation has wrapped to a natural conclusion, resist the urge to take one last jab at your parents. You'll just open up a whole new can of worms. Choose your battles wisely.

I Hate You

Jatina and her family are going to her grandparents' for Sunday evening dinner. For some time, Jatina and her stepmom have argued over Jatina's choice of clothes. Jatina feels that what she wears is none of her stepmom's business.

"Oh, no. You're not wearing that around my parents. It's totally immodest."

"Chill out, Mom. What's wrong with this outfit?"

"Just look at you. That blouse is way too revealing."

"I don't have anything else to wear."

"Oh, c'mon. How many times have I taken you shopping lately? You've got lots of nice things to wear. What about that cute green outfit we just got you?"

"Eeuuww! That's ugly. And since when did you become my fashion consultant? I'll wear what I want."

"Not around my parents, you won't. Now, you can either put on something else, or you can stay home this weekend. It's your choice."

"Ugh, Mom. You're so weird. **I hate you.**"

I hate you is just a convenient phrase we hurl at our parents when we're mad or frustrated and nothing else comes to mind. I don't think we really mean it most of the time. I remember sometimes telling my mom I hated her, when I got really upset. Sometimes she'd ignore it. Other times I could see it really hurt. I regret ever having said it.

When you're angry with your parents, you're better off letting out a BIG HUFF, biting your tongue, or SHOUTING... **ARRGH!!** like a pirate.

HOW TO BREAK BAD NEWS TO YOUR PARENTS

A mother enters her daughter's bedroom and sees a letter on the bed. With the worst feelings of premonition, she reads it, her hands trembling.

Dear Mom:

It's with great joy that I'm telling you that I've eloped with my new boyfriend. I found real passion and he's so nice, with all his piercings and tattoos and his big motorcycle. But it's not only that, Mom, I'm pregnant and Biff said that we'll be very happy in his trailer in the woods. He wants to have many more children and that's one of my dreams. I've learned that marijuana doesn't hurt anyone. We'll be growing it for us and his friends, who are providing us with all the Ecstasy we may want. In the meantime, we'll pray for science to find the AIDS cure for Biff. He deserves it.

Don't worry Mom, I'm 16 years old now and I know how to take care of myself. Someday I'll visit so you can get to know your grandchildren.

Your daughter,

Judy

P.S. Mom, it's not true. I'm at the neighbor's house. I just wanted to show you that there are worse things in life than my report card that's in my desk drawer. I love you!

The hardest communication challenge of all is when you have to break bad news to your parents. So, if you just wrecked the family car, an approach like the one above might work well for you. It tends to put the little things into perspective.

When You Have to Raise Your Parents —

Most parents are doing the best they can. Despite all their shortcomings, they love you and want the best for you. But some teens aren't so lucky and have parents with major problems. A few of you have parents that are totally absent from your life, are drug addicts or alcoholics, sleep around with every passing stranger, or are abusive with their words or fists. They may still love you, but they've lost control of their lives. Their addictions and habits are stronger than their love.

I'll never forget getting a letter from a young Vietnamese kid named Trinn.

Dear Sean:

I am eleven and I am in sixth grade and I have a problem. My dad takes drugs and my mom goes out a lot and she is cheating on my dad. I wish I could take control of my family. Can you give me some ideas or clues about what I should do?

I wasn't sure what to say. I finally wrote back and told him that he could only make choices for himself, not for his parents, and to do the best he could. If you're in a similar situation to Trinn's, here are a few things to consider.

GET HELP

If your parents are hooked on drugs or alcohol, they obviously need help, such as seeing a therapist or going through a rehab program. One of the signs of addiction is denial. They won't admit they have a problem. And they won't want your help. Consider talking to a grandmother or grandfather, an aunt or uncle, or an adult friend. Or talk with a school counselor or trusted teacher. Tell them what's going on and see if they can help you. If you're afraid your mom or dad will get angry or violent if you tell on them, visit the Help Desk in the back to find a few hotlines you might call.

If you're in a home where you are beaten or sexually molested, you must get help immediately. No one deserves to live under those conditions. Contact a relative or anyone you can trust, and tell them what's happening. You may need to move out of your home or call the police directly. If you're scared, visit the Help Desk in the back for a few other organizations you can contact. They have experts on these situations and can help you talk through the issue, and offer options and solutions.

LOVE AND FORGIVENESS

If your parents are totally dysfunctional, you don't want to follow in their footsteps, but you can still love them and, however hard it may be, forgive them. Such was the case with a young girl named Liz Murray. I heard her share her life story and was touched by her deep love for her parents even though they completely neglected her and her sister.

Liz and her younger sister lived with their parents in the Bronx, New York. Both parents were drug addicts. Liz remembers the countless times kind strangers would carry her mother back from the bar, blood and vomit coating her ragged clothes. She would have to bathe her mother and get her into bed. Their apartment was smelly and filthy, and seldom was there food in the house because her parents spent their welfare checks on drugs.

"The first of the month was a holiday, and the mailman was Santa Claus," says Liz. You see, that is when the welfare check would arrive. The whole family would go together to cash the check and Liz and her sister would get Happy Meals. Then the two girls would wait outside a building while her parents bought their drugs.

Her life, already a mess, unraveled further when her mother was diagnosed with HIV. Her family was separated, and Liz, a young teen, was sent to a group home. After many unpleasant experiences there, at the age of 15, she stuffed all that she owned into a backpack and headed out on her own. She sometimes slept at friends' houses. Often she slept on park benches or, when it was cold, in the subway. Sometimes a couple of weeks would go by between baths.

Liz took care of her deteriorating mother until she died of AIDS. Liz was 16, and this was her wake-up call. "I saw these broken adults around me," she said. "Maybe if I didn't take charge of my life, I would become one of them...I had nothing and became terrified, and this fear drove me back to school."

Despite being homeless, Liz poured herself into her studies. She took morning classes, night school, and Saturday classes. She studied everywhere—in hallways, stairwells, subways, you name it. After two years, she completed high school.

She then applied for a college scholarship sponsored by the *New York Times.* The application board was so impressed with her extraordinary life story she was awarded one of the six scholarships and was accepted at Harvard University. Since then, she has written a book about her experiences, *Breaking Night,* and helped direct a Lifetime Television movie, *Homeless to Harvard.*

To me, the most amazing thing about this whole story is how Liz treated her parents throughout the whole ordeal. She had every right to hate them, but showed love in return. "Love is the answer," says Liz when asked why she now takes care of her father after he neglected her for years.

"I'm not angry with my parents. They cared about me, and I loved them back. They were addicts since before both my sister and I were born, and probably should have never had kids. I'm grateful to them. They taught me things—they showed me which way not to go. But I also have good memories. I remember my mother coming into my bedroom at night, tucking me into bed. I remember her singing. If I could tell her anything today, I'd say, "Don't worry about me anymore. I'm gonna be fine, and thank you for everything. And, I love you."

BREAKING THE CYCLE

Life's not fair. How is it that one kid grows up in a home where they are loved and made to feel like they are somebody and another kid grows up in a home where they are abused and made to feel worthless? If you're the latter, you may ask: "What did I do to deserve this?" Well, you didn't do anything to deserve it. It's not right, and it's not your fault.

You *can* do something about it. How? By breaking the cycle. If your parents are messed up, and their parents were messed up, you can break the cycle by not repeating these negative patterns in your own life, and by passing on good habits to your own kids someday.

You may be in a family that is drowning in sickness from drugs, violence, abuse, molestation, or neglect. It may have gone on for generations. But you can stop it from being passed on to your kids. You can rise above your childhood. Perhaps that's why you were born into this family, to heal the sickness within it, to be a purifying influence, to be the stable one, the example that others can look to. If you've been abused, you can pass on love. If you've been neglected, you can show great care. If you were raised in a contentious home, you can build a peaceful one. You can change everything downstream.

Jesse was raised in a violent home but is now well on his way toward becoming a cycle-breaker.

When I was a small child, my mother was an alcoholic. She often left me in the car while she passed out inside the house. I was very aware that my mom and dad couldn't work out their problems without violence. I remember vividly my mother falling to her knees as she was being punched at full force by my father. I felt helpless and all I could do was cry. I remember Mom crying too and pleading, "Don't let Jesse see this, please."

While I was still young, my parents were divorced. Because my mother was always drunk, Dad got custody of me, or "owned" me, as he liked to say. He beat me constantly during those years.

The last summer I was at my father's house he was making me work doing hard labor, shoveling, carrying rocks and blocks close to 16 hours a day. One day I threw my shovel down and said I needed a break. He punched me and knocked me down. He then jumped on top of me and beat me senseless. I called the police that night for help.

When I turned 16, I took my father to court so I could move back in with my mom. She was definitely still an alcoholic but hid it to get custody of me. Mom would try to sober up but it never lasted more than six months at a time. While drunk, she would just lay on the bed for days, unable to function. When she was like this, she never cared about anything, even me. I never had anyone to tell me I did a "good job" and I had no support. I didn't care about school, work, or life so I struggled and failed everything. I was miserable and became almost suicidal at one point.

At the end of tenth grade, Mom got really drunk and Dad found out about it. He went to court and I had to go back and live with him again, which really scared me.

Fortunately, my father had remarried a decent woman who was concerned about my struggles in life and took an interest in me. She also gave me a self-help book that really sparked me. My life immediately began to change for the better.

I had to make new friends because I could see the ones I had weren't the best influence on me. Eventually, I stopped hanging out with them, as I realized they would have led me to a path of drugs. I took the initiative to go to my counselor and get help in school. For the first time, I had the desire and drive to finish high school instead of dropping out as my friends did. My counselor helped me get into college.

I started to believe that if I kept working hard and kept holding on, things would be better. I repeated that over and over to myself, and, for the first time, I had hope.

My new goals are to work hard, finish school, and one day have a good job and the money I need to support my family. More than anything, I want my kids to feel safe and supported in our home where they know their parents love them.

YOUR #1 INFLUENCE

There are a lot of myths about teens. One of the big ones is that teens don't like their parents. Not true. Most teens like their parents, want to get along, and wish they could spend more time with them. In fact, you rank parents as the #1 influence in your lives, above friends, media, faith, heroes, or whatever else.

Tabitha is an example of what I'm talking about. "My family isn't perfect," she says, "but we are all close to each other. I talk to my parents about most stuff, although I don't tell them everything. We eat dinner together at night. We fight sometimes but eventually get along. I rarely stay at friends' houses; I feel more comfortable at home. My friends come to my house to hang out because my parents make them feel like family. Everyone is always welcome at my house."

There are so many fun things you can do with your parents. You can shoot hoops, go to a ball game, attend a concert, camp, hike, fish, go out to eat, bake cookies, watch the stars, go on Sunday drives, watch your favorite reality show, or listen to music. Even if you have only one thing in common, take advantage of it, as did Nicole.

I remember getting into some pretty big fights with my mom. It seemed like we could never get along. But one thing that we did have in common was our love of the theater. We both loved comedies and musicals. Once or twice a month, my mom would buy tickets for us to go to a play together. We would usually go to dinner before and have a chance to talk one on one. I remember always being in a good mood on these nights and being able to really open up to her and tell her about school and my friends and stuff. She would usually just listen on those nights. We made a connection that way. Looking back now, I see that she probably created those opportunities for us on purpose.

You've probably figured out by now that you can't choose your parents. Sorry, but you're stuck with them. That's why what you choose to do about that feeling which exists between you and them is one of the 6 big decisions. So, what's it going to be? Are you going to show respect or disrespect? Build the relationship or run away from it? Talk through your problems or fight about them?

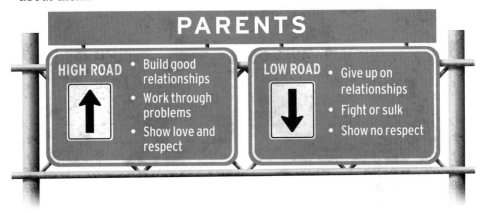

PARENTS

HIGH ROAD
- Build good relationships
- Work through problems
- Show love and respect

LOW ROAD
- Give up on relationships
- Fight or sulk
- Show no respect

I think you're better off taking the high road, however hard it may seem at times. If your relationship is nonexistent, start making deposits today, no matter how small. Say **"Please,"** "Thank you," **"I love you,"** and "How can I help?" often. From time to time, you'll have to swallow your pride and obey unreasonable orders. Ten years from now, you'll be so grateful if you have a sweet relationship with your mom and dad. So, never give up on your parents, just like you hope they never give up on you.

● ● ● COMING ATTRACTIONS ● ● ●

Everything you've always wanted to know about dating and sex is in the next chapter. You wouldn't want to miss that, would you?

BABY STEPS*

1. In the space below, write down three huge deposits you could make into your parents' Relationship Bank Accounts.

   GINORMOUS PARENT DEPOSITS

   _____

   _____

   _____

2. Clean your room cleaner than it's ever been. Then blindfold your mom or dad and tell them you have a surprise.

3. Today, use all four of the Magical Expressions at least once with your mom or dad:

   Please   Thank you   I love you   How can I help?

4. Is there an issue you and your parents constantly argue about? If so, go to them and say, "Help me understand your point of view." Then listen. Repeat in your own words what they are saying and feeling until they feel understood.

5. What is your favorite thing to do with your mom or dad? A movie? A Sunday drive? Eating out? Make plans together to do it again sometime soon.

   Favorite thing to do with Mom or Dad _____

6. Invite your parents to be part of your life. Sometime this week, really open up and share what's going on in that head of yours.

7. If your home is short on love, suggest a *family-only night* to your parents. Set apart one night each week to do something fun together as a family.

8. If you don't see one of your parents too often, write him or her a note and express your love.

9. Download a ringer on your cell that reminds you to be nice to your parents when they call, such as James Taylor's "Shower the People."

10. If your parents are alcoholics or hooked on drugs, or if you are in an abusive situation, get help! Don't wait! Carefully consider the help sources suggested in the Help Desk.

---

* To keep an online journal of your Baby Steps progress, go to www.6decisions.com.

DATiNG & SEX

DO WE HAVE TO
TALK ABOUT THIS?

Top 10

Things You Oughta Know About Dating and Sex...

MENU

10. Never, ever, ever use or give in to "If you really loved me you would..." If they really loved you, they would not manipulate you.
— LOGAN KENDELL, 19, POCATELLO, IDAHO

9. Love is not measured by how many you have dated or how many you have slept with. It's not a competition.
— METTE FOGED, 19, COPENHAGEN, DENMARK

8. You stay in charge.
— HWA YOUNG LEE, 15, SUNG NAM-SI, KOREA

7. You don't need to be head over heels with the person before you go on a date, you might be pleasantly surprised.
— JENNIFER HASTIE, 19, GULLANE, SCOTLAND

6. Don't make any decisions if you are in doubt.
— BAASANJAV, 16, UVS, MONGOLIA

5. Recognize that how you behave might affect not only you but also your family.
— TAKU WADA, 19, AKITA PREFECTURE, JAPAN

4. Date people your own age.
— JANET, 17, LONG BEACH, CALIFORNIA

3. Don't ever think life is over because your boy/girlfriend broke up with you.
— SOPHIA IACAYO, 18, MANAGUA, NICARAGUA

2. Don't have sex until you're married; you won't regret it.
— NICK ADAMS, 16, WINCHESTER, VIRGINIA

1. Dating is hard sometimes. Oh, wait! It's always hard.
— RACHEL TURNER, 17, BRIELLE, NEW JERSEY

Relationships are hard. It's like a full-time job, and we should treat it like one. If your boyfriend or girlfriend wants to leave you, they should give you two weeks' notice. There should be severance pay. The day before they leave you, they should have to find you a temp.
— Bob Ettinger, author

Here are some of the all-time cheesiest lines from old movie classics:

"Love means never having to say you're sorry."
Jenny Cavilleri (Ali MacGraw) in *Love Story*

"Kiss me. Kiss me as if it were the last time."
Ilsa Laslow (Ingrid Bergman) in *Casablanca*

"Ditto."
Sam (Patrick Swayze) after Molly (Demi Moore) says "I love you" in *Ghost*

"Do I love you because you're beautiful, or are you beautiful because I love you? Are you the sweet invention of a lover's dream, or are you really as beautiful as you seem?"
Prince Charming to Cinderella in *Cinderella*

"I'm just a girl standing in front of a boy asking him to love her."
Anna Scott (Julia Roberts) in *Notting Hill*

"I always just hoped that, that I'd meet some nice friendly girl, like the look of her, hope that the look of me didn't make her physically sick, then pop the question and…um…settle down and be happy. It worked for my parents. Well, apart from the divorce and all that."
Tom (James Fleet) in *Four Weddings and a Funeral*

"Shut up…just shut up. You had me at hello." Dorothy (Renée Zellweger)
responding to Jerry's (Tom Cruise) statement *"I love you. You complete me,"*
in *Jerry Maguire*

We're all romantics at heart, so, if you're like most teens, you probably skipped right to this chapter. Everyone wants to know all they can about love and romance, dating and sex. Welcome to the world of drama! Excitement and trauma included. Get ready and hold on.

Of all decisions you'll make as a teen this is probably the most important one. Why? Because these choices have big consequences that not only affect you, they affect many others. Once again, there is a high road and a low road. You can take the high road by dating intelligently, treating sex like it's a big deal, and holding out for true love and commitment. Or you can choose the low road by dating brainlessly, treating sex like a toy, and fooling around as if there were no tomorrow. The good news is, you can glance down each road beforehand and learn from the successes and slip-ups of those who went before.

I really debated whether I should write this chapter because it's so darn touchy, especially the sex part. On one hand, I don't want to be careless or casual about something so delicate. On the other, I need to be brutally honest and share the facts. I'll do my best to find the right balance. Of course, the best place to go for info on dating and sex is your parents. I don't pretend to take their place. Just think of me as a supplement. The approach I've taken toward sex is neither religious nor political. It's a principle-based and practical approach that applies to teens universally.

DATING AND SEX CHECKUP

Perhaps this little checkup below will give you some idea of how you're doing in this area. Total your score below and see what it tells you.

CIRCLE YOUR CHOICE	NO WAY!				HECK YES!
1. I carefully choose who I go out with and don't date just anybody.	1	2	3	4	5
2. I have decided beforehand what I will and won't do on a date.	1	2	3	4	5
3. My relationships with the opposite sex are based upon genuine friendship, not just the physical side of things.	1	2	3	4	5
4. I feel good about the decisions I'm making when it comes to dating and sex.	1	2	3	4	5
5. My romantic relationships are healthy.	1	2	3	4	5
6. I'm well informed about STDs, pregnancy, and the emotional risks of having sex.	1	2	3	4	5
7. I have not centered my life on a boyfriend or girlfriend.	1	2	3	4	5
8. I have the courage to say *no* to things I don't want to do.	1	2	3	4	5
9. I treat my body with respect.	1	2	3	4	5
10. I'm waiting until I'm in a long-term, committed relationship before having sex.	1	2	3	4	5
TOTAL					

Add up your score and see how you think you're doing.

 You're on the high road. Keep it up!

 You're straddling the high and low roads. Move to higher ground!

 You're on the low road. Pay special attention to this chapter.

This chapter is made up of three sections. The first one is all about that game we call dating. It's called **Intelligent Dating**. Next, we'll discuss **The Four Great Sex Myths**. Aren't you curious to see what they are? Finally, we'll take a look at the meaning of true love in **Love Waits**. Here goes...

Intelligent Dating

Intelligent Dating: dating successfully; being selective about who you date; hanging out and having fun; remaining steady through the natural highs and lows of romance; keeping your own standards.

Brainless Dating: dating ineffectively; dating anyone who has a pulse; becoming centered on your girlfriend or boyfriend; having your heart broken repeatedly; doing what everyone else seems to be doing.

Dating. Even the word conjures up all kinds of emotions—good and bad. Everyone is always talking, thinking, reading, praying, and worrying about it.

By *dating* I simply mean the process by which guys and girls get to know each other. Don't get hung up about my choice of the word *dating.* I could use words like: *going out, hanging out,* or *seeing someone.* Your grandparents called it courting. Their grandparents called it something else.

In the world of dating, everyone seems to fall into one of the following six camps. Sometimes they straddle two. Pick which camp you're mostly in.

Camp **I Wish**: *You don't date and you wish you did.*

Camp **Who Cares?**: *You don't date and you really don't care.*

Camp **This Rocks!**: *You really enjoy dating and you wonder why everyone else doesn't.*

*Camp **Help!**: You're stuck in a bad dating relationship you can't get out of.*

*Camp **Never Again**: You just had your heart broken and don't want to start dating again.*

*Camp **Hanging Out**: You don't really date, you just sort of hang out. You see dating as an old-fashioned ritual.*

*Camp **Curious**: You're too young to date, but you're really curious about it.*

Regardless of where you are, you can become an intelligent dater by following the principles in this section. Let's start by answering some questions.

6 UNIVERSAL DATING QUESTIONS

1. WHAT SHOULD I EXPECT?

Expect lots of drama. Dating is complicated and emotional, full of highs and lows. Watching my brothers and sisters play the dating game was like living in a soap opera. Cynthia, my oldest sister, fell in and out of love on a regular basis. She had so many boyfriends: Mark the meat man, Steve the scholar, Vic the Virginian, Castellano the Italian, Lennon the ripped, and Jake the Greek God. Cynthia even had a life-sized photo of Jake in her room. Weird!

My brother and I used to sneak into her bedroom and read her journal. I'll never forget the entry where she wrote in big bold letters: "I love to kiss!" As a young kid, I was shocked that my sister had actually **kissed** someone. Sick!

And then there was my older brother Stephen, who had a jealous streak as wide as the Grand Canyon. He fell in love with a girl named Vicki. One night he made me hide with him behind some shrubs near her home, like spies, to see if Vicki's date tried something at the door.

And I can't forget my little sister, Colleen, the ultimate drama queen. She'd literally be on cloud nine one minute and bawling the next over some guy. I get exhausted even thinking about it. Yes, dating is dramatic.

Expect fickleness, pickiness, and indecisiveness. Let's face it, when it comes to romance, teens are indecisive, fickle, choosy, nitpicky, fussy, and unpredictable. This is normal. You're young. You aren't sure what you want. So you have a right to be this way.

As a teen, I was as fickle as a chameleon. I liked a different girl every week. I'd be attracted by the simplest thing, like the way some girl flipped her hair. And I'd get turned off by the stupidest thing, like the time I stopped liking this girl because it bugged me that she wore T-shirts all the time. I wasn't trying to hurt anyone. I was just immature. I didn't know how to communicate my feelings, like lots of other teenage boys. I like how comedian Conan O'Brien said it:

"A study in the *Washington Post* says that

women have better *verbal skills* than men.

I just want to say to the authors of that study: '**Duh.**' "

Girls aren't too different from boys. Christie, a senior in high school, sounds just like I felt:

I'm completely stressed out about guys. I've had a boyfriend for about nine months and want a change. He sometimes gets mad when I hang out with my friends and go to parties. His being like this is ruining our relationship and I'm considering breaking up with him. On top of all this I have a secret crush no one knows about. Now I'm stuck in a hard place and there's no way out. I'm not sure how to handle all this.

Christie is unsure and indecisive about who she likes. Her boyfriend might be feeling just the same way. To some degree, everyone's playing mind games with each other. Can you see why it's not smart to take dating and romance too seriously while you're young? Now's the time to explore, get to know lots of different people, and be free to change your mind.

"FM-96 dedication line? The next time you test the Emergency Broadcast System, I'd like to dedicate it to my boyfriend because our relationship is a *disaster*!"

© 1999 Randy Glasbergen.

Expect to make a fool of yourself. If you're like most teens, you're going to make dumb mistakes from time to time. Common dating blunders include:

- *Saying something really* **stupid** *like, "So what's your name again?"*
- *Being so* **shy** *that you can hardly carry on a conversation.*
- *Giving your date the* **COLD SHOULDER** *when you don't really mean it.*

- **Leading on** *your date to believe you're in love with them when you're not.*
- **Passing gas** *(it happens, believe me!)*

Michael shared this.

It was homecoming and I was excited for my first date. My friend Steve asked Lori and I picked a cute girl named Kaitlyn. We have a tradition at our school of doing a predate activity so several of us went up the canyon in the afternoon and roasted hot dogs and marshmallows and played some games. I kept noticing that Steve kept hanging around Kaitlyn and talking her ear off. It was obvious that he was more interested in my date than his. He sat down next to her with me on the other side while his date sat down alone.

It kind of ticked me off, but since it was my first date I didn't know what to do so I didn't say anything. I could tell Steve's date, Lori, felt really stupid and didn't know what to do either. It was awkward for everyone. Steve didn't seem to even notice.

The next day, Steve was in a really bad mood. When I asked why, he said he had just gotten yelled at by Lori's friends who said he acted like a jerk. Lori felt so bad she didn't even want to go to the dinner and dance with him. He didn't know his flirting was so obvious, and realized he had made a complete fool of himself. He felt really bad that he made Lori so uncomfortable. To top it off, his date cost him seventy-five bucks, and all he got out of it was a bad reputation.

Yup, Steve blew it and you might blow it too, occasionally. In fact, some dates might be downright miserable. That's OK, just learn from it. Dating will teach you communication and adaptation skills you'll need to survive in the real world. For example:

- *Are you so shy that it makes your date uneasy and they have to carry the entire conversation?*
- *Do you laugh at your date's expense when you're trying to be funny?*
- *Do you come across as rude or sarcastic?*
- *Do you have the social skills to meet your date's parents and answer their questions so they like you?*
- *Did you pay attention to your parents' lessons on manners, such as how to eat a steak without picking it up off the plate, and not talking and chewing at the same time?*
- *Do you know how to dance, how to order politely at a restaurant, how to plan a fun night that doesn't include Xbox, and to have options if things don't work out?*
- *If something goes wrong on a date, can you handle it, or do you lose your cool?*

If you're struggling with any of these, be patient and keep practicing. Dating will help you work the kinks out.

2. WHO SHOULD I GO OUT WITH?

When you're choosing someone to date, what's the first thing you notice about them? Their personality? Right—let's get real. The first thing you go for is their looks. You can't help it. Being attracted to someone is where it all starts, but there is so much more to a person than looks.

My friend and colleague Durelle Price teaches a seminar on intelligent dating in which she compares dating to choosing a car. Have you ever gone with someone to buy a car, maybe a parent or friend? Did they walk onto the car lot and wait for the salesperson to choose a car for them? Absolutely not! Usually they did a ton of research beforehand and developed a mental wish list of things they've gotta have and things they can do without. They might decide that the make, color, and reliability of the car are must-haves and that they could do without the sunroof, fuel economy, and warranty.

Intelligent daters put the same brain matter into choosing a date. They don't just let it happen to them. They have a wish list of character traits and interests they've gotta have. They also have a list of things they can do without. So what is it that you must have? Do you have to have good looks? Do you have to have someone who's nice? Fun? Smart? Focused? Nice to children? Liked by your parents? Spiritual? Do you want someone who brings out the best in you?

What can you do without? What if your date isn't that popular? Or doesn't dance well, or doesn't have a car? Can you do without those? What if they've got a bad reputation or use drugs? Is that something you could do without?

Spend a few minutes and fill out the list below.

My Dating Wish List

GOTTA HAVE	CAN DO WITHOUT
1.	1.
2.	2.
3.	3.
4.	4.
5.	5.
6.	6.

Bottom line—begin with the end in mind. A key step to becoming an intelligent dater is to get clear on what's really important to you and where you won't compromise. Don't date just anyone. Be choosy.

3. WHAT IF I NEVER GET ASKED OUT?

If you're 19 and you've never been kissed or if you're a senior in high school and never been on a date or only a few, big deal.

Consider yourself LUCKY you haven't had to deal with all the drama.

If you really want to date, there'll be plenty of time for that in the years ahead. Dating is not a contest to see who can land the most boyfriends or girlfriends or collect the most kisses.

I know a young woman who won the talent pageant at her high school. She's an incredible pianist and dancer and is strikingly beautiful. I also know that upon graduating from high school, she'd only been on a couple of dates. She was a little shy and preferred spending time with her friends and family. Now that she's in college, she's starting to date more.

There are lots of great guys and girls who don't date much in their teen years and that's perfectly OK. They'll have many opportunities ahead. So don't stress out about it or feel like something's wrong with you.

Never forget, there are many alternatives to dating and different ways to get to know other boys and girls. Just be friends, hang out in groups, and do stuff together without officially labeling it a "date."

However, if you really want to date, but aren't, here are a few questions you may want to ask yourself:

- *Am I friendly with everyone?*
- *Instead of waiting to be asked, could I ask someone instead?*
- *Am I making up excuses for not dating?*
- *Am I doing everything I can to make myself attractive?*

You don't have to have the perfect genes or body type to be attractive. A leading dating service did an informal survey of singles to find out what they considered to be the biggest turn-ons. Here's what they found:

TOP 10 TURN-ONS

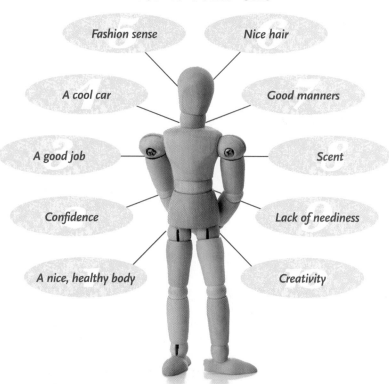

It's interesting that all items on the list are completely within your control—except maybe the cool car.

4. WHAT IS THE BIGGEST MISTAKE TEENS MAKE WHEN DATING?

HAVE YOU MET MY GIRLFRIEND, SHEILA?

This one's easy. It's becoming centered on your girlfriend or boyfriend.

There's nothing wrong with having a boyfriend or girlfriend, but if you begin to center your life on them, you're begging for a breakup. Too often, what started as a friendly relationship turns into a possessive relationship. Your boyfriend or girlfriend becomes the most important thing in your life, and you can't think about anything else. You become addicted to them, as it were. Here are three signs that suggest you might be girlfriend or boyfriend centered:

- *Your mood each day is dependent on how your girlfriend or boyfriend treats you.*
- *You become possessive and jealous.*
- *You stop spending time with your friends and family and spend virtually all of your time with your boyfriend or girlfriend.*

When I was 16, all I could think about was Mandy, Mandy, Mandy. She was a flirt, and I got terribly jealous and possessive. I think she enjoyed the control she had over me, owning the remote control to my emotions. I didn't like what being Mandy-centered did to me. It cut me off from my friends and family and I stopped having fun.

It's ironic, but true, that the more you center your life on a girlfriend or boyfriend the more unattractive you become to them. You usually end up losing the very person you build your life around. Stephanie shared this:

I've had a problem with being boyfriend centered. My ex-boyfriend was my world, my 100 percent center—nothing else existed. I did not realize it because I wanted to be with him 24/7. The more I wanted to be with him, the less he wanted to see me. The closer I got to him, the more he pushed me away.

Looking back, I realize how unattractive that made me. There was no chase, no fun, no wondering about anything because it was already there, in his face, all the time. Relationships are more fun when they're surprising and spontaneous, not planned and obsessive. I was the one who always felt like I needed to have those sickening where-do-we-stand talks.

Eventually, Stephanie and her boyfriend broke up because he couldn't take it anymore. You see, when you center your life on a boyfriend or girlfriend, it becomes your paradigm, the pair of glasses through which you see the world. As a result, the other important things in your life, like school, friends, and family, get distorted.

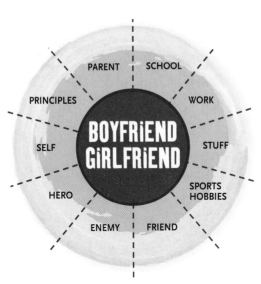

You can like and date someone without centering your life around them. As discussed in earlier chapters, the only true center is one based on principles, the natural laws that rule the universe. By maintaining the proper center, you'll be stabler, more confident, and less dependent upon how others treat you. Remember, very few of us wind up marrying the people we date in high school. So even though you may be convinced your current boyfriend or girlfriend is *the one*, they most likely aren't.

5. HOW WILL I KNOW WHEN IT'S TIME TO BREAK UP?

There are four types of relationships: Win-Win, Win-Lose, Lose-Win, Lose-Lose. If your relationship is based on anything other than Win-Win, you need to fix it or break it off.

Win-Win: **The relationship is good for both of you. Enjoy it!**

Example: Kiran and Sonia date each other but also date other people. They have a lot of fun together. Their relationship is based on friendship. They bring out the best in each other.

Win-Lose: **The relationship is good for you but bad for them. Fix it or get out!**

Example: Jasmine gets lots of social mileage out of her boyfriend, Carlos. He's popular and all her friends tell her how lucky she is. She expects Carlos to be totally devoted to her and to call her every day. Carlos, on the other hand, feels totally controlled by Jasmine and doesn't want to be tied down. He just wants to have fun and be free.

Lose-Win: *The relationship is bad for you but good for them. Fix it or get out!*

Example: Laura's been going with Quinton for three years now. He was sweet to her at first but is now verbally abusive and controlling. Quinton likes having a girlfriend who's all his. Laura feels locked in and doesn't know how to get out.

Lose-Lose: *The relationship is bad for both of you. Get out fast!*

Example: Jackson and Emery are totally centered on each other. They constantly fight and accuse each other of cheating and flirting. They keep breaking up but keep getting back together because they're dependent upon each other. They often tell each other "I love you!" and "You're such a jerk!" within the same conversation.

THEM

	LOSE	WIN
YOU — WIN	**UNHEALTHY** RELATIONSHIP Fix it or get out of it!	**HEALTHY** RELATIONSHIP Enjoy it!
YOU — LOSE	**SiCK** RELATIONSHIP Get out fast!	**UNHEALTHY** RELATIONSHIP Fix it or get out of it!

Another way to know when it's time to break up is to watch for red flags—warnings that something isn't right. Take them seriously. Here are five red flags to consider.

Ultimatums. In college, I had a girlfriend who would call me the night before I'd be playing a game on national TV and say, "Are you committed to me or not? You need to decide by tomorrow morning or I'm leaving."

Well, tomorrow would come and she'd back off. But then, two weeks later, she'd give me another ultimatum. Finally, I could see the red flag, and we broke up. I only wished I'd done it sooner.

Often, the ultimatums are more serious, such as: "You'd better stop flirting with him or you're going to pay for it," or "You'd better sleep with me or I'm leaving you." Ultimatums are a sign of immaturity and control and should warn you to break it off.

2 **The savior complex.** This is when you feel you want to change someone or save them from themselves. Observe how Joie got sucked into this and can't see her way out:

> I was with a guy for two years. Most of the two years was horrible. He had lots of problems and I tried to change him. I have learned you can't change anyone. I would drive around looking for him making sure he was all right. For some reason, I can't leave him alone. It finally caught up with him, and he is in jail. I still love him with all my heart and would do anything for him. I hope after he gets help he will be a better person and we can work out our problems.

Guess what, Joie? You said it yourself. You can't change people. They can only change themselves. Move on.

3 **Lies.** If someone's lying to you, your relationship is based on hot air. My friend Annie interviewed a girl named Astrid about her boyfriend. Here are a few lines from that interview:

Annie: *Does your boyfriend Carson go to school here?*

Astrid: *No, he went to school at Riverside. He says he graduated early but I don't know if he graduated or dropped out.*

Annie: *What does he do?*

Astrid: *Um, he says he works. Like, he's not very honest.*

Annie: *I'm gonna ask you a funny question. Is this the kind of person you want to end up with?*

Astrid: *Yeah. No. But he's not...he's honest with me. Well, he like, lies about things to make himself look better.*

Hello! Astrid, can't you see the big red flag?

4 **You'll never find anyone else who will love you.** If you ever hear these words, realize there's a red flag the size of your bedspread being flown in your face. A young girl shared this.

When I was 14 years old I had a crush on Andy. He was seventeen, drove a red sports car, was tall, and, from what I could tell, was a pretty quality guy.

When we first started hanging out, everything was fine. He was a perfect gentleman, he respected me, and I thought he loved me. Well, Andy's gentleman stayed around for only a while. Before I knew it, he became abusive in every way imaginable. He used to tell me that I would never find anyone else who would love me. I actually believed him.

After almost a year of abuse, I finally got out.

5 **If you leave me, I'll hurt myself.** This is another red flag. When Benjamin was 17, he started dating a girl. Everything was fine at first, but, after a few months, she began to threaten to kill herself. Benjamin was shocked at first and very concerned. He hoped she'd never mention it again. But, throughout the next couple of months, that's all she could talk about. After a while, he grew numb to her threats and began seeking advice from others. "When she discovered this," said Benjamin, "she gave me the ultimatum to stop telling people or she was really going to do it.

"I was fed up, and I really didn't know what to do next. I couldn't break up with her because I feared the worst. One thing was for sure, I couldn't continue my life with the constant fear of her committing suicide. Her threats were taking over my life."

After seeking professional advice, Benjamin realized that she wasn't really serious about hurting herself, but was just trying to get attention. After confronting her, he was able to end the relationship peacefully.

Now, of course, if anyone is talking about committing suicide, you need to take it seriously and get them professional help. What you shouldn't do, however, is feel that you have to stay in the relationship. Find a way to exit gracefully.

I've only touched on a few red flags, there are a dozen more. Above all, listen to your conscience and trust your instincts. Get advice from those who love you most. Steer clear of dangerous liaisons.

6. HOW DO I GET OUT OF AN ABUSIVE RELATIONSHIP?

My friend Durelle Price, whom I mentioned earlier, has developed a terrific program that focuses on helping teens identify and get out of abusive relationships. The information that follows is hers, which I've adapted with permission.

It starts with a little name-calling, a push, or a slap. You might think it's an isolated incident. Most likely an apology will follow. You don't want to believe it could ever happen again. But the truth is, this isolated incident is actually the tip of the iceberg—the first glimpse at a pattern of abusive behavior that will inevitably follow.

As comedian Jim Carrey put it,

"YOU KNOW WHAT THE TROUBLE ABOUT REAL LIFE IS? There's no danger music."

No one ever asked to be abused, and no one deserves it. All any of us really want is to be loved and accepted, just like Michelle. She was zapped—love struck by Justin, a hot, star athlete at their high school. Justin could be very sweet. He told her how beautiful she was and how much he loved her. Lots of girls wanted to go out with him, but he chose her. Early in their relationship they went to a party and the guy at the front door told her she had pretty eyes. Before she could say thank you, Justin punched the guy flat to the floor.

She had a terrible feeling in her stomach, but her friends all said, "Wow, you are so lucky. He loves you so much!" A few years later they'd decided to get married.

A week before the wedding, they had a minor disagreement. Suddenly, Justin dove across the room and grabbed Michelle by the throat.

It was the longest 20 seconds Michelle had ever experienced. Just as quickly as it began, it ended. He dropped to his knees, threw his arms around her waist and pleaded with her to forgive him. As the tears streamed down his face, he blamed it on being nervous about the wedding and swore he'd never do anything like that again.

Michelle didn't know what to do. She'd been taught to forgive, right? She was humiliated and confused. She

THE TIP OF THE ICEBERG

NAME CALLING
SLAP   PUSH

ISOLATION   STALKING
THREATS WITH WEAPONS
BELITTLING   BEATING   RAPE
PRESSURE TO HAVE SEX   EMOTIONAL ABUSE
KICKING
STRANGLING

didn't tell her sister. She sure didn't tell her mother and she didn't even tell her best friend. She prayed it would never happen again. A week later they were married. Now she was trapped.

Over the next several years, the physical and emotional abuse went from bad to worse before Michelle finally gathered the courage to leave Justin. He continued to stalk her for years.

Michelle's story is not uncommon. In fact, one out of three teenage girls report experiencing physical violence at the hands of a dating partner. If this is happening to you, don't accept it. And please don't think, "Well, this is the way guys are." Believe me, there are lots of decent guys who aren't like that.

Use this Get-Out-Quick checklist to see if you're in an abusive relationship.

Does your boyfriend or girlfriend...

☐ MAKE you cry all the time?

☐ DO or SAY things that make you feel stupid, embarrassed, or worthless?

☐ KEEP you from spending time with your family and friends?

☐ KEEP you from doing things you want to do, like keep a job or join a team?

☐ ACT super jealous or possessive?

☐ SHOVE, SHAKE, SLAP, or HIT you?

☐ THREATEN to hurt or kill you or themselves?

☐ LIE or HIDE things from you?

☐ Always EXPECT to get their way?

If you said yes to even one of these, it's time to say **"I'M OUTTA HERE!"**

There's a right and wrong way to break up with an abusive person. Here's what the wrong way looks like.

Jamal had been verbally abusive—putting Cheri down and making her cry all the time. She knew she needed to break off the relationship. He was alone in his grandmother's house when she came by with his sweater and CD case. He knew immediately she was there to break up. When he opened the door, he grabbed her by the hair, pushed her up against the door, and called her terrible names. Cheri was hurt and frightened.

Cheri made several mistakes in her plan to break up with Jamal:

- *She went alone.*
- *She met him in a private place.*
- *She underestimated what he was capable of.*

Now, let's look at the right way to break up with someone who is abusive.

Devon could no longer accept Crystal's possessive and jealous behavior. She would follow him everywhere and watch him from a distance. She would scream accusations at him, then slap him when he tried to defend his innocent actions.

So Devon told his minister, his friends, and his family about the abusive behavior. Devon called Crystal on the phone and told her the relationship was off. He told her not to call or approach him again. It was hard. He kept remembering what it was like in the beginning when Crystal was so sweet. His minister helped him deal with his feelings. His friends and family continued to provide support as he sought to get over it.

Devon's breakup plan was smart:

- *He broke up with her on the phone.*
- *He told his friends, family members, and a minister about the abuse.*
- *He sought help to deal with his feelings after the breakup.*

6 GUIDELINES TO INTELLIGENT DATING

Our society has created two rules of dating that we tend to buy into without even thinking.

PAIR UP:

Having a girlfriend or a boyfriend is the only way to be happy.

GET PHYSICAL:

The more you like someone the more physical you have to get. You can only show love with your body.

The result is broken hearts and a cycle of short-term relationships You don't have to buy it. You can say good-bye to our culture's brainless approach to dating.

What follows are six guidelines for dating success gleaned from the wisdom of your peers. These will guard you from becoming boyfriend- or girlfriend-centered, keep your relationships healthy, shield you from abusive relationships, and increase the fun factor.

1. DON'T DATE TOO YOUNG

Talk with any teen who began dating when they were really young. They almost always wish they had waited. Start too young and you'll run into problems, such as getting taken advantage of, getting physical too soon, or not knowing how to end the relationship. Waiting until you're 16 before dating is a good rule of thumb.

2. DATE PEOPLE YOUR OWN AGE

This guideline is a cousin to the first one. It especially applies to girls. Dating guys two, three, or four years older than you may be flattering, but isn't healthy. I can't tell you how many times I have heard stories like the one below, shared by a young girl from Allen East High School.

I had my first serious relationship when I was in sixth grade. I can't even begin to say what attracted me to him, but somehow he pulled me in. Before I knew it I was in over my head. He was a few years older and I think I liked that an older guy was interested in me.

This guy had a lot of problems. He was very controlling and liked to push me around. He would never let me do things with my friends or talk to other guys. It took me a long time to realize that this was not normal, especially at my age. I was scared of him and I didn't know who to tell. The relationship went on until the end of my freshman year in high school.

It's so easy to get taken advantage of when you date older people. Why take the chance?

3. GET TO KNOW LOTS OF PEOPLE

Romance seems to run in our veins. We'd all like to find our soulmate and live happily ever after. So, it seems only natural to fall in love with the first person we can. However, by doing this we create expectations and cut ourselves off from other relationships.

Kip had never paid much attention to Hope before. After all, she was his neighbor. But when she showed up at a summer party, looking hot, it was as if he was meeting her for the first time. He called her for a date and pretty soon they were a couple and spent a lot of time together. Kip was a junior in high school and Hope, a sophomore, was the first person Kip had ever really liked. He fell hard for her.

That summer, Kip's family went on vacation for three weeks. When he got back, Kip found out that while he was gone Hope had gone out with two of his friends and had even kissed one of them. Kip was furious and felt betrayed! He thought they had an understanding between them that they were only dating each other.

When Kip confronted her she said, "Well, you were gone for so long and I like him, too! It's not like we're boyfriend and girlfriend or anything." That killed Kip because in his mind they were exactly that.

Kip vowed never to speak to her again and didn't for months. Hope, on the other hand, didn't understand what all the fuss was about. She moved on and dated many others while Kip fumed. It was a long time before he could trust another girl or start dating again.

See what can happen when you get all serious and start to believe that the first person you fall for is your one and only love? Your middle or high school years are not the time to settle into a serious relationship.

My dad used to tell us:

"THE RULE OF OUR HOME IS THAT YOU CAN never date the same person twice in a row."

It was his way of making sure that we got to know lots of people and avoided getting trapped into a single relationship. I must confess that I broke Dad's rule more than once (sorry, Dad!), but, overall, his approach kept me from getting too wrapped up with just one person.

Ashley's situation is very common.

I'm in high school and I've had a boyfriend for about two and a half years now. So, I've never experienced other guys or real dating. This really stresses me out. I'm never quite sure if I'm making the right decision by only dating one person. He's a safety crutch for me. That's part of the reason I stay with him.

I really wish I could've met this wonderful person after high school, then things might be different. Since I can't change that, I really wish we could just date other people and see what happens after high school.

Don't be in such a hurry to have a girlfriend or boyfriend. Now's the time to date different people, have fun, and not get too serious. There will be time in the future to narrow down your choices and start dating one person seriously. But not when you're a teenager! You don't want to join the adult world too soon; it's not half as much fun. Enjoy your days of singleness while ye may.

4. DATE IN GROUPS

Dating in groups, whether it's on a double date or with a larger group, has many advantages. Usually, it's more fun. There's safety in numbers. You'll meet more people, and there are fewer expectations. Aaron, a high school senior, shared this experience.

My best friend and I go on double dates all the time. There has only been one time that we have had any difficulty. The date started out pretty normal. We picked up the girls and headed to the bowling alley. Everyone was having a good time. Then things started to get a little hairy. Chris's date decided that she wanted to sit on his lap, so she did. Then my date decided to follow suit.

Because we barely knew them and weren't looking for relationships at all, this made both Chris and me more than uncomfortable. It was then that we learned the true value of knowing what the other is thinking. It is simply a matter of communicating with your eyes. We decided to just sit at the scoring table after our turns. This worked like a charm. By treating the situation delicately, we were not only able to make ourselves more comfortable, but we were also able to spare the girls the embarrassment of something more direct.

5. SET YOUR OWN BOUNDARIES

Decide now the kind of people you will and won't date. Decide now how far you're willing to go, what's off limits, and don't let anyone talk you out of it. Don't wait until you're making out to decide; by then it's too late. If you haven't decided beforehand what your boundaries are, stuff happens you didn't plan on.

The greatest form of protection there is against heartbreak, inflated expectations, disease, pregnancy, or unwanted advances are the personal standards you set for yourself. If someone has a bad reputation, for heaven's sake, don't go out with them. One safe rule of thumb is: Only date people who respect your standards and make you a better person when you're with them. Consider the message of the movie *A Walk to Remember*.

Landon Carter is the reckless leader who is skating through high school on his good looks and bravado. He and his popular friends at Beaufort High publicly ridicule everyone who doesn't fit in, including the unfashionable Jamie Sullivan, who wears the same sweater day after day and gives free tutoring lessons to struggling students.

By accident, events thrust Landon into Jamie's world and he can't help but notice that Jamie's different. She doesn't care about conforming and fitting in with the popular kids. Landon's amazed at how sure of herself she seems and asks, "Don't you care what people think about you?" As he spends more time with her, he realizes she has more freedom than he does because she isn't controlled by the opinions of others, as he is.

Soon, despite their intentions not to, they have fallen in love and Landon has to choose between his status at Beaufort...and Jamie. "This girl's changed you," his best friend yells, "and you don't even know it." Landon admits, "She has faith in me. She wants me to be better."

He chooses her.

After high school graduation, Jamie reveals to Landon that she's dying of leukemia. During her final months, Landon does all he can to make her dreams come true, including marrying her in the same church her mother and father were married in. They spend a wonderful summer together, truly in love.

Despite Jamie's dream for a miracle, she dies. Heartbroken, but inspired by Jamie's belief in him, Landon works hard to go to medical school. But he laments to her father that he couldn't fulfill her last desire, to see a miracle. Jamie's father assures him that Jamie did see a miracle before she died, for someone's heart had truly changed. And it was his.

Now that's a movie to remember!

Never apologize for having high standards and don't ever lower your standards to please someone else. Lift theirs instead. Here are some examples of dating standards some teens have set:

- **always** date in pairs or groups
- only date people with **good reputations**
- **stay away** from **compromising situations**, like car parking, getting drunk or stoned, or babysitting with your date while your parents are out
- keep your **clothes on** and your **hands off**

If you don't set your own boundaries, someone else will do it for you.

6. HAVE A PLAN

Sixteen-year-old Metta shared this:

Guys, I'm telling you, if you want to impress a girl, you have to make some effort. I went on a really lame date last week. AJ asked me if I wanted to go bowling with a bunch of other couples. That sounded like a lot of fun, and I was really looking forward to the date. Well, when AJ and another couple came to pick me up they were 30 minutes late. I was bugged by that, but, oh well. And then when we all got to the bowling alley we couldn't get any lanes for 60 minutes.

We finally ended up going to AJ's house, where he and the guys spent two hours playing Xbox while the girls sat around talking. What a waste of time! Needless to say, I'll never go out with AJ again.

When you go out, have a plan as well as a backup plan in case things don't work out. I asked a few teens the question: What is the best date you've ever been on and what specifically did you do? Here's what a few of them said:

"My friend Chris and I played doubles in tennis with a couple of girls our age." — Aaron

"When my date came to pick me up to go skiing, my whole family invited themselves along. My date never complained, and, rather than be embarrassed, decided to make it a really great day for everybody." — Annie

"Me and my date played hide 'n' seek with other couples in the mountains." — Hank

"We went iceblocking (racing on blocks of ice), watched the movie *Ice Age,* and went out for ice cream." — Keli'i

"We walked around in the city, went to a museum, then he took me on a tour of the fire station where his dad worked. Most of all, he just took me to places that I would enjoy and was respectful." — Shannon

You don't need to have a lot of money to plan fun dates. Here's a list of 20 cheap but fun dating ideas you can do in pairs or groups:

Fun 'n' Cheap Dating Ideas*

1. Bake cookies together and deliver them to another friend.

2. Go to your niece's or nephew's soccer or baseball game.

3. Play board games with a group of friends or family.

4. Attend a community or church youth activity together.

5. Get together as a group and take turns watching everyone's favorite funny movie clip.

6. Make popcorn and watch a movie at home.

7. Have a picnic.

8. Go for a hike or rock climbing.

9. Attend a school play, then go for ice cream.

10. Play miniature golf.

11. Visit an art, science, or historical museum.

12. Go listen to a local band.

13. Play bigger and better. Start off with a pencil and go door-to-door in a neighborhood you know exchanging the item for something bigger and better. Meet up to see who wound up with the biggest and best item.

14. Go water-skiing or snow skiing.

15. Attend a free community event (check the newspaper to see what's going on).

16. Have a karaoke party.

17. As a group, go to the beach or the mountains and roast marshmallows.

18. Get camcorders, divide into teams, and have each team make a short film. Get back together and show all the films. The best film wins a prize.

19. Go to a golf driving range and hit a bucket of balls.

20. Borrow a telescope and look at the stars.

---

* If you want to share your creative date idea or learn what fun dates other teens are doing, go to www.6decisions.com.

To guys out there who are never really comfortable with the whole dating thing, just remember the classic words of Alex "Hitch" Hitchens from the movie *Hitch*:

"So tonight, when you're wondering what to say, or how you look, or whether or not she likes you, just remember, she is already out with you. That means she said YES when she could have said no. That means she made a plan when she could have just blown you off. So that means it is no longer your job to try to make her like you. It is your job NOT to mess it up."

The Four Great Sex Myths

Myths are beliefs that are widely held, but just because everyone believes something, that doesn't make it true. Here are a few common myths.

Myth: *Eating chocolate causes acne breakouts.*
Fact: Contrary to popular belief, there is no link between eating chocolate and acne breakouts.

Myth: *Daddy longlegs are the most poisonous of all spiders but their mouths are too small to bite you.*
Fact: There are several spiders that have been branded with this nickname—the harvestman, the crane fly, and the pholcid house spider. The first two aren't poisonous, and there is no scientific evidence to suggest the pholcid spider has particularly potent venom.

Myth: *Swallowed chewing gum takes seven years to digest and pass through your system.*
Fact: Chewing gum, though largely indigestible, will make its way through your digestive system at the same rate as anything else you eat.

So it is with the subject of sex. Lots of myths exist—popular beliefs that are false and unsupported by facts. Let me introduce you to four of the great ones. Before going there, however, take this quiz to see how much you know about the topic. I'll give you the answers to the questions as we go.

THINGS YOU ALWAYS WANTED TO KNOW ABOUT SEX BUT WERE AFRAID TO ASK

1. True or False. The vast majority of high school kids are having sex.

2. True or False. Having sex as a teen is becoming more and more common.

3. STD stands for
   a) Scare Teens to Death
   b) Some Tough Dude
   c) Sexually Transmitted Disease
   d) Soft, Tender, and Delicious

4. Each year, one in ___ sexually active teens gets an STD.
   a) one thousand
   b) one hundred
   c) fifty
   d) four

5. True or False. The younger a person begins having sex the more susceptible they are to a sexually transmitted disease.

6. True or False. Sexually transmitted diseases always have symptoms or signs that can be noticed.

7. True or False. You can pick up an STD from oral sex.

8. Approximately ___ teenage girls get pregnant each year in the U.S.; 80 percent of these pregnancies are unplanned.
   a) 7
   b) 300,000
   c) 3,000,000
   d) 6 gazillion

9. True or False. A girl can get pregnant the first time she has sex.

10. What percent of guys who get girls pregnant marry these girls?
    a) 100 percent
    b) 50 percent
    c) 20 percent
    d) 10 percent

11. The only protection that is 100 percent safe is
    a) taking birth control pills consistently
    b) using condoms every time
    c) practicing abstinence
    d) taking showers twice a day

12. True or False. About one in ten teens who have had sex wish they had waited.

13. After having sex, many teens
    a) have regrets
    b) get depressed and suffer from low self-esteem
    c) feel disappointed, hurt, betrayed
    d) any of the above

MYTH 1 EVERYONE'S DOING IT

Fact: Everyone's not doing it.

Some teens have sex before marriage because they think everyone is doing it and they just want to be normal. Well, guess what? About half your fellow teens aren't having sex. This number varies by country. In the United States, it's about half, in Europe it's higher, in Asia, it's lower. It may be higher or lower in your school.

> ## Question 1 Answer: False
>
> The majority of teens aren't having sex. About half are.

So, if you've decided to wait to have sex (or if you've had it but choose not to going forward) and you're feeling like you're not normal—take heart. You've got lots of company.

You might be thinking, "Well, the only people who aren't doing it are those who can't." Not true. There are lots of scholars, dancers, cheerleaders, athletes, popular kids, and normal teens who have decided to wait. And the number who are waiting is on the rise. Why? I think teens are beginning to see that teenage sex is not all that it's cracked up to be. And then there are all those diseases you can pick up.

Remember the Gamma Girls we spoke about on page 98? These are the girls who are involved in a variety of activities, are self-confident, and think popularity is overrated. If there is one thing about them that stands out, it's

> ## Question 2 Answer: False
>
> Having sex as a teen is becoming less common, not more.

that they have decided to wait until marriage to have sex.

Another person who waited was NBA star A. C. Green, who holds the NBA record for most consecutive games played. After playing in the NBA for 16 seasons, he married his wife as a virgin at the age of 38. Do you find that hard to believe? A. C. stayed true to his goal of waiting until marriage by following a few key rules he set for himself:

- **I control what I see and hear.** *I don't watch television and movies that show people having sex, or listen to music that tells me to have sex.*

- **I stay away from pressure situations.** *I don't invite a woman to my house after midnight to hang out or to watch a movie.*

- **I use the buddy system.** *I often bring a friend with me instead of being alone with a woman. It's easier to control myself when someone is there with me, making me accountable.*

MYTH 2

YOUR SEX DRIVE IS SO STRONG YOU CAN'T CONTROL IT

Fact: You can control your urges.

Man is an amazing creature! We splice genes, build skyscrapers 100 stories high, and fit a thousand million transistors on a silicon chip the size of a fingernail.

I have a friend, Erik Weihenmayer, who climbed Mount Everest—blind! I've read about Joan of Arc, the courageous 14-year-old French girl turned warrior, who saved France from its enemies and was later burned at the stake. I remember watching the TV news coverage of a plane crash in an icy river, and seeing a man pass the lifeline again and again to others until, exhausted and freezing, he sank below the surface, giving his life for people he didn't know. These are examples of the triumph of the human spirit.

So, when I hear someone say, "Teens are going to have sex because they can't control their hormones," I want to throw up. I mean, c'mon. It's not like we're a bunch of dogs in heat. Teenage guys, especially, get a bad rap for having no control of their bodily functions.

No responsible adult will ever tell you that having sex as a teen is a good thing. But many *will* say, "You can't stop teens from having sex, so teach them to be safe about it."

That's why they teach you about protecting yourself from disease and pregnancy in school. It's done with good intentions. The assumption is you aren't capable of controlling your urges.

That's where I differ. If we can split the atom, we can control our urges. We're human beings, not animals, after all. And we have the freedom to choose. Consider these stories shared by two teen boys from a Web site called greattowait.com.

I KNOW, BUT I'VE DECIDED TO KEEP IT IN THE GARAGE FOR NOW.

Craig: *Would a guy ever turn down sex? I did. My ex-girlfriend wanted to have sex, but I refused. She kept pressuring me. I don't know whether she thought I would stay with her if she did it or what. At the time, it really confused me. I liked her, but I wasn't ready to be tied down or get more involved. I guess she got what she wanted with her next boyfriend, although they're not together anymore. Last month, she came over to me and told me that I was the only boy she'd ever dated who respected girls and didn't try to use them. She said, "I wish I was still going with you."*

Ray: *I have been dating my girlfriend about six months. When we first started dating I told her that I had made the decision not to have sex now. She respects that. But I must admit it gets hard sometimes...When I get feelings that tempt me to go all the way, I make myself pull back and get those urges under control. I tell myself: "I can wait. I can wait." Believe me I spend a lot of time saying those three words to myself—but it's working.*

You see, between what happens to us (the stimulus) and what we do about it (our response) is a space, and in that space lies our freedom to choose. This is what it means to be proactive.

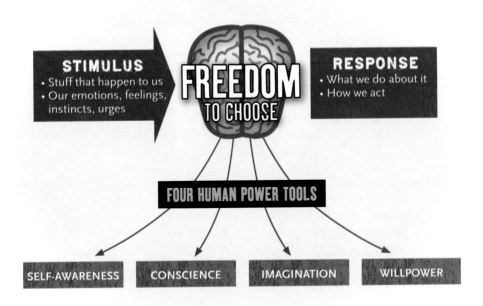

Craig and Ray were able to keep their commitments by using their power tools, also known as self-awareness, conscience, imagination, and willpower.

SELF-AWARENESS: I can stand apart from myself and observe my thoughts and actions. *(Craig and Ray knew it would take a lot of character strength to wait.)*

CONSCIENCE: I can listen to my inner voice and know right from wrong. *(Craig and Ray felt that waiting was the right thing to do.)*

IMAGINATION: I can imagine the future and the consequences of my actions. *(Craig and Ray could visualize that having sex now would tie them down and change the nature of their relationships.)*

WILLPOWER: I am free to choose and act in the face of strong influences. *(Craig and Ray chose to wait in the face of their urges.)*

Controlling Your Impulses

There are three notable things about our sex drive. First, it is strong. Second, it is constant. And third, it is good. Without it, no one would want to settle down and have children and the world would soon run out of people. It just needs to be used at the right time and with the right person, and it needs to be controlled, just like any other impulse.

I mean, what kind of world would we have if we responded to every passing urge? If you got angry with someone, you'd simply punch 'em. If you felt like sleeping in, you'd skip school or whatever and sleep in. Heck, if I gave free rein to my urges I'd weigh 420 pounds, because my instinct is to eat everything I see. At the movies I always get the urge to buy popcorn, a hot dog, a 36-ounce soda, licorice, and nachos for dessert. But I have to control myself because I don't want to weigh 420. Shouldn't we apply the same logic to our sex urges?

It takes a little discipline, but it's well worth it. As business philosopher Jim Rohn puts it, "We must all suffer from one of two pains: the pain of discipline or the pain of regret. The difference is discipline weighs ounces while regret weighs tons."

I just don't buy the idea that waiting to have sex is unrealistic. It's not unrealistic. Millions of teens worldwide have waited and are waiting and so can you. Self-control is stronger than hormones.

Yes, your sexuality is an important part of your life. But it's not the be-all and end-all of your existence, as our culture may lead you to believe. There are more important aspects to little ol' you than your sexuality, like your intellect, your personality, your hopes and dreams. As one teenage girl put it, "We are so much more than our urges."

DISCIPLINE

REGRET

MYTH 3 · SAFE SEX IS SAFE
Fact: There's no such thing as safe sex!

My greatest fear in life is being mauled by a bear. Every summer since I was little, my family has gone to my grandparents' cabin near Yellowstone Park, which happens to have lots of bears. Now, I've never actually seen one, but I've always had this premonition that I'm going to be mauled by one. I've even bought several books on how to survive a bear attack. My family thinks I'm weird, but at least I'm ready.

Now that I've shared my secret fear, what are you most afraid of? A shark attack? Being struck by lighting? An airplane crash?

Well, it's always helpful to put your fears in perspective, which is exactly what David Ropeik did for the Harvard Center for Risk Analysis as presented in *Prevention* magazine.

Big Fears versus Real World Risks

THE FEAR	THE REAL RISK
Deadly shark attack	1 in 280 million
Deadly anthrax attack	1 in 57 million
Deadly airplane accident	1 in 3 million
Shot by a sniper	1 in 517,000
Losing your job	1 in 252
Home burglary at night	1 in 181
Developing cancer	1 in 7
Catching a foodborne illness this year	1 in 4
Catching a sexually transmitted disease	1 in 4
Developing heart disease	1 in 4
Dying five to ten years early if you're overweight	1 in 4
Death from tobacco-related illnesses (smokers)	1 in 2

What struck me most about this chart is that it didn't include bear maulings, and that...

if you are a sexually active teen, you have a 1 IN 4 chance of picking up an STD this year.

Question 3 Answer

STD stands for sexually transmitted disease.

Is that unbelievable or what?

Even more shocking is a report from the Centers for Disease Control and Prevention that estimates half of all sexually active young Americans will get an STD by the age of 25. That's one out of every two! After what I've learned about STDs, believe me, you don't want one.

Now, before you start thinking, "Oh no, another old person trying to scare me out of sex," let me finish. Sex in

Question 4 Answer

Each year, one in four sexually active teens gets an STD.

itself is not bad or wrong. In fact, it's a wonderful thing, at the right time and with the right person, like with the person you're going to spend your life with, but it's very risky at the wrong time and with the wrong person.

GROSS ME OUT!

In 1950 there were two well-known types of STDs. Today there are more than 25. In the U.S. alone, more than three million teens pick up an STD annually. Given that there are only about 28 million teenagers, that's a bunch! The effects of these STDs are as ugly as their names: gonorrhea, syphilis, crabs, warts, chancroid, chlamydia, pelvic inflammatory disease, human papilloma virus, herpes. Eeeeuuuw! STDs can cause cervical cancer, genital warts, sterility, infertility, and diseases that can be passed on to unborn and newborn babies. They are a source of pain and depression, and can

Question 5 Answer: True

The younger you are, the more susceptible you are to sexually transmitted diseases.

ultimately kill you! The younger you are, the more susceptible your body is to picking something up, because teens have a lower level of antibodies, which fight infection, than adults.

Sounds extreme, doesn't it? Well, I was stunned, too. Some of this stuff may gross you out, but you need to know the facts. Here's a little info on four common STDs. Much of this information comes from reliable public information sources as well as from Dr. Meg Meeker's excellent book called *Epidemic: How Teen Sex Is Killing Our Kids.*

Herpes: The Incurable STD. Herpes is **INCURABLE**. It's also gross. Although the painful symptoms may come and go, the virus stays in your body for life. This virus is particularly nasty because it never disappears; it

> ### Question 6 Answer: False
>
> Sexually transmitted diseases can often lie dormant for years without signs or symptoms.

just goes underground, hiding in some of your nerve cells. It may lie dormant for months or years until something, like stress, causes an outbreak and then the virus causes ulcerated, painful lesions or blisters around your genitals or mouth. Is that a disgusting image or what? Even when herpes is inactive for eight or more years, you can still pass it on to a sexual partner.

Herpes is extraordinarily painful and humiliating. Infected mothers may give birth to babies who suffer brain damage or have become physically malformed because of the disease. Carriers report feeling like lepers and damaged goods; they never realized having casual sex would affect them for life.

"I thought she had sex with me right away because she liked me," said Allen. "But she just wanted to tell people she'd done it with me. Even though I'd like to forget her I never will. Why? Because, for the rest of my life, every time I'm involved in a relationship, I'm going to have to tell the person that I have one of the worst kinds of STDs, Herpes Simplex 2. It has no cure. I get rashes and blisters on my private areas and everything itches. I need to rest a lot—when I get stressed out, the blisters appear. I wonder if someone will ever want to be with me knowing that I have this and could pass it on to them. I am so angry at the girl who didn't warn me and gave me this disease. Having sex was supposed to mean I would feel really good. But I feel ashamed of myself. It wasn't that she was easy, I was easy."

OH, THIS IS MY STD. HE COMES WITH ME ON ALL MY DATES.

Human Papilloma Virus (HPV): The Most Common STD. HPV is the most prevalent STD. An estimated 20 million Americans are infected with HPV. Dr. Meeker, who specializes in treating teens with STDs, describes asking a group of teens: "Can sex give you cancer?" She was almost laughed off the stage. "Cancer? You can't get cancer from having sex!" students hooted. How she wished they were right.

HPV is the second leading cause of cancer deaths among women; approximately 5,000 women die each year from this disease. The virus works by infecting mucous membranes in the body, and young girls are especially vulnerable.

While HPV causes silent damage to internal organs you may never know about for years, it's also responsible for genital warts on young men and women. These venereal warts can become quite large and painful, and must be treated with either medication or surgery. Sick! Although treatable, HPV, like herpes, is **INCURABLE**. You have it for life.

HIV and AIDS: The Deadliest STD. Mark writes: "You hear about AIDS all the time but I thought it wouldn't ever happen to anyone I know. Then my sister's best friend got AIDS. This girl was a cheerleader, she got good grades, she had a great personality. Now she gets all these infections...I asked her how she got AIDS, and you know what she said? 'I trusted someone.'

Who knows, maybe the guy didn't know he had it...We all know she's going to die."

Why does AIDS get all the press? Because it's by far the deadliest. AIDS is the leading cause of death for African-American males between the ages of 15 and 44.

You can become infected with HIV if you come into contact with it in blood, semen, vaginal secretions, or breast milk. You can get it through heterosexual activity, not just homosexual activity, and it's spreading among women also. Today, 80 percent of all transmission occurs sexually, not through sharing drug needles or contaminated blood.

Like herpes, you may test negative for HIV and still have the virus.

Syphilis: The Baby STD. Syphilis continues to spread and many teens who have it may not even know it. Babies can contract syphilis while in the uterus. If a mother is not treated, there is a 20 percent chance that the baby will be either stillborn or miscarried, a 25 percent chance that the baby will die shortly after birth, and a 33 percent chance that the baby will have permanent brain or body damage.

Chains of Contagion

In a recent study published in the *American Journal of Sociology,* researchers tried to document every sexual contact among high school students over an 18-month period. The purpose was to learn how STDs travel through teen populations. The survey was conducted at a high school (they called it "Jefferson High") in a midwestern U.S. town with about 1,000 students. The result was a map that took the researchers by surprise. It showed that of the 832 kids surveyed, 288 of them were linked in a giant sexual network. Many others were linked in smaller networks. This is how STDs are spread.

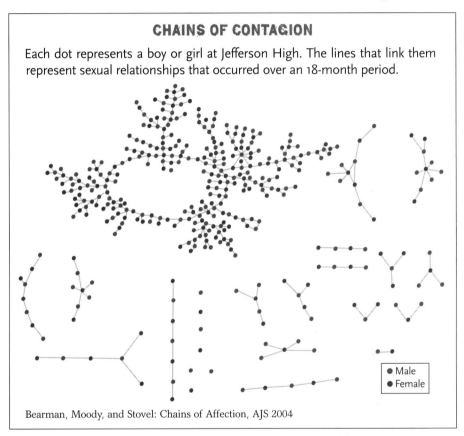

CHAINS OF CONTAGION

Each dot represents a boy or girl at Jefferson High. The lines that link them represent sexual relationships that occurred over an 18-month period.

● Male
● Female

Bearman, Moody, and Stovel: Chains of Affection, AJS 2004

Here are a few key facts from that study:

- *The more we pass ourselves around, the greater the likelihood of picking up something. If you were part of the chain of 288 students, you risked contracting an STD from everyone in the chain, even if you only had one partner. In other words, if you have sex with someone, you're having sex with everyone else they've had sex with.*

- *Several hundred students at Jefferson High had no sexual partners and were at no risk of catching an STD.*

- *The long and complex chain could easily be snapped by a single person who opts out. Think how quickly STDs could be reduced or eliminated through smart choices.*

The Ever-Changing Tide

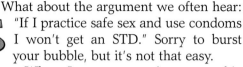

What about the argument we often hear: "If I practice safe sex and use condoms I won't get an STD." Sorry to burst your bubble, but it's not that easy.

When I was young, it was no big deal to lie out in the sun all day and get burned, but now experts tell you that even a couple of really nasty burns can cause skin cancer years later. Likewise, during the 1990s, experts used to say that safe sex could be practiced by using condoms. Now, some of these experts are saying using a condom is not safe sex at all, but only less dangerous sex.

Dr. Patricia Sulak, who is a doctor and professor at Texas A&M University's College of Medicine, is one expert who changed her mind. "I used to think all we had to do was dump condoms in the schools and be done with it," she said. "But after reviewing the data, I've had to do a 180 on kids and sex."

In the past few years, guess what they've discovered? *There is no clear scientific evidence that using condoms provides significant protection from several STDs,* including the incurable and most common one: HPV. Surprise! One reason for this is because some STDs like HPV are passed by skin to skin contact of the genital area, not just the part the condom is covering.

Likewise, birth-control pills help to prevent pregnancy, but do nothing to protect against STDs.

In addition, condoms often aren't used properly, may slip or leak, and, even with the best of intentions, most couples don't have the discipline to stick with them.

So, the next obvious question you may be thinking is: What about oral sex? Is that safe? I'll let Rhonda Katz, an expert on teens and sex, answer that question for me.

Question: *I've heard...that there's a lot of oral sex happening among teens. The kids think it's safe and not really sex...What are the risks of oral sex?*

Answer: Oral sex carries the risk of contracting (and spreading) serious diseases—gonorrhea, syphilis, herpes, HIV, chlamydia, and others. STDs can easily infect your mouth and throat, and mouth herpes (cold sores) can infect genitals. Most girls don't use condoms for oral sex, making the risk of STDs even greater...Having herpes sores on your mouth is not only embarrassing, but you run the risk of spreading it by oral sex or even kissing.

If you've been shocked and grossed out a little by all this stuff—good! Hopefully, you'll do something about it. If you've been sexually active, perhaps you'll want to turn over a new leaf.

You may know someone with an STD, or maybe you suspect you've got one. If so, please see a doctor and get tested immediately. You may need help and the sooner you can get it the more options you'll have. See the Help Desk for more info.

> **Question 7 Answer: True**
>
> You can pick up an STD
> from oral sex.

I don't know about you, but that's about all the STD talk I can take.

UH-OH!

Birth control can fail—it often does. That's why millions of teens throughout the world get pregnant each year, unplanned. If you're sexually active, chances are good that you'll either get pregnant or get someone pregnant, even if you use protection.

> **Question 8 Answer: 3,000,000**
>
> Approximately **3,000,000** teenage girls get pregnant in the United States each year; eight of ten of these pregnancies are unplanned.

It can also happen in just one encounter. I know of an Australian girl who found out she was pregnant on the same day she got accepted to study music at a premier university. She only did it one time with her boyfriend but that was enough. As a result, she never went to college and her life took a totally different course.

Girls: You and your partner are not both pregnant—just you are. It will change your life forever. Jerusha, who became a mother at 16, shared what it was like during a regular day at Young Mothers School:

> **Question 9 Answer: True**
>
> A girl can get pregnant
> the first time she has sex.

All of the girls were at different stages. Some were newly pregnant, some were about to give birth, and some had one- and two-year-olds. At first, it was very distracting because you would sit in class with these girls and their babies. You would be in the middle of taking a test and sometimes four or five babies would be screaming right next to you.

This is what a typical day was like for me and my baby Kristin.

6:30 A.M.: I'd wake up and get myself ready.

7:00 A.M.: I'd get Kristin up, feed her, give her a bath, do her hair, get her dressed, pack us both a lunch, and pack the diaper bag.

8:00 A.M.: I'd leave for school.

8:15 A.M.: I'd try to get Kristin settled in the nursery—she'd often cry and not want me to go—I'd cry because it was so hard to leave her.

8:30 A.M.: School starts. I'd try to do my homework, but wonder if Kristin was doing okay without me. Often, I'd get called out of class to change her diaper, then I'd have to leave her screaming again which killed me.

12:00 NOON: At lunch I'd have to hurry and pick her up, feed her in a high chair, clean up the big mess she'd make, and if I'd get lucky, eat some lunch myself and get her back to the nursery all within 30 minutes. She'd get upset all over again when I'd have to leave.

And this is just the first half of Jerusha's day.

Guys: If you get a girl pregnant and she has the baby, you've just fathered a child. Whether you marry the girl or not, that baby is yours! Whether you do the responsible thing and take care of the child or the irresponsible thing and abandon it, you're obligated to that child for life. Are you ready to be a daddy to a living, breathing human being who needs love and attention?

> **Question 10 Answer: 20 percent**
>
> **20 percent** of guys who get a girl pregnant wind up marrying the girl.

Read how an unplanned pregnancy impacted Dylan.

I remember the day my girlfriend told me she was pregnant. One minute I had no worries, then the next I had a lifetimeful. Don't get me wrong, I wouldn't give up my daughter for anything. But now, while my buddies hang out and have fun, I go to work trying to make enough money to support my child. Having sex used to make me feel grown-up. But there's a big difference between feeling grown-up and being grown-up. I'm just now learning what it means to be responsible for the life of another person. One way or another, my future is always going to be tied to this girl because of my baby.

Whole People

So far, we've only talked about the physical risks of sex, like disease and pregnancy. There are also serious emotional risks, like heartbreak, regret, guilt, depression. Remember that we are made up of four parts: body, heart, mind, and soul, and all four parts are connected into one great whole. Like the four tires of a car, if one is out of balance, all four wear unevenly. Realize that having sex, a physical thing, also impacts your heart, mind, and

Question 11 Answer: C

Abstinence as a teen is the only protection that is **100 percent** safe from disease, pregnancy, and emotional scarring.

soul, whether you want it to or not. Don't ever think that you can get physical with someone and not have it affect how you feel about yourself. Having sex as a teen

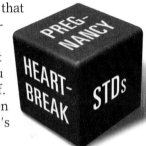

is like playing Russian roulette with your future. There's risk at every roll.

After everything we've talked about, can you see why I can safely say there's no such thing as safe sex?

IT'S NO BIG DEAL
Fact: It's a Big Deal!

You're not going to get married for another ten years or so, so what's the harm in having a little fun, as long as you're not hurting anyone and no one's getting pregnant? Right?

I can't blame anyone for believing that sex is no biggie. After all, the media treats sex as a disposable form of entertainment that can be bought, sold, rented, or traded, and is available everywhere, 24/7, and in all forms, including live, virtual, mobile, audio, or print. During your teen years alone, you will see and hear about 98,000 sexual references and innuendoes on TV. Whoa! That's a lot of smut.

Of course, some will argue that what you see in the movies and on TV doesn't really affect you. Then, these same people will turn around and pay millions for a 30-second commercial during the Super Bowl. If a 30-second commercial can get you to change your shampoo, surely 98,000 impressions can influence the way you think. As Alisia said,

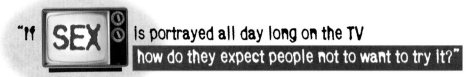

"If **SEX** is portrayed all day long on the TV
how do they expect people not to want to try it?"

In the movies, everyone's doing it, usually on the first date. When you see it enough times, you start to think that's just the way things are and it's OK. We forget that movies lie about the way things really are.

For instance, when's the last time you saw a show where a couple slept together, then felt guilt or regret, or one of them picked up an STD? Have you ever seen a romantic movie that shows the betrayal a woman feels when she finds out she's pregnant and her boyfriend wants nothing to do with her? You never see it because it's neither fun nor romantic. Let's not be so quick to buy Hollywood's line that sex is no big deal. It's a lie.

Intimacy and Commitment

With roughly 7 trillion cells working in concert, your body is an extraordinary thing that should be respected, not a merry-go-round on which everyone gets a ride. It doesn't make sense to share the most intimate parts of yourselves until you are fully committed to each other. Intimacy without commitment is like getting *something for nothing;* it goes against a basic principle. What is a committed relationship? A marriage is the best form I know. With a marriage, you get a legal document, a public celebration, a ring, a recognized union, and a deep promise to love each other through health and sickness.

What about a high school relationship where you're truly in love? Does that count as committed? Not really. Although there may be a very strong bond, there is no real commitment. There is no legal agreement, no celebration over your union, no shared rent payment. You aren't doing the dishes, cleaning the laundry, or paying the bills together. You break up, move, go to college, start liking someone else, and so on.

Some teens think that if you haven't actually done it (sexual intercourse) then you haven't had sex and can still be classified as a "technical virgin." Hey, let's be real. Sex is sex.

I'm sorry for being so direct, but whether it's intercourse or outercourse, manual, dry, or oral sex, or whatever else you invent, if you're unzipping things, taking off clothes, reaching inside clothes, exchanging fluids, or handling each other's "private parts" (as little kids like to call them), it's intimate and it's sex. Although some forms of sex may not be as risky physically, they're every bit as risky emotionally.

Everyone disagrees with what the terms *hooking up* or *friends with benefits* really mean, but basically they are nothing more than no-strings-attached sexual encounters of some type. In reality, it's just a way to use each other's bodies for pleasure without any expectations or commitment—fast, easy, and unfulfilling.

Depression: The Emotional STD

I was interested to see what a doctor had to say about the emotional impact of sex. After treating thousands of teens over two decades, Dr. Meeker is convinced that teenage sex causes severe emotional problems, even calling depression the *emotional* STD. She writes:

"While many teenage boys claim sex is fun, in private, many admit that they lose respect for themselves after a sexual encounter. They may boast about their sexual exploits and appear to have gained more self-confidence, but privately they admit that something changed inside them after they started having sex. They have less self-respect, having given up their sexual intimacy to someone they didn't care deeply about.

"Girls have the potential to feel an even greater loss of self-respect. Society has encouraged her to expose every inch of her body she can get away with, and in doing so teaches that their bodies are not worth protecting. She may give herself sexually (which means a lot to her) to a guy she deeply cares about and he may not receive it with respect and she soon learns he's not so interested in her, just in sex.

"Protecting our virginity, like self-preservation, must be hard-wired into us because I have watched hundreds of teens grieve the loss of their virginity. Inwardly, we all sense and know down deep that virginity is something precious and private and when we surrender it and then experience disappointment or rejection we feel a great loss of something we can't get back."

> ### Question 12 Answer: False
>
> About *half* of teens who had sex wished they would have waited.

Lucian, featured in a *Newsweek* article, shared the emotional impact on him and how he rebounded.

Lucian had always planned to wait until marriage to have sex, but that was before a warm night provided him with an unexpected opportunity. "She was all for it," says Lucian. "It was like, 'Hey, let's give this a try.'" But the big event was over really fast and lacked any feeling of love or intimacy. "In movies, if people have sex, it's always romantic," he says. "Physically, it did feel good, but emotionally, it felt really awkward. It was not what I expected it to be."

Lucian was plagued by guilt. "I was worried that I'd given myself to someone and our relationship was now a lot more serious than it was before. It was like, 'Now, what is she going to expect from me?'" Lucian also worried about disease and pregnancy and promised himself never again.

Lucian, now an engineering major at a university in Canada, considers himself a "renewed virgin." His parents had always stressed chastity but it didn't hit home until after he'd done it. "It's a pretty special thing, and it's also

Question 13 Answer: D

After having sex, many teens have regrets, become depressed and suffer from low self-esteem, or feel disappointed, hurt, and betrayed.

pretty serious," he says. "Abstinence has to do with 'Hey, are you going to respect this person?'" Now, when he dates, he restricts himself to kissing. "Not because I think everything else is bad. But the more you participate with someone, the harder it's going to be to stop...I'm looking forward to an intimate relationship with my wife, who I'll truly love and want to spend the rest of my life with," says Lucian. "It's kind of corny, but it's for real."

YES, SEX IS A VERY BIG DEAL.

Love Waits

Every summer I go water-skiing at a beautiful, but freezing, lake in the Rocky Mountains. I've learned how to ski starting on the dock instead of in the water. I stand on the dock holding the ski rope while the boat slowly pulls out. When most of the slack in the rope is out I yell "hit it" and the boat floors it. Then, just as the slack tightens I step off the dock onto the water and start skiing.

This took dozens of tries to master. I learned that if you step off too soon and have too much slack, you sink into the glacial water and start hyperventilating. If you step off too late and have no slack, you get jerked off the dock and your arms practically get ripped out of their sockets. If you time it just right, you step smoothly onto the water and start skiing without getting wet. It's the best feeling in the world.

Sexual intimacy is kind of like that. If you do it at the wrong time, you either sink in the frigid water or get your arms ripped off. If you do it at the right time and with the right person, it's the greatest feeling in the world. It's all in the timing.

I remember reading an interview with a 21-year-old guy who was attending college who said:

"Chastity has been an enormous concern to me. I have failed at it because I couldn't answer the question, 'Why wait to have sex?' I gave in because I didn't have a solid answer."

Good question. If you don't have a solid answer to the question "Why wait?" consider these reasons.

WAIT FOR THE CHILD

As author Jeffrey R. Holland states, two of the most important things in life are how people come into the world (birth) and how they go out of the world (death). We're so careful about how people leave the world. We have stiff penalties for murder. We do all we can to prolong life. We mourn when people die. But we're so careless when it comes to how people enter the world. Millions of babies are born each year all over the world through unplanned pregnancies—millions more are aborted.

Your ability to create life is like a match. It can do much good or much harm. A match can give light to everyone in a dark room. It can also burn down your home.

Each time you have sex you are playing with fire. There's always a chance that a baby could come of it. And it's so unfair to the child to be born without a committed father or to a mother who hasn't even finished high school. Some girls get pregnant just because having a baby gives them attention and someone to love. Maybe so. But it's so unfair to the baby. They need every advantage they can get to make it in this world. If you want your child to be raised in poverty, then have a baby as a teen. It is the surest indicator.

Lots of kids are raised without fathers. Luckily, there are many moms who do an amazing job as single parents. If you don't have a father in your life, you can be a cycle breaker and become the father you always wished you had to your own kids. You probably know of James Earl Jones, the voice of Darth Vader in the *Star Wars* films. Recently he received an award by the National Fatherhood Initiative. He stood up and said, "This award means more to me than any acting award I have ever received. I never knew my father. My father never knew his father. But my son knows me."

Don't take the chance of bringing a child into this world until you're ready to be a great father or mother. Give your child the best possible chance to succeed. Wait for the child.

INSTRUCTIONS:
MOM AND DAD, PLEASE READ CAREFULLY

I'M A 100 PERCENT GENUINE BABY. CLOTHE, PROTECT, AND FEED ME OFTEN. THE MORE TIME AND ATTENTION YOU GIVE ME, THE BETTER I GROW. I LIKE TO PLAY, SING, DANCE, TALK, GO ON WALKS, AND SCRIBBLE. SOMETIMES I NEED DISCIPLINE. BEST RESULTS WHEN RAISED BY A MOM AND A DAD.

SIZE MAY VARY.

WAIT FOR THE RELATIONSHIP

Relationships move forward in two different ways. Both start with **attraction.** Lots of different things attract or turn us on, a look, a gesture, the sound of a voice. Where the relationship goes from there is up to us.

The **selfish lust** route usually starts with **infatuation**, which feels like real love but is merely a flash in the pan. These obsessions usually burn out quickly. Before long, we start looking for our next flame. The **material** stage is when you get physical because it feels good and seems like the logical next step in the relationship. You say it's love but it's really lust. **Breakup** is what inevitably happens when the relationship is based primarily on the physical.

If you want to build solid boy-girl relationships, you take the **selfless love** route. It starts with a foundation of **friendship**, getting to know and like someone, regardless of what you might get from them physically. **Bonding** is when you start to understand and care for someone on a deeper level, learning their hopes and dreams, their fears and faith. It may involve some light hugging and kissing, based on affection, not lust. **Commitment** is when you desire to share your lives together in a committed, long-term relationship, commonly known as **marriage**. At this stage sex is good and fulfilling.

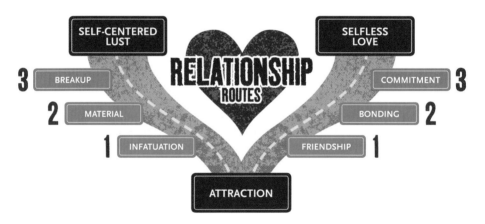

Hoon, a 17-year-old from Seoul, Korea, had to choose which relationship route to take.

I had been dating my girlfriend for over six months. Like most guys my age, I was pretty curious and full of wonder about having sex. I heard from friends that it was great. So, I naturally thought I would have sex when the time came.

One day, it was just me and her alone in the apartment and after watching TV I started doing business. When I kissed her, I looked into her eyes. They were filled with fear. It startled me. So I had to ask, "Is anything wrong?"

"No, nothing," she said. "I'm just so nervous. We're not old enough yet."

She was 20 years old and I wasn't even her age yet, but I assumed that we were old enough. What she then told me completely changed my ideas about having sex. She wanted to save herself for someone who she would get married to. She was also thinking about the trouble that pregnancy could cause us. She also confessed she didn't want hasty sex to become an obstacle in our relationship.

Her words showed me what sex would really mean to us, and I gave her a big hug to show her I loved her and I felt warm all over.

So, how far is too far? Everyone will tell you that once you start kissing passionately and get turned on it's really difficult to turn off and things naturally tend to progress. So it's smart not to move beyond short hugs and light kisses. If you want to keep healthy relationships and if you want to avoid the risk of pregnancy, STDs, and emotional scarring, live above the bar. Stay on the side of affection and save passion for later.

Live Above the Bar

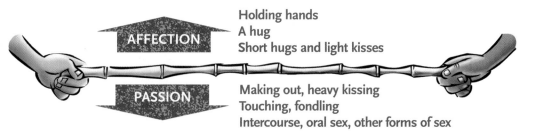

AFFECTION
Holding hands
A hug
Short hugs and light kisses

PASSION
Making out, heavy kissing
Touching, fondling
Intercourse, oral sex, other forms of sex

Living above the bar won't just happen. You'll have to make it happen. How? By making your own rules. When I started dating seriously in college I had to set rules for myself to live above the bar, like not dating girls that had fast and easy reputations. One teen boy said, "They teach you all the facts about sex, but don't teach you any rules." Well, here are three common sense rules to help you live above the bar.

- *Set goals and write a personal mission statement that spells out what you want to achieve. These will give you strength to say no to things you don't want to do.*

- *Avoid compromising situations where it's easy to let your guard down, like being alone in a bedroom.*

- *Don't fill your mind with racy music, movies, or pornography of any kind that will influence your thoughts and actions.*

For a moment, imagine the person you hope to marry. What do they look like? Are they funny, intelligent, kind? How do you hope they are living their life right now? Would it bother you if you knew they were hooking up each weekend or had five, ten, or fifteen different partners over the past several years? Or would it make you smile if you knew they were holding out for you? Why not live your life as you would want them to live theirs? Wait for the relationship.

WAIT FOR THE FREEDOM

When's the last time you flew a kite? Did you notice that when a kite is flying high it's the tension from the string that keeps it up? If you cut the line, which is the restraining force, the kite would drop to the ground.

So it is with love. Restraint keeps love and relationships alive. At times we wonder why we shouldn't give way to our raging hormones. The answer is that rules and restraints don't restrict us, but actually increase our freedom. If you aren't sexually active, consider the freedom your choices have already granted you. You are free from worry, regret, disease, pregnancy, complications, or taking on responsibilities you're not ready for.

Here's how Maisey from a California high school put it:

I'm not having sex right now. I believe that I should just wait until I get married. I don't want to live my whole life wondering about an STD. I want to be free to do whatever I want to do. I have a friend. She's had sexual intercourse, and she was worried about HIV or something. And I was like, "Wow. You're so young and you're already worried about that." I don't want to be worried about that, and I don't want to be worried about having a kid and not being able to have fun.

> ...AND IF ANYONE KNOWS WHY THESE TWO SHOULD NOT BE WED, SPEAK NOW OR FOREVER HOLD YOUR--

> **YOO-HOO!**

When it comes to romance, unless you have a plan, anything can and usually does happen. More than 50 percent of senior girls who have had sex said it was something that just happened. Girls, I've got to single you out because most likely you're the ones who are pressured by your boyfriends to say "yes" to sex or other stuff. Maybe you've already felt this pressure, and didn't know what to say.

Well, I've got some good ammunition for you. Kristen Anderson, in her book *The Truth about Sex by High School Senior Girls*, gives you some smart comebacks to classic lines boys have used since the beginning of time to wear you down. These could also apply to guys getting pressured by girls.

LINE: "Come on, please? Let's take our relationship to the next level."
COMEBACK: "I think sex will ruin what we have going now, not make it better."

"Explain why not. I don't understand."
"I just don't want to." (That's all the explanation you need to give.)

"Maybe we should just break up until you grow up."
"Maybe we should just break up until **you** grow up."

"You're going to wait until you're married? I don't know if I'll ever get married."
"That's too bad 'cause then you'll never get to have sex with me."

"Of all the girls who like me, I picked you."
"I think you have good taste."

"You've had sex before. What's the problem now?"
"The problem is I did something I regret now. I don't want to go through that again."

"Just relax and let go."
(If you are tense or nervous, it's for a reason. Your mind and body are trying to
tell you something. Respect your intuition and call things off.)

"If you loved me, you'd do it."
"If you loved me, you wouldn't pressure me."

Whatever you do, don't change your mind in the heat of the moment. A
true lady or gentlemen won't ask you to do something you don't want to do.
Wait for the freedom.

Worth Waiting For

Below are two letters from teens who were willing to share their reasons
for waiting.

To: Guys who think they have to have sex to be accepted
From: A guy who says no and is comfortable with it

*When I entered high school, everyone knew that my mom was the sex educa-
tion teacher in school, and so kids assumed I held the same beliefs she did. I have
always been taught by my parents that my body is a temple and that sex is reserved
for marriage. Besides that, the facts my mother has on STDs are terrifying and
reason enough for me to keep my commitment to be abstinent until I get married.*

*After high school, I was offered a scholarship at Temple University to play soccer.
Our team has a great group of guys, but I didn't know anyone so I had to reestab-
lish myself socially. At first, some of the people I got close to respected my beliefs,
but didn't know if I was serious about abstinence because they didn't know anyone
like me. But now, I have great friends with similar standards, and it's good to
associate with others who feel the same about sex before marriage.*

I have had a few girlfriends and gone on many dates and never had a problem with sex because they knew of my feelings beforehand and respected them. We connected on different levels than just sex so I really got to know them well. Sometimes they have asked how I can abstain from sex. I always tell them that if you really believe in something, then you wouldn't want to break your oath, would you? I look forward to marriage and raising a family with someone who I have saved myself for.

To: Girls who are feeling pressure to have sex
From: Sue Simmerman, a girl who's been there

My decision not to have sex was not difficult in middle school, but when I entered high school it definitely became more of an issue. A lot more of my friends began having sex with older guys.

I had the same boyfriend from eighth grade all the way through high school, and my first year of college (five-and-a-half years), so rather than saying no to a lot of people, I was just saying no to him. I must admit, I almost gave in a few times for the mere fact that I was SOOOOOO SICK *of having the same conversation and argument over and over again.*

Sometimes, out of frustration, I would finally say, "Fine, whatever. I'll do it then!" But then I'd quickly think about it and say, "You know what? I'm not giving in to you and letting you ruin that experience for me since it will be out of sheer frustration that I'd be doing it!" Then I would apologize for my beliefs, which I hated doing and totally regretted afterward. Fortunately, I finally realized it was a very unhealthy, immature relationship and I found the courage to end it.

I am 19 years old now, and there is not a day when I have regretted my decision to stay abstinent. I'm actually happier with it as the years go by. I have a new boyfriend who completely respects my decision and doesn't hassle me about it and we have a wonderful relationship.

If there is a girl out there who is struggling with the decision to remain abstinent or not, I would say from experience to hold true to what you want for yourself. If your friends or boyfriend don't accept your decision or make fun of you, I know it's a cliché, but they're not your real friends anyway.

Here's my list of advantages for waiting:

1 *I can give the person I marry a gift that no one else will ever have.*

2 *I have escaped the emotional trauma that I've seen some of my friends go through because of having sex with different people and even being taken advantage of.*

3 *I escaped a bad reputation.*

4 *I have learned a tremendous amount of self-respect.*

5 *I have learned self-restraint.*

6 *I know that my decision is pleasing to God and my family.*

7 *I have not had the worries that many of my friends and peers have had about pregnancy and disease.*

The Domino Effect

Perhaps you've passed yourself around too much. Perhaps you've been in an abusive relationship and lost your self-esteem. Maybe you've gotten pregnant or gotten someone pregnant. Now what?

Whatever you do, don't be like a line of falling dominos, where one mistake leads to another and another and another. Sometimes when we slip up we think: "Well, I've already blown it. Who cares what happens now?" Just remember, one mistake isn't as bad as two or three mistakes. If you've done something you regret, stop the dominos from falling by taking control and not making another mistake.

Remember, today is not forever. The desperate situation you may be in now will get better if you go to work on it. Things change, people forgive, hearts can be made whole, and life can be good again.

See how Andrea Small stopped the dominos from continuing to fall in her life.

I became a mother of a little girl when I was only 15. By 16, we lived in a small downtown apartment and I was working to support us. I didn't have even a year of high school education, but I spent tons of time at a local Barnes & Noble reading books on every subject. I got my GED and scored high on the SAT, so I enrolled in college, one year earlier than if I had remained in high school. A year later, I began at the University of Virginia.

I worked my way through college at a coffee shop with my daughter in day care. At night, she had to listen to me read from my Norton Anthology of English Literature *instead of* Goodnight Moon *because I had to get my homework done!*

Well, the years have gone by, and that little girl turns 14 soon and has been on the honor roll for every grading period of her entire life! She is now the oldest of four beautiful, brilliant children who are all succeeding in school.

I feel I have learned that you can't live forever on one success or failure. You will always encounter new challenges, and life is never what you thought it would or should be. I'm just glad life isn't boring.

I could go on with stories of teens who have turned around their lives after making a mistake: an unwed mother who gave up her baby for adoption to a loving couple because she wanted a better life for her child; an unwed father who married the girl he got pregnant and became a dedicated husband and father; and a promiscuous teen who earned a bad reputation but did a sex-180 and took a totally different approach to relationships.

If you've been sexually active up to now and you're starting to regret it, it's never too late to wipe the slate clean and start over. Anthony Maher grew up in a home where his parents taught him about the importance of good values. "I knew at a very young age what was right and wrong concerning relationships," says Anthony. "So when I was a freshman in high school, I made a half-hearted commitment to remaining sexually pure until marriage. I thought it would be easy. What I didn't know was by continuing to surround myself with those who were sexually active I was setting myself up for failure.

"It was my senior year, and in one moment of bad judgment I lost something I will never get back again. Instantly, I knew I had let myself down."

At that point, Anthony made a commitment to what he calls "secondary virginity." But this time he meant it. He's now a 22-year-old professional soccer player who has remained true to his commitment.

"I'm no longer the 16-year-old high school student who thinks remaining a secondary virgin will be easy. Now, I feel I have a strong foundation that includes defining my commitment, surrounding myself with friends with similar values, and keeping on guard. I believe with all my heart that by doing this, I will provide myself with the best chance to have a great marriage and all that goes with it."

TWU WUV

Here we are at the end of the chapter. I hope I haven't offended you with my opinions and bluntness. My only wish has been to equip you for your quest for true love.

As for me, I've always struggled over making big decisions so I really wondered if I'd ever get married. Talk about a big decision! Then, in college, I met a girl I really liked named Rebecca.

To my utter surprise, I fell in love, made a decision, and got married. One of the best things was that before getting married we had a great dating relationship based on friendship and affection, not on passion. It made all the difference!

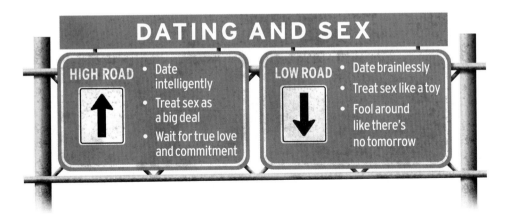

DATING AND SEX

HIGH ROAD
↑
- Date intelligently
- Treat sex as a big deal
- Wait for true love and commitment

LOW ROAD
↓
- Date brainlessly
- Treat sex like a toy
- Fool around like there's no tomorrow

There are two roads to choose from. I hope you'll choose the higher road by dating intelligently, treating sex and intimacy like it's a big deal, and holding out for true love and commitment. I promise you that you'll never regret it. Believe me, you don't want to have your heart broken, you don't want to feel used, you don't want to be raising a kid when you're still a kid, and you don't want to tell your future fiancée, "Sorry, but I have this strange sexual disease I picked up my junior year. Oops!"

So, choose wisely.
Be careful with your kisses.
And remember that
Love is definitely worth waiting for.

● ● ● COMING ATTRACTIONS ● ● ●

If you've ever wondered what's meant by the words hooch, snuff, roach, stackers, glass, skag, whippets, toot, and Georgia homeboy, you'll soon find out. Keep reading.

BABY STEPS*

1. Plan an original and fun date. For ideas, go online and search under *"cool dates for teens."*

2. If you know someone in an abusive relationship, share your book and have them read the "Intelligent Dating" section. Be supportive and remind your friend that no one deserves to be abused.

3. Watch the movie *A Walk to Remember*. As you watch it, ask yourself: What kind of standards do I want to live by?

4. Share *"The 6 Guidelines to Intelligent Dating"* with another person—a sibling, parent, or friend.

5. Write down five solid reasons for waiting to have sex.

   _____

   _____

   _____

   _____

6. Post it: "Timing is Everything!"

7. Make your own list of comebacks to someone who is making unwanted advances. Practice them in the mirror or on your most intimidating stuffed animal.

8. Draw a line on your mirror with lipstick or a crayon to remind yourself to Live Above the Bar. Stay on the side of affection and save passion for later.

9. If you're currently in a relationship that is based on the physical side of things, switch it to a relationship based on friendship. If it's a healthy relationship, it will endure. If it's based on infatuation, it won't. Either way, you win.

10. Imagine the person you will marry someday. How do you hope they're living their life right now, especially when it comes to dating and sex?
    I hope my future love is...

    _____

    _____

    _____

* To keep an online journal of your Baby Steps progress, go to www.6decisions.com.

DECISION 5

ADDiCTiONS

It's Not Hard to Quit...I've Done It a Dozen Times

Top 10
Things You Oughta Know About Addictions...

10. Addictions can be good and bad. Be addicted to getting your homework done and on time.
Jason Ormond, 16, Orem, Utah

9. Addictions are expensive to buy, dangerous to health, damage a family, make people die, and are difficult to get rid of.
Joy Wu, 16, Singapore

7. The key to most things in life is that everything must be done in moderation. Anything in excess, even exercising, subtly eats away at you and your personality.
Paul Jones, 19, Wales

8. Drinking is NOT a social norm.
Muhammad Faiz Gin Abdul Rahmat Mordiffi, 18

6. Addiction is a sign of a bigger problem. You'll never overcome addiction unless you search out the real problem and deal with it.
Martin Palmer, 19, Honolulu, Hawaii

5. If one is addicted to something, then he is a slave to that addiction.
Shahd Bakir, 16, Ramallah, Palestine

4. Be strong enough to leave friends who pressure you.
Logan Kendell, 19, Pocatello, Idaho

3. Smoking kills you and your friends... just don't smoke— it stinks.
Aimee Peyton, 17, Tacoma, Washington

2. The friends you make through addictions only like you because you are part of the addiction. They are not true friends.
JENNIFER HASTIE, 18, GULLANE, SCOTLAND

1. Taking drugs is not stylish or cool. It is dangerous and reckless and it will take your life away.
Kanchan Kaicker, 15, Gurgaon, India

Smoking kills. If you're killed, you've lost a very important part of your life.

— Brooke Shields, actress

Below are some of the greatest last lines said by people just before they took their final breaths.

FAMOUS LAST LINES

"I wonder where the mother bear is."

"I'll hold it and you light the fuse."

"So, you're a cannibal."

"Don't worry. I'm sure it's dead by now."

"Gee, that's a cute tattoo."

"I think it's trying to communicate."

Here are some other famous last lines said by teens as they started down the path toward addiction.

- *"No, dude, this stuff is completely natural and safe. That's why it's called herbal."*
- *"One time isn't going to hurt me."*
- *"Everyone's doing it."*
- *"I could quit any time."*
- *"You only live once."*
- *"It's my life. I'm not hurting anyone."*

There are so many things you can become addicted to including tobacco, alcohol, illegal drugs, prescription drugs, food, sleeping, eating disorders, overspending, compulsive behaviors, obsessions, TV, video games, Internet surfing, instant messaging, sex, pornography, card games, gambling, or even self-mutilation like cutting. Many of these are minor and won't really harm you, such as playing endless card games or craving a certain kind of candy. They're really more like preferences than addictions. Other addictions are severe and can alter your brain, make you do stupid things, or even kill you.

We live in an addiction-infested society. In the surveys I sent to your fellow teens, drinking, smoking, and drugs were always mentioned as one of the top challenges teens face. In many schools, it was *the* top challenge.

So, why are addictions such a big deal? Consider this.

During World War II, Viktor Frankl, a Jewish psychiatrist, was imprisoned in the death camps of Nazi Germany. His parents, brother, and wife died in the camps or were sent to the gas ovens. Frankl himself was tortured repeatedly and suffered beyond words, never knowing from one moment to the next if he too would be led to the ovens.

One day, alone in a small room, he began to become aware of what he called "the last of human freedoms"—the freedom the Nazis could not take away from him. They could kill his family, they could torture his body, but he alone could decide within himself how all of this was going to affect him. *He was free to choose his response to whatever happened to him.*

To keep his hopes alive, Frankl would imagine himself lecturing to his students after his release from the death camps. He'd see himself talking about the very experiences he was then going through in the camps. Over time, he became an inspiration to the prisoners around him and helped many find meaning in their suffering. In the end, Frankl survived the war, and went on to become a great teacher and author, just as he had visualized.

Next to life itself, the power to choose is your greatest gift. And if you become addicted to something, you give up your power to choose—your freedom. You become the slave and the addiction becomes your master. When it says "jump," you say "how high?" That's why what you choose to do about addictions is clearly one of the most important decisions you'll ever make. You can take the high road by respecting your body, saying "no" the first time, and avoiding addictions like the plague or take the low road by abusing your body, thinking "one time won't hurt," and getting hooked on something harmful.

In this chapter, we'll focus on the more serious addictions, the ones that can really mess you up. I apologize in advance for the heavy tone of this chapter. It's just that there's nothing fun about addictions, except maybe

the creative slang words used for drugs (smack, X, roofies, poppers) and the silly introductory comment made by Brooke Shields when she was being interviewed as a spokesperson for an anti-smoking campaign.

This chapter has three sections. **Three Brutal Realities** is about the life altering impact addictions have on you and others. **The Truth, the Whole Truth, and Nothing but** will give you the cold, hard facts and hopefully answer most of your questions about the most common drugs. In **Striking at the Root** we'll explore how to avoid and overcome addictions. It also identifies what I call the drug of the 21st century.

ADDICTIONS CHECKUP

Before reading further, take this little quiz to see which road you're on.

CIRCLE YOUR CHOICE	NO WAY!				HECK YES!
1. I have made up my mind that I will never use drugs.	1	2	3	4	5
2. I am free of any compulsive behaviors such as gambling, shopping, overeating, web surfing, or endless TV watching.	1	2	3	4	5
3. When it comes to choices about alcohol, tobacco, and drugs, I make my own decisions and don't give in to peer pressure.	1	2	3	4	5
4. I have been alcohol and tobacco free for the last 30 days.	1	2	3	4	5
5. I avoid situations where there's going to be heavy drinking or drugs.	1	2	3	4	5
6. I stay away from Internet porn.	1	2	3	4	5
7. I hang out with friends who share my views about substance abuse.	1	2	3	4	5
8. I encourage my friends to stay away from harmful substances.	1	2	3	4	5
9. I never let my friends drink and drive.	1	2	3	4	5
10. I am free of any eating disorders such as anorexia or bulimia.	1	2	3	4	5
TOTAL					

Add up your score and see how you think you're doing.

 You're on the high road. Keep it up!

 You're straddling the high and low roads. Move to higher ground!

 You're on the low road. Pay special attention to this chapter.

Three Brutal Realities

When it comes to addictive substances or activities, there are three brutal realities we all must face.

Brutal Reality 1: They Can Become Stronger Than You

I used to think that drug abusers and addicts were weak and selfish. As I've learned more about it, I regret my lack of understanding. Addiction strikes the best and brightest among us. No one is immune. There are many fine people who are also alcoholics, compulsive gamblers, or drug addicts. They're really not much different from you and me. Same hopes. Same dreams. The only thing that separates them from the rest of us are a few choices they made, usually during their teens.

I have a good friend named Phil. He's a great guy—smart, genuine, honest. I never knew he'd been an alcoholic for years.

When Phil was thirteen, he struggled with low self-esteem. One day Phil smuggled a bottle of liquor from his dad's friend's truck. He stashed it away in his coat waiting for the right moment to give it a try. A week later, after begging his mom for permission to attend a local dance, Phil found his chance.

The small container fit nicely inside my cowboy boot as I walked into the dance hall. I made a beeline to the men's room. I took a drink. My face flushed. Suddenly, I felt a wave of relaxation and euphoria. My shyness and self-consciousness seemed to disappear. A door swung open in my mind that encouraged a strong craving for more. Alcohol, I thought, was the missing ingredient to raise my self-esteem.

Throughout his teenage years, Phil began drinking more and more, frequently stealing and lying to get what he needed. On several occasions, he got completely plastered and one time he and his friends drove their car off a cliff and were almost killed. Yet even that wasn't enough to stop him.

"As my college years passed," said Phil, "I was seldom at peace unless I was drinking. By the end of my third year, I was carrying a bottle of whiskey to class in a briefcase and spending most of my free time at a nearby tavern."

A few years later, Phil got married and began a family. His drinking continued and began to erode his marriage, family, and career. Phil adored his young daughter and kept promising her that he would stop. She'd write him short notes to encourage him. Here's one of them.

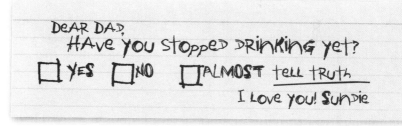

DeAR DAD,
HAve you stopped DRiNKiNG yet?
☐ YES ☐ NO ☐ ALMOST tell tRuth
I Love you! SuNie

But Phil *couldn't* stop. "Promises, prayers, good intentions, and tons of willpower had little effect on controlling my craving. The alcohol's power felt greater than my power. I couldn't stop drinking—not for my wife, my parents, my career, my church, or my children—not for anything!"

Months later his daughter wrote,

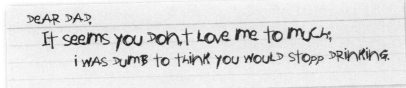

DeAR DAD,
It seems you DoN,t Love me to much;
i wAS DumB to think you wouLD stopp DRiNKiNG.

Phil eventually lost everything: his marriage, his daughter, his job, his health, his self-esteem, his freedom to choose. I'll tell you the rest of the story in just a bit.

Here are a few real statements from teens about the power of addiction:

- *"I used to be able to run a mile in under six minutes. Now I'm lucky to make it in eight. And I'm wheezing all the way. I want to quit, but it's not that easy."*

- *"It began to be so habitual we did not think we could stop."*

- *"I wish I had never started, but most smokers say that."*

- *"My friends use drugs and alcohol like it's no big deal. I've asked them if they are addicted, and they all say that they are not, and could quit at any time. But they seem to do them every day."*

As we talked about earlier, between your impulses and what you do about them is a space, and in that space lies your freedom to choose. Yet, in the case of an addiction, your freedom to choose is pushed aside by the power of your addiction. There is no more space.

Don't ever underestimate the power of addiction. It can become stronger than you.

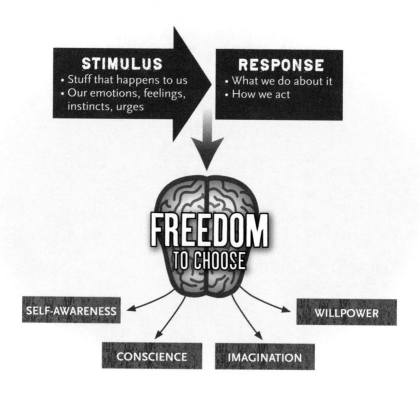

Brutal Reality 2: It's Not Just About You

Some teens think that what they do with their lives is nobody else's business. "You do your thing and I'll do mine." The reality is, when it comes to smoking, drinking, and doing drugs, it's not just about you. It impacts everyone around you whether you like it or not.

Who does it impact exactly? Let's pretend that Inger begins to drink and smoke pot thinking that it's nobody's business as long as she doesn't hurt anyone. However, because of her example, one of her friends starts smoking pot too. Her mom finds out and gets upset, and it begins to cause friction at home. Inger's younger brother, Kip, thinks that if Inger is doing it, then it's okay for him to do it, too. Inger's boyfriend doesn't like what smoking pot does to Inger and decides to dump her. Ultimately, she gets caught with drugs and is sent to a youth detention center for three months, paid for by public taxes. And the story continues. You get the picture.

Who an Addiction Impacts

A friend of mine told me about how drugs impacted her family.

I was eight years old when my brother started using drugs. I can't remember a time during my childhood when I wasn't scared—scared to be alone with him, scared of him hurting me as he threatened to, scared of him killing himself, scared of my parents not ever figuring out how to deal with it.

He said it was his life—to leave him alone—that his choices didn't have anything to do with us. He was wrong. Even though he was the only one addicted, we were impacted and consumed just as much. We felt the desperation when he didn't have enough money to get a fix, the pain from all of the times he went through withdrawal, and the severe guilt from hurting those he loved most.

Years later, he is the one who is scared—scared he will never have an education, never catch up with other people his age, never be able to hold down a job, never be able to stay married, never be able to restore the relationships he damaged, and never be able to truly stay clean. Even though he is clean, he has to fight a mental battle...every day.

My parents are scared too—scared for him for all the same reasons he is scared. And, even though he is an adult, they still feel responsible and want to help, yet feel just as helpless as when he was a teenager.

Have I ever done drugs? No. But they have certainly abused me, my family, and everything around me.

Brutal Reality 3: Drugs Destroy Dreams

I saw a great ad the other day. It read, "Think about how much you can do with your life. Now think how smoking pot could stop you." You can't afford an addiction. It costs too much, in terms of time, money, brain cells, focus, relationships, and happiness. And it only gets worse when you become an adult.

I met a young lady named Kori. A junior in high school, Kori is full of energy. She has devoted her life to teaching kids to stay off drugs. "I want to help kids not make the same mistake I made," she said, "a mistake that cost me years of my life, years that I can't get back. I have to live the rest of my life with horrible flashbacks, nightmares, and memories."

"What in the world happened to you?" I asked. She told me her story.

Up until she was about 11 years old she had a great life, with a loving mother and father, an older brother and sister, and a younger brother. "As soon as my dad came home from work each night we all sat down at the dinner table, said grace, and ate. We were a family."

About a year later Kori began to be unhappy with things. Her older brother was a big jock and the perfect son and her younger brother was the baby. Kori felt lost in the middle and neglected. She also felt she couldn't measure up to expectations. "My parents expected perfection out of me, out of my family. I was pretty much just angry at the world because life wasn't being fair."

It wasn't long before Kori ran away from home and moved in with four other teens. These new friends consisted of Tom and his girlfriend, Emma, who were both 19, Mark, who had been kicked out of his house, and Jay-Jay, who was a young teen and a runaway like Kori. Even though she tried to block out everything from her previous life, Kori continued to call her mom regularly.

They all began experimenting with alcohol and weed. Soon they progressed to more serious drugs. "We all became junkies. We tried every drug that was available to us. Most of our paychecks went to buying more drugs," said Kori.

Then, one night Tom brought home something they'd never tried before: heroin. They all gathered around the table and took turns sharing the needle. Mark went first, followed by Kori. She then passed the needle to Jay-Jay, who had already been drinking and smoking a lot that day.

"It's a memory I'll never forget," said Kori. "Jay-Jay strapped up his arm, loaded the needle, and began. After 15 seconds, he froze, turned blue, and died right on the spot. Everyone started to freak out. I just sat there, stunned, and stared at my lifeless friend...then I called 911."

The police came and Kori and her friends were all put into state custody and sentenced to go through drug rehab. After being released a few months later, Kori returned home a changed person and began a new life.

"So, what happened to all your friends?" I asked.

"That's the sad part," said Kori. "The multiple consequences that can happen to people who do drugs happened to the five of us. Today, Tom has brain damage. He seems like he's all there, but he can't do normal things. Like he can't write in cursive anymore and he's just now relearning to tie his shoes. Tom's former girlfriend Emma has HIV and doesn't leave the house. She just sits around all day and her mom takes care of her. Mark is 18 years old, still hooked on drugs, and has a five-year-old daughter. Jay-Jay died that night."

"So, it looks like you're the only one who survived this whole ordeal," I said.

"Well, sort of. My doctor told me that because of the drugs I have the heart and lungs of a 37-year-old, even though I'm only 17. He said it'd be really surprising if I make it to 50. How am I supposed to tell my mom that she gets to bury me? I made a lot of stupid choices. So, I've pretty much devoted the rest of my high school career to helping other kids stay off drugs."

What a sad story! Five teens who got hooked on drinking and drugs. Five terrible outcomes. Who knows what they could have made of their lives? Perhaps Tom could have become everyone's favorite high school teacher. Maybe Emma might have matured into a gifted musician. And Jay-Jay could have grown up to be a great dad to his kids—kids who he will never get to take fishing or read books to. That is what drugs do. They destroy dreams.

THE ANATOMY OF AN ADDICTION

At this point you may be thinking, "Yeah, but these are extreme stories, Sean. I haven't run away from home and I'm not into hard-core drugs. I just wanna have a little fun. It's not like I'm going to get addicted or anything. I know kids who drink and get high from time to time and they're just fine."

You're right. Many teens who drink, smoke, and do drugs won't become addicts. But a high percentage will. You see, everyone responds a little differently to addictive substances. While one teen can take a drink and be fine, another can get hooked after just one shot. Besides, even if you never become an addict, drugs can do immense damage to your body and brain, even after just one try. So why take the chance?

Most substance abuse problems start with the gateway drugs of tobacco, alcohol, and marijuana. These substances are dangerous in and of themselves and, more often than not, lead to more dangerous drugs. Almost imperceptibly, addiction sets in. My friend Phil calls it *the wedge of addiction*. It starts so small—a drink, a cigarette, a joint. You want more. You want harder stuff. And that wedge keeps going deeper and getting wider until it breaks you in half.

You can always tell an addict. Just watch for these three signs:

- *They will deny they have an addiction and claim, "I can quit anytime I want."*
- *They will knit a tapestry of lies to cover up their problem.*
- *They will center their lives on their addiction, always living for the next high.*

There's no getting around it. The realities of addiction are brutal.

The Truth, the Whole Truth, and Nothing but———

I believe that if you know the truth you'll make smarter choices. So below, I've put together key facts you really should know about the most common drugs today. Most of this information is adapted from **www.health.org**, a reliable source on teens and drugs.

The Truth About ALCOHOL

a.k.a. (also known as)—booze, sauce, brews, brewskis, hooch, hard stuff, juice

Did You Know?

Alcohol messes with your brain. Alcohol leads to a loss of coordination, poor judgment, slowed reflexes, distorted vision, memory lapses, and even blackouts. Mixing alcohol with medications or drugs is especially dangerous and can be fatal.

Alcohol kills. The three leading causes of death among teens are motor vehicle crashes, homicides, and suicides. Alcohol is a major factor in each. In

I'M NOT COMING IF HE'S COMING.

fact, alcohol kills many more teenagers than all the other illegal drugs combined.

Alcohol is a contributing factor in more than 75 percent of all date rapes. Dating and drinking don't mix well. Duh!

Alcohol makes you do stupid things. When I was in high school, I was recruited by Stanford University to play football. One weekend I was invited to visit their campus in Palo Alto, California. My host was a big, 240-pound Stanford football player. His job was to show me a good time so I'd want to go to the school and play football there. Although he knew I didn't drink, the first thing he did when I arrived was take me to a frat party where everyone was getting wasted. I drank a lot of 7-Up. Afterward, he and his friends took me to the infamous *Rocky Horror Picture Show.*

During the movie, my host became incoherent and passed out, having downed too many bottles. He then began to vomit uncontrollably in this passed-out state. I thought he was going to die. After calling an ambulance, his friends and I carried his massive body to the ambulance outside the theater. He spent the night in the hospital. His job was to show me a good time but he only made a fool of himself and turned me off completely.

I like what snidelyworld.com has to say.

- *Consumption of alcohol is a major factor in dancing like a retarded imbecile.*

- *Consumption of alcohol can cause awakening in bed with a person whose identity you are unable to recall and whose physical appearance you discover to be aesthetically repulsive when sober.*

- *Consumption of alcohol may cause you to thay shings thike lisss.*

FAQs (Frequently Asked Questions)

Q: Aren't beer and wine safer than liquor?

A: No. One 12-ounce beer has about as much alcohol as a 1.5 ounce shot of liquor, a 5-ounce glass of wine, or a wine cooler. And beware of those sweet-tasting alcopops that are loaded with calories and are nothing more than cheap beer.

Q: Why can't teens drink if their parents can?

A: Teens' bodies are still developing and alcohol has a greater impact on their minds and bodies. People who begin drinking before age 15 are four times more likely to develop alcoholism than those who begin at age 21.

The Truth About TOBACCO

a.k.a.—smokes, cigs, butts, chew, dip, snuff

Did You Know?

Tobacco is addictive. Cigarettes contain nicotine—a powerfully addictive substance. Three-fourths of young people who use tobacco daily continue to do so because they find it hard to quit.

Nicotine is poisonous. Nicotine is the tobacco plant's natural protection from being eaten by insects. Drop for drop it's three times deadlier than arsenic. Within eight seconds of the first puff, nicotine hits the brain and begins the addictive process.

Tobacco kills. Smoking is the most common cause of lung cancer and is also a leading cause of cancer of the mouth, throat, bladder, pancreas, and kidney. Smokeless tobacco can cause mouth cancer, tooth loss, and other health problems. Because your body is still growing, smoking is especially bad for teens. And shockingly, roughly one-third of teens who become regular smokers when under age 18 will eventually die from a tobacco-related disease. Yikes!

DON'T BELIEVE **US** ABOUT HOW GREAT SMOKING IS?

LISTEN TO THESE TEEN TESTIMONIALS:

NOW MY TEETH MATCH MY TAN!

(COUGH)...MY FRIENDS SAY I HAVE A COOL RASPY VOICE!...(COUGH)...AND IF YOU STAND UPWIND, YOU CAN'T EVEN SMELL MY BREATH! ...(COUGH, COUGH)...

NOW THAT I'M GETTING CHEMOTHERAPY FOR MY LUNG CANCER. I DON'T HAVE TO SHAVE ANYMORE! THANKS, BIG TOBACCO!

Ashley, a 14-year-old, watched her grandfather die from lung cancer.

"It's a horrible thing to see," she says. "The cancer just took over his body."

Her grandfather began smoking as a teenager in the Navy. Ashley understands how a teen in the 1940s might have been tricked into taking up cigarettes. But she can't see how today's teens fall for it.

"With all the information that's out there, with all the people who have died from smoking, it just puzzles me that kids keep doing it," she says. "You know that if you put that cigarette in your mouth, it might kill you. But you do it anyway. That just doesn't make sense."

FAQs

Q: Isn't smokeless tobacco safer to use than cigarettes?

A: No. There is no safe form of tobacco. Smokeless tobacco can cause mouth, cheek, throat, and stomach cancer. Smokeless tobacco users are 50 times more likely to get oral cancer than nonusers.

Q: Isn't smoking sexy?

A: Only if you think bad breath, smelly hair, yellow fingers, and coughing are sexy. Ads portray smoking as sophisticated, but think carefully about who created the ads and why the tobacco industry spends $1.2 million in advertising per hour trying to get you hooked.

The Truth About MARIJUANA

a.k.a.—weed, pot, grass, reefer, ganja, Mary Jane, blunt, joint, roach, nail

I appreciate Garrett's courage in sharing his story.

I had a rough time growing up as my brothers were taken away from our parents because of their drug use. I should have learned from their mistakes, but instead I too began to abuse drugs and alcohol.

On a hot summer night, my best friend Hannah came over to my house and we started smoking marijuana. Around midnight, we left the house with a few other friends to get some alcohol. All of us were too drunk and high to drive but I thought I could handle it.

Driving home, I thought I saw something in the road and turned sharply to avoid it. I overcorrected and the car flipped over and over. Passengers were thrown all over.

Everyone was seriously injured. One girl went into a coma for three weeks, the owner of the car had to go to a rehabilitation center but, the worst thing of all, my best friend Hannah died that horrible night. I can never see her again, and her family has lost a daughter because of me. Even to this day I still remember hearing the desperate sounds of my friends moaning and crying in that mangled vehicle. I have to live with that for the rest of my life.

I was charged with manslaughter, and now I am committed to a state youth correction facility where I will live for years, but at least I have a chance after I'm released to start again. Hannah never will. I have sworn never to drink or do drugs again in her memory.

Did You Know?

Marijuana drains motivation and harms babies. Marijuana is known to drain your motivation. In men, it can lower sperm counts and cause impotence; in women, it can mean an increased risk of miscarriage and can cause developmental problems for a child whose mother smoked pot while she was pregnant.

Marijuana is not always what it seems. Marijuana can be laced with other dangerous drugs without your knowledge. Blunts—hollowed-out cigars filled with marijuana—sometimes have substances such as crack cocaine, PCP, or embalming fluid added.

FAQs

Q: Isn't smoking marijuana less dangerous than smoking cigarettes?

A: No. It's even worse. One joint affects the lungs as much as four cigarettes.

Q: Is the marijuana used today stronger than when my parents were teens?

A: Yes. The marijuana smoked today is much stronger than when the drug became popular in the 1960s. On top of that, in the old days, they smoked joints, just a little bit rolled up. Today, they're smoking blunts or bowls (pipes) and consuming a lot more of the drug.

The Truth About
PRESCRIPTION DRUGS

a.k.a.—(OxyContin, Percocet, Lortab): 80s, OC, hillbilly heroin, Percs, juice
(Valium, Xanax, Ativan): barbs, candy, downers, roofies, tranks
(Adderall, Concerta, Ritalin): JIF, skippy, smarties, bennies, black beauties

"I started using Lortab for a legitimate medical problem," said Lee. "I was sent to a doctor who prescribed it legally. I had enough pills for 30 days. They made me feel better and got rid of the pain. After 30 days, I wanted more. The doctor prescribed more without even a checkup. This went on for six months. I was hooked. Finally, that doctor would not give me any more so I found someone who would, illegally. They were super expensive but I needed them. Soon, I needed a bigger high, so I switched to OxyContin and Ambien. I wanted to stop but couldn't. I went to my parents and they took me to our family doctor.

"I stayed off for three months then went back. I got so bad financially and mentally that my dad knew I was out of control. He took the week off work and took me to a clinic. It was a five-day program. I couldn't see anybody. When my mom called to make sure I was okay I cried and begged her to come get me and take me home. And I'm 18 years old!

"I will be dealing with this the rest of my life. And I will always live with the knowledge that I drained my folks' savings in just one short week—and I know we're not done! One addiction leads to another. I struggle with wanting alcohol and still crave the feeling of wanting more OC. I never thought this would happen to me."

It starts so innocently. It seems so harmless. But as Lee discovered, addiction can suck you in faster than you can blink.

WATCH OUT FOR THE SUCK ZONE, MAN. ONCE YOU'RE IN, YOU'LL NEVER GET OUT.

Did You Know?

Painkillers and heroin are close cousins. Heroin, one of the most dangerous and addictive street drugs, contains similar ingredients to prescription painkillers. Both are opiates and both are treacherous.

Prescription drug abuse can be life threatening. The abuse of prescription drugs is known to cause all sorts of problems, including respiratory depression, fatal seizures, irregular heart rate, cardiovascular system failure, high body temperature, hostility, feelings of paranoia, or worst of all, constipation.

FAQs

Q: Aren't prescription drugs safer than street drugs?

A: No. Many teens think prescription drugs are safe because they have legitimate uses and come in nice bottles, but taking them without a prescription to get high or self-medicate can be as dangerous and addictive as street drugs.

Q: Aren't teens getting these drugs from doctors?

A: No. Most teens get prescription drugs from classmates, friends, and family members, or they steal the drugs from people who are taking them legitimately. Some sell their prescriptions to desperate teens to make a quick buck.

The Truth About CLUB DRUGS

a.k.a.—(Ecstasy): E, X, XTC

> *(GHB): Liquid X, grievous bodily harm, Georgia homeboy*
>
> *(ketamine): K, Special K, Ket, Vitamin K, Kit Kat*
>
> *(Rohypnol): roofies, R-2*

Club drugs refer to a wide variety of drugs often used at all-night dance parties (raves), nightclubs, and concerts. If you could take a pill that would make you...

- *Do poorly in school*
- *Lose interest in your favorite hobbies, sports, or activities*
- *Become hostile and uncooperative*
- *Develop sleeping problems*
- *Clench your jaw and grind your teeth*
- *Have anxiety and panic attacks*

...would you be interested? Well, that is what you get with Ecstasy, one of the more prevalent club drugs. The short-lived bang it may give you just isn't worth it.

> I CAN PREDICT THINGS. IT'S KINDA LIKE I HAVE ESPN!

Did You Know?

Club drugs do weird things to your body and brain. Ecstasy is a stimulant that increases your heart rate and blood pressure and can lead to kidney and heart failure. GHB is a depressant and can cause drowsiness, unconsciousness, and breathing problems. Club drugs can damage the neurons in your brain, impairing your senses, memory, judgment, and coordination. Higher doses can cause severe breathing problems, coma, or even death.

Club drugs and date rape are like peas in a pod. Club drugs like GHB and Rohypnol are sedatives. In other words, they make you unconscious and immobilize you. Rohypnol can cause a kind of amnesia—you may not remember what you said or did after taking the drug, making it easier for someone to take advantage of you. Scary!

FAQs

Q: If somebody slipped a club drug into your drink, wouldn't you realize it immediately?

A: Probably not. You can't smell or taste most club drugs. Some are made into a powder form that makes it easier to slip into a drink and dissolve without a person knowing it.

Q: Are there any long-term effects with taking Ecstasy?

A: Yes. Studies on both humans and animals have proven that regular use of Ecstasy produces long-lasting, perhaps permanent damage to the brain's ability to think and store memories.

Q: If you took a club drug at a rave, wouldn't you just dance off all of its effects?

A: Not necessarily. Some of Ecstasy's effects, like confusion, sleep problems, depression, and paranoia, have been reported to occur even weeks after the drug is taken.

A friend of mine from Ireland told me about a friend of his who learned about club drugs the hard way.

A boy I know named Michael, the oldest of ten children, came home one night intoxicated with E. When he saw the family's pet Labrador in the kitchen he strangled it to death, convinced that it was the devil. The dog bit him and there was blood all over the kitchen. The siblings who ran in to watch the aftermath of the scene were traumatized. Michael is now in drug rehab recovering from addiction.

The Truth About **STEROIDS**

a.k.a.—arnolds, gym candy, pumpers, stackers, juice, roids

Anabolic steroids are synthetic derivatives of testosterone, the male sex hormone. They don't build muscle in and of themselves, but they allow you to work out harder and longer and recover faster. People take steroids to get that pumped-up look and to be better in sports. On the outside you look great with all those big muscles. On the inside you're being eaten alive.

FOX News ran a story called "Breaking Point: The Truth About Steroids." It featured Patrick, who began taking steroids as a teen.

Patrick was still in high school when he decided he needed to change his body image.

"So many people, especially teenagers, feel self-conscious about their bod-

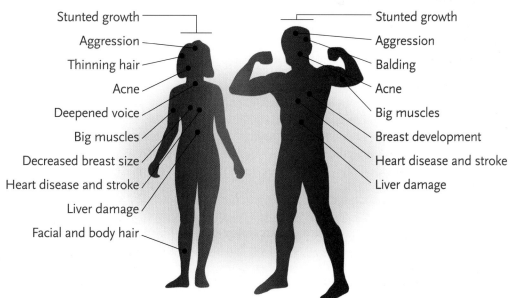

ies, and if it bothers you that much, you're willing to go to any extreme to change that," says Patrick.

He went to the gym seven days a week, but...working out wasn't enough. So he, like millions of other young men...started taking illegal anabolic steroids.

"People would go, 'Wow, look at you, you're the picture of health.'" he says. "And I'd laugh."

Before long, his blood pressure was through the roof, his hair was falling out, and his temper was uncontrollable.

"I was a textbook specimen of 'roid rage,'" he says. "You wake up pissed off, and the rest of the day you get more and more angry."

Patrick stopped using steroids three years ago, but the damage may already be done.

Did You Know?

Steroids change your appearance—not necessarily in a good way. How can you tell if someone is doing steroids? It's easy. Besides bigger muscles, just look for acne, yellowing of the skin, bad breath, and rage. In guys, look for baldness, the development of breasts (oops!), and impotence.

In girls, look for growth of facial hair, deepened voice, and breast reduction. How feminine! Boys start turning into girls and girls into boys.

Steroids can stunt your growth. If taken at a young age, steroids can stunt your growth. God may have intended you to be 6'0" but you may end up being a muscular 5'10" instead.

FAQs

Q: Are steroids addictive?

A: Yes, they can be. Withdrawal symptoms include mood swings, suicidal thoughts and attempts, fatigue, restlessness, loss of appetite, and sleeplessness.

Q: How long do steroids stay in your system?

A: It varies from a couple of weeks to more than 18 months.

Q: How can I excel in sports if I don't use steroids?

A: If you eat well, use vitamin supplements, sleep well, and work out hard, you can develop big muscles naturally. Millions of athletes, and the best athletes of all time, have excelled and are excelling without doing 'roids. Besides, steroids are now banned in virtually every major collegiate and professional sport.

The Truth About **INHALANTS**

a.k.a.—glue, kick, bang, sniff, huff, poppers, whippets, Texas shoeshine

Inhalants include a large group of chemicals that are found in such household products as aerosol sprays, cleaning fluids, glue, paint, paint thinner, gasoline, propane, nail-polish remover, correction fluid, and marker pens. None of these are safe to inhale—they all can kill you. Chemicals like amyl nitrite and isobutyl nitrite (*poppers*) and nitrous oxide (*whippets*) are often sold at concerts and dance clubs.

Did You Know?

Inhalants cause brain damage. Inhalants are substances or fumes from products that are sniffed or huffed to cause an immediate high. Because they affect your brain with much greater speed and force than many other substances, they can cause irreversible physical and mental damage before you know what's happened.

Inhalants affect your heart and body. Inhalants starve the body of oxygen and force the heart to beat irregularly and more rapidly. People who use inhalants can experience nausea and nosebleeds; develop liver, lung, and kidney problems; and lose their sense of hearing or smell. Chronic use can lead to muscle wasting and reduced muscle tone and strength.

FAQs

Q: Since inhalants are found in household products, aren't they safe?

A: No. Even though household products like glue and air freshener have legal, useful purposes, when they are used as inhalants they are harmful and dangerous. These products are not intended to be inhaled.

Q: Doesn't it take many huffs before you're in danger?

A: No. One huff can kill you. Or the tenth. Or the hundredth. Every huff can be dangerous. Even if you have huffed before without experiencing a problem, there's no way of knowing how the next one will affect you.

Q: Can inhalants make me lose control?

A: Yes. Inhalants affect your brain and can cause you to suddenly engage in violent, or even deadly, behavior. You could hurt yourself or the people you love.

The Truth About COCAiNE

a.k.a.—coke, dust, toot, snow, blow, sneeze, powder, lines, rock (crack)

Did You Know?

Cocaine affects your brain. The word *cocaine* refers to the drug in both a powder (cocaine) and crystal (crack) form. It is made from the coca plant and causes a short-lived high that is immediately followed by opposite, intense feelings of depression and edginess, and a craving for more of the drug. Cocaine may be snorted as a powder, converted to a liquid form for injection with a needle, or processed into a crystal form to be smoked.

Cocaine is addictive. Cocaine interferes with the way your brain processes chemicals that create feelings of pleasure, so you need more and more of the drug just to feel normal. People addicted to cocaine start to lose interest in other areas of their life, like school, friends, and sports.

Cocaine can kill. Cocaine use can cause heart attacks, seizures, strokes, and respiratory failure. People who share needles can also contract hepatitis, HIV/AIDS, or other diseases. Even first-time cocaine users can have seizures or fatal heart attacks.

Combining cocaine with other drugs or alcohol is extremely dangerous. The effects of one drug can magnify the effects of another, and mixing substances can be deadly.

FAQs

Q: Isn't crack less addictive than cocaine because it doesn't stay in your body very long?

A: No. Both cocaine and crack are powerfully addictive. The length of time it stays in your body doesn't change that.

Q: Don't some people use cocaine to feel good?

A: Any positive feelings are fleeting and are usually followed by some very bad feelings, like paranoia and intense cravings. Cocaine may give users a temporary illusion of power and energy, but it often leaves them unable to function emotionally and physically.

The Truth About METHAMPHETAMiNES

a.k.a.—Speed, meth, crystal, crank, tweak, go-fast, ice, glass, uppers, black beauties

In an article in the *San Francisco Chronicle,* Christopher Heredia tells the story of a teen named Sam who liked to write poetry and download music off the Internet. Sam's family lived a typical suburban life and she seemed to be happy. Until she did meth, that is.

"When Sam first tried crystal meth with her Walnut Creek high school friends last year, she was scared. But she liked it. She did it again. And again.

"Sam had always hated her body, and now she was losing weight. She finally belonged. She'd been depressed, and the meth was holding that at bay.

"Yet not much later, she started fighting with her parents and her friends. Sometimes she spent days on end in her room, fearful that the police were about to knock at her door. She was sure they were coming to get her. She couldn't sleep. She weighed only 100 pounds—down from 145.

SHE WAS A SKELETON IN THE MIRROR. HER HAIR WAS FALLING OUT. SHE FELT ALL ALONE.

Over the next several years, Sam battled an addiction to meth and continually fought with her parents. Eventually, she was placed in a family treatment center where she made various pacts with herself and her family, "Today is my last day using speed."

She relapsed two more times. But today she has been clean for almost a year. Says Sam,

"I thought meth was fun. In reality, it was not fun...I have goals and plans and deadlines and clean days to keep track of. I can't use. I could die. Things will be the same if I use again."

Did You Know?

Meth is totally unpredictable. Because of the many different recipes for making crystal meth you can never know how the drug will affect you from use to use. While one time you may experience no adverse side effects, the next time may kill you. There is no standard way of making crystal meth.

Meth affects your brain. In the short term, meth causes mind and mood changes such as anxiety, euphoria, and depression. Long-term effects can include chronic fatigue, paranoid or delusional thinking, and permanent psychological damage.

Meth affects your body. Over-amping on any type of speed is pretty risky. Creating a false sense of energy, these drugs push the body faster and further than it's meant to go. It increases the heart rate, blood pressure, and risk of stroke.

Meth is addictive. Meth is a powerfully addictive drug that can cause aggression and violent or psychotic behavior. Nearly half of first-time crystal meth users and more than three-quarters of second-time crystal meth users report addiction-like cravings.

FAQs

Q: Isn't methamphetamine less harmful than crack, cocaine, or heroin?

A: No. It's more dangerous. Some users get hooked the first time they snort, smoke, or inject meth. Because it can be made from lethal ingredients like battery acid, drain cleaner, lantern fuel, and antifreeze, there is a greater chance of suffering a heart attack, stroke, or serious brain damage with this drug than with others.

Q: Isn't using crystal meth like using diet pills?

A: No. Although crystal meth is known to cause extreme weight loss the effects are not permanent. Many regular meth users experience *adaptation*—the weight loss stops as the body becomes used to the effects of the drug. When this happens users may even start to gain weight.

THE BOTTOM LINE

There are still a ton of drugs that we haven't covered like LSD, heroin, PCP, and more, but you're probably tired of reading about all this stuff. After a while, it all starts to sound the same. Bottom line, if you know someone who is using drugs, urge them to get help. If you're using them, stop! Talk with an adult you trust. Drugs are bad for you, ruin your life, and rob you of your money. Cocaine users, for example, will spend hundreds, even thousands of dollars each week to support their habit. Just think of all the clothes and entertainment you could buy with that.

So, as comedian Geechy Guy said, "You should just say no to drugs. That will drive the prices down."

"That's my little brother. He's all messed up on Skittles and Mountain Dew."

©The New Yorker Collection 2002
David Sipress from Cartoonbank.com. All Rights Reserved.

Striking at the Root

No one ever starts out thinking, I can't wait to become an addict. You do it because you have a deeper need that is not being met.

Philosopher Henry David Thoreau put it this way. "For every thousand hacking at the leaves of evil there is one striking at the root." In other words, we too often focus on the symptoms of drug abuse instead of getting to the root of the problem. To tackle addiction, you must strike at the root. It's usually one of six things.

The Roots of Addiction

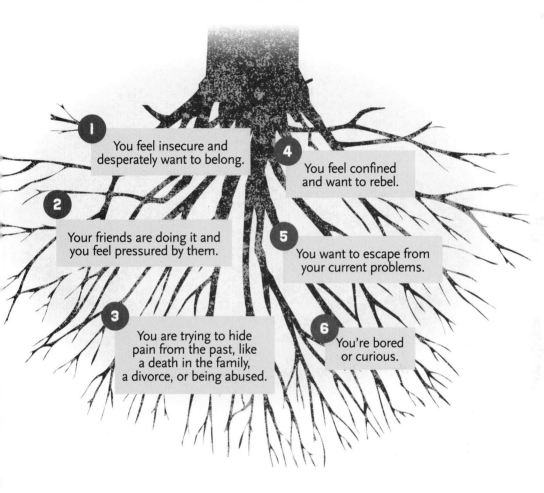

1 You feel insecure and desperately want to belong.

2 Your friends are doing it and you feel pressured by them.

3 You are trying to hide pain from the past, like a death in the family, a divorce, or being abused.

4 You feel confined and want to rebel.

5 You want to escape from your current problems.

6 You're bored or curious.

Take Amanda, for example. Amanda's family moved when she was 13 and had just entered seventh grade. It was a big disruption in her life.

"At this time I got in with a group of kids at school that smoked and used LSD. The smoking was something that bonded us. I was confused and just wanted to belong. I didn't think about the product of my choices."

So if you're depressed, angry, hurting, rebellious, fearful, insecure, or have some other hole in your life that needs to be filled, instead of filling it up by drinking or doing drugs, try something more satisfying and enduring. Just as you can become addicted to harmful substances or practices, you can also pick up positive addictions, and get high naturally! Here's a short list of positive addictions that may help you fill the potential holes in your life.

The Anti-Drugs

- **Exercise.** *Working out releases endorphins, which are the body's natural painkillers and positive mood-makers. Have you heard of runner's high, that euphoric feeling you get while running? Truly, nothing can clear your head like a good workout can.*

- **Sports.** *Competing in sports is healthy, consuming, and addictive. Sports will help you meet new people and keep you so occupied you won't have time for the drug scene.*

- **Music.** *I have a friend who discovered he had a great gift for music at about age 13. Despite never taking a lesson, he became the best guitarist in the school. His music consumed him and, when he was down, he'd play his guitar instead of drowning himself in drugs.*

- **Service.** *Losing yourself in service to others has always been the best way to forget your own troubles.*

- **Hobbies.** *Find something you love to do and get good at it. Whether it be photography, cooking, or astronomy, hobbies produce a natural high without the big crash afterward.*

- **Learning.** *Get turned on by learning. Read voraciously. Take advanced-placement classes or college courses at your school. Pour your heart into it.*

- **Family.** *No one cares more about you than your family, including cousins, aunts, uncles, and grandparents. When you're hurting, cast your burdens upon them, instead of looking for another outlet.*

- **Faith.** *Practicing your religion or beliefs alone or with others can give meaning and purpose to your life and offer you standards to live by.*

- **Friends.** *In times of trouble, lean on good friends. Talk through your problems with them instead of the bottle.*

- **Journal writing.** *Your journal can become your best friend, your solace, the place where you can let out all your emotions and not be judged.*

At some point during your teen years, you may feel immense peer pressure to drink, smoke, or do drugs. Perhaps you already have. Perhaps you've given in a time or two and wish you were stronger.

So where do you get the power to resist? I'd suggest learning the 3 Knows and the 5 Nos.

THE 3 KNOWS

Know the Facts. Some decisions can be made based just on facts. Smoking wreaks havoc on your body and is terribly addictive. Alcohol makes you do stupid things. Drugs kill brain cells. Addictive substances hurt everyone around you. What more do you need to know?

Know Yourself. To have the strength to say no you need to have something more important to say yes to. For example, if you want to attend and do well in college, you'll need all the brain cells you have. If you're an athlete, you need to be totally focused. At most schools, you'll get kicked off the team if you're caught drinking or doing drugs. If you plan to have a family, you can't afford an addiction of any kind. Eventually it will rear its ugly head and hurt those you love most.

When you're faced with a tough decision, ask yourself: Does this fit with who I am and who I want to be?

By knowing what she wanted out of high school, it was easy for Chelsea to resist peer pressure and stick to her plan.

Sadly, there's a lot of drug and alcohol abuse in my school. Some of the people I hang out with will say, "So do you want to smoke?" I'm like, "Uh, no." I can't allow some nasty toxin into my body that's just gonna eat it up. I try to stay away from parties 'cause I've heard some stories. I do my own thing. I'll hang out with my friends and the people I know I can trust, who won't try to pressure me into doing stuff.

One of the goals I strive for is to leave a legacy for people to remember me for. My brother left a legacy in this school when he graduated and his face is plastered on a plaque because of his many awards for service and sports. I want to be remembered in the same way for giving my time and efforts that have an impact on our school.

Know the Situation. Don't flirt with danger or put yourself in situations where you may not be strong enough to resist. A recovering alcoholic does not take a job as a bartender. Likewise, if you have the tendency to give in to the crowd, for heaven's sake, don't go to that party where everyone's going to get stoned. Plan ahead or somebody else will do your planning for you.

The Russian army once had a very interesting tradition. After a soldier completed basic training, a big party was held for him at the barracks.

Russian barracks are five to six stories high, with large windows, big enough for a man to stand in. The way a soldier proved his manhood was by drinking all night, getting absolutely stoned out of his mind. The soldier then stood on the windowsill with his back to the five-story drop and drank one more bottle of beer. If he could do it without falling, he was a man.

The moral of the story is ➤

> **He who stands on a windowsill to see how far out he can lean without falling is a moron.**

THE 5 NOS

At 18, Alby was arrested for dealing drugs and landed in a maximum-security jail. It all started on a summer day on a street corner in Yonkers, New York, when Alby was 13.

"You need to get your mind right. Hit this blunt," a friend said.

Alby didn't have the strength to say no. He felt he had to smoke the blunt to fit in. He was desperate to belong. His parents had never been there for him. They were drug addicts themselves and were lousy parents. So he smoked it, and kept smoking it, eventually becoming an addict and a dealer. If only he had been stronger.

In truth, one of the reasons teens don't say no is simply because they don't know how. They haven't said no before, and when put on the spot, they cave. If you're prepared, your chances of resisting go way up. Here are five ways to say no. Pick one that looks like it will work for you and practice it out loud in front of the mirror several times. Then, when the real thing happens, it will feel natural.

Be direct. If you have enough self-confidence, just tell them straight up. And don't apologize. It might go something like this.

"You need to get your mind right. Hit this blunt."

"No, thanks."

"Oh, c'mon man. It's not going to hurt."

"Maybe not, but I just don't want to. I have my reasons. Is that cool with you?"

Use humor. Sometimes using a touch of humor can do the trick.

"Hey, try some of this. It's really good."

"No, thanks, I like my brain cells."

Blame it on your parents. If you get in a tough situation, blame it on your strict parents. This is one of the better approaches.

"It's your turn. Give it a try."

"Nah, my parents would kill me."

"Who's going to tell them?"

"You don't know my parents. They find out everything."

Suggest an alternative. Some teens drink and do drugs because they're bored and can't think of anything better to do. So always have some handy alternatives ready to go.

"Here, take one."

"Don't we have something better to do?"

"Like what?"

"Let's go see that new movie that just came out. I hear it's good. I'll drive."

Get up and go. If you're ever in a messy situation that just doesn't feel right, trust your instincts and get away fast. Don't worry about what they might think of you.

"Hey, where ya going?"

"I've gotta go. I'll explain later. See ya."

So many addicts have said, "If only I would have said no the first time my life would be so different today." Be strong that first time. Don't tell yourself, "One time isn't going to hurt me." That's what they all said. Never do once what you don't want to do all the time.

LET YOUR REPUTATION SPEAK FOR ITSELF

If you don't drink or do drugs, eventually your reputation will speak for itself and you won't be invited into the circles or the parties of those that do. Consider this a compliment. And don't worry; you're not missing out on anything. You may even get made fun of from time to time, but you can handle it, as did Josh Kennedy, a high school senior and an extraordinary musician.

One of my friends asked me if I wanted to go to this party. I said, "Yeah, I'd love to go." Later, he said, "No, I don't think you want to go." So, I was uninvited. My friends know I don't drink so they don't invite me to parties where there is drinking. It was nice to know that maybe I was setting an example for him.

My faith is a big part of the reason for not drinking. Every once in a while, people make sarcastic comments about me not drinking. One girl calls me a wuss because

I don't go to parties. She thinks I'm missing out. But when I see what happens to these people—the hangovers, the casual sex, getting plastered and not even knowing how to get home—I don't feel I'm missing out on anything. Besides, I really don't care what they say.

DEFEATING AN ADDICTION

Perhaps you're heading down the path of addiction. Maybe you're already hooked. Whatever your situation, remember that it's much easier to break an addiction now, while you're still a teen, than it will be later.

Because drug addiction is a brain disease, it is difficult to overcome. Drug abuse literally changes the way your brain functions. Drugs impact your moods, alter your brain cells, change how you think, even affect the way you walk and talk. We're talking major stuff here.

Some teens are able to quit cold turkey just by making up their minds. Others may be able to quit after one treatment at a rehab center. Many have to undergo extensive treatment or therapy over several years. Some are never able to conquer it.

My friend Phil, whom I told you about earlier, battled alcoholism for years. He'd go to a rehab center, make promises to himself and to others, become sober for a few months, and then, one night, drink himself into oblivion.

He experienced a never-ending cycle of triumphs and crashes. At last, after losing everything and hitting rock bottom, he found the strength to try one more time. Using the 12-step process of Alcoholics Anonymous and through turning his life over to God, he was finally able to conquer his addiction, and has been sober for many years.

Today, Phil is happily remarried, at peace, and devoted to helping others overcome their addictions. He even wrote a book about his experience, appropriately titled *The Perfect Brightness of Hope*. However, he still considers himself an alcoholic; he knows he is only one drink away from returning to his old ways.

I'm no expert on overcoming addictions but some key principles include:

1. **Admit it.** Admit that you have a problem or are on the path toward having a problem.

2. **Get help.** Seek help from your parents, a good friend, a support group, or a counselor. Because drug abuse is such a widespread problem there are all kinds of treatments, programs, and support groups that can help. You're so much better off if you don't try to battle it alone. Amanda shared how she got hooked on drugs in an effort to rebel against her parents. Later she came to them for help. "When I was 17, I came to my parents on my own and told them I was addicted to drugs and the only way out for me was if I left the state for a while and got away from my friends." Her parents were very supportive and made arrangements so she could live away for a while to get out of the bad environment. Later, Amanda returned, free of her addiction, and is now going to college.

3. **Do it now.** If you think you may have a problem you probably do. Don't procrastinate. *It will only get harder the longer you wait.*

The Turning Point

Above all else, if you're ever confused about what to do, follow your conscience, that intuition or gut instinct inside you.

Curtis decided at a young age that he didn't want to drink or do drugs. Week after week, he'd go with his friends to parties and was always the designated driver afterward.

Curtis recalls, "Most of the parties had big crowds. Even with all those people around, that was the loneliest time in my life. Those times would lead me to think there had to be something better for me. The parties got bigger, the drinking was heavy, and the cigarettes were traded in for marijuana and other drugs."

Soon, Curtis gave in and began drinking too.

After a big blowup with his dad, Curtis ran away from home and moved in with his friends. One night he had a wake-up call.

"Me and my friend returned to the apartment one evening to find our friends and some others already drinking. They gave me a bottle. I took one drink and nearly threw up. I sat down and looked over the people there. At that moment thoughts began striking deep into my heart. I realized I wanted something great out of life. I knew the people in that room could not provide it. They could barely take care of themselves let alone understand, support, or love me.

"If I wanted to dream and believe again, I had to end the drinking. I had to get far away from these people. Even if I had to be on my own for the rest of my life, I would be better off. I wanted to be somebody."

Curtis returned home the next day. He was afraid his dad would be angry. Instead, his dad cried for joy. Today Curtis and his dad are good friends and Curtis is on a new path.

Breaking the Cycle

Many teens who drink, smoke, or do drugs have parents and grandparents who did the same. It is a pattern that too often repeats itself. If this is the case, you have the opportunity to break the cycle and pass on good habits to your future children. What a great contribution this would be, not only to your future family, but to those who went before and were unable to kick the habit.

THE DRUG OF THE 21ST CENTURY

There's another addiction we haven't talked about yet: pornography. I call pornography a *drug* because it's as addictive as cocaine. Just ask any porn addict or a therapist who works with them. I use the term *of the 21st century* because, although pornography has always been around in some form, it grew to full-fledged maturity with the rise of the Internet in this century. A generation ago, porn was hard to get. Today, it comes to you.

The pornography industry is a mega-billion-dollar industry and growing. The people who run it don't care about you. They just want your money. They know it's addictive and have found ways to entice and trap you. One such technique is called mousetrapping, which forces users to remain on the Web site. Attempting to exit the site will automatically open a new browser window, endlessly, and the only way to escape may be to reboot the computer.

Have you ever watched one of those nature films where a crocodile is hiding in a pond? The thirsty gazelle trots around the pond, afraid to get too close, while the vicious, one-ton croc waits silently below the surface. Eventually, the gazelle overcomes its fear, meanders to the pond, and begins drinking. Suddenly, the gaping jaws of the crocodile reach up and grab its prey, pulling it beneath the surface and eating it alive.

So it is with porn. If you get too close it will reach up, sink its teeth into you, and pull you down beneath its murky waters so fast you won't even know what happened. It's especially tempting for guys, even though girls are getting into it more and more.

Let's take a closer look.

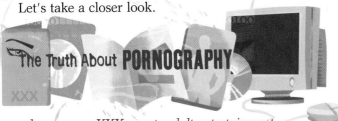

The Truth About **PORNOGRAPHY**

a.k.a.—porn, XXX, smut, adult entertainment

Did You Know?

Porn works just like a drug. Dr. Judith Reisman writes that pornography creates chemical reactions in your brain just like a drug does: "Viewing pornography triggers adrenaline and the production of testosterone, oxytocin, dopamine, and serotonin. It's a drug cocktail you're hit with."

Porn is highly addictive. "Pornography is very, very addicting," said Wes. "I'd rank it right up there with nicotine. I was hooked the moment I saw it!

"I became so engrossed that it was ruling my life! That was all I ever thought about. I shut out my family to be with the porn.

I let my grades slip. At home I stashed it in my closet and then I'd do some homework, then look at porn some more until dinner.

"After dinner I'd watch movies with sex and nudity on cable until 3:00 A.M. I'd fall asleep and wake up at 6:00 A.M., look at more, go to school, and do it all over again. I was trapped and digging deeper and deeper. I didn't know how to get out.

"Once, I got busted, but I went back to it a week later, lying to my mom, telling her I wasn't using the computer anymore. That's the power porn has over me. My advice is to stay as far away from pornography as you can."

This addiction usually starts at a young age. Dr. Victor Cline, a clinical therapist who for 25 years has treated hundreds of men for pornography and sex addictions, said this: "I found that nearly all of my adult sexual addicts' problems started with porn exposure in childhood or adolescence (eight years and older)."

The more you look at it the more you're going to want it, until, like Wes learned, it pretty much consumes your waking hours, your ambitions, your everything, just as if you were hooked on meth.

FAQs

Q: Isn't looking at pornography normal?

A: **No.** There's nothing normal about any kind of addictive material. One of the most abnormal aspects of porn is how it impacts relationships. It can cause you to start seeing people as objects for your own pleasure. It may ruin your relationships with boyfriends and girlfriends, because no one could ever live up to the perfect images on the computer screen, in magazines, or on TV. You'll start to prefer cyber-relationships to real ones. It will change you into a person you are not, and, like a drug, lead you to do things you normally wouldn't.

It also has an abnormal desensitizing effect. You'd never want to become so overstimulated through porn that you can no longer get turned on by little things, like holding hands, a simple kiss, the curve of her neck, or the line of his jaw. But that's exactly what happens. "Labor to keep alive...that little spark of celestial fire, conscience," or so said President George Washington. Nothing will squelch that spark faster than porn.

Q: What's the harm in viewing pornography?

A: Many reliable studies and numerous experts in law enforcement and counseling will tell you that pornography is a significant contributing factor in child abuse, rape, violence against women, drug abuse, broken marriages, and broken lives. Dr. Cline cites four levels of pornography addiction: *addiction, escalation, desensitization,* and the last one, *acting out.*

Gene McConnell, the founder and president of Authentic Relationships, experienced all four levels. He was brave enough to share his story.

When Gene was six years old, he was sexually molested by a babysitter, and carried this secret with him for years. At the age of 12, he was exposed to pornography. He described the experience as a drug injection straight into his veins. He was immediately hooked. For the next several years, he got into heavier and more deviant forms of pornography.

Gene writes: "One day, I came upon a magazine that dealt with rape, torture, and abduction. I started fantasizing what it would be like to actually rape someone, and instead of getting the help I needed I kept silent until I had an opportunity to act upon what I had been reading and fantasizing about.

"I was headed to my car parked in a dark parking lot when I saw a young woman and I followed her to her car. I forced my way in with the intention of raping her, and I had my hands to her throat. But as I looked into her eyes I saw deep fear in them...I realized I was about to destroy another person's life. It woke me up. I released her and said, 'I am so sorry, please forgive me,' and let her go."

The girl managed to get Gene's license plate as he walked in a daze to his car. Subsequently, Gene was sentenced to 45 days in jail for aggravated assault. He was glad, however, since this brought his problem to light. Today Gene is a changed person and is out and about speaking on the harmful nature of pornography addiction to youth and adults.

Ted Bundy, the serial killer who was eventually executed for his crimes, said this: "I've met a lot of men who were motivated to commit violence, just like me. And, without exception, every one of them was deeply involved in pornography."

Two Wolves

One of the best books I was ever forced to read in school was *Lord of the Flies*, by William Golding. Perhaps you read it too. It's the story of a bunch of boys who are marooned on an island after their plane crashes. No adults are present. Within a few days they begin taking sides and fighting with each other. Some of the boys remain civil, but many of them slowly turn savage. The story illustrates that all of us have two sides, the light and dark, the kind and brutal, the civil and savage, and it is our choice as to which side we will be on.

It reminds me of the fable of the two wolves.

"Grandson, I feel as if I have two wolves fighting in my heart. One is the vengeful, angry, violent one and the other is the loving, compassionate one."

"Grandfather, which wolf will win this fight going on in your heart?"

"Dear Grandson, only the one that I am willing to feed."

That's the way it works. If you feed your baser side by taking in all kinds of mental trash, the savage in you will grow stronger. As the philosopher Kuhn put it, "You can't entertain the animal inside you without becoming fully animal."

On the other hand, if you starve it, it will die. How do you do that? You feed the good wolf, instead. Fill your head full of movies, music, and images that entertain, inspire, and uplift you. Hang out with friends who bring out the best in you.

Pornography is a behavioral addiction as strong as cocaine. Avoid it. Be smart and self-aware. Throw it away or turn it off. Put your computer in the family room where everyone can see it, not in your bedroom. If you view porn with certain friends, don't be alone with them. Tell them you're becoming addicted and can't look at it anymore.

If you are hooked, get help, just as you would with a drug addiction. Studies show that it is difficult to overcome on your own. Don't let anyone tell you it's normal or harmless or that boys will be boys. We all know better.

Pornography is usually viewed in secret. But that which is done in the dark will eventually be brought to light in the form of broken relationships, low self-esteem, and unfulfilled dreams.

ADDICTION FREE

There are so many other addictions we haven't discussed, like the SAD syndrome, or screen addiction disorder. The screens we're talking about include the TV screen, computer screen, cell phone screen, movie screen, video game screen, iPod screen, and more. And then there's gambling, eating disorders, cutting, and other compulsive behaviors. Each of these can be very dangerous and can consume you. We could go on and on. But we don't need to, because, the fact is, addictions are all the same. While I was researching this chapter I was shocked at how similar all of the stories were. They seemed to follow the same pattern, every time. These six steps were almost always present:

DESCENT INTO ADDICTION

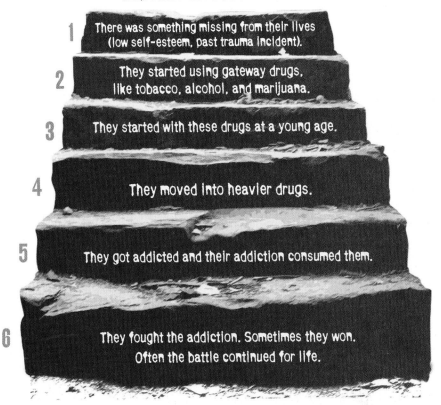

1 There was something missing from their lives (low self-esteem, past trauma incident).

2 They started using gateway drugs, like tobacco, alcohol, and marijuana.

3 They started with these drugs at a young age.

4 They moved into heavier drugs.

5 They got addicted and their addiction consumed them.

6 They fought the addiction. Sometimes they won. Often the battle continued for life.

I'm convinced that if we could eliminate all of the addictions in the world it would double the wealth of the world overnight. I mean, just think about the amount of wasted time, money, and energy that is put toward coping with the terrible wake of addictions.

LUCKY COW   *MARK PETT*

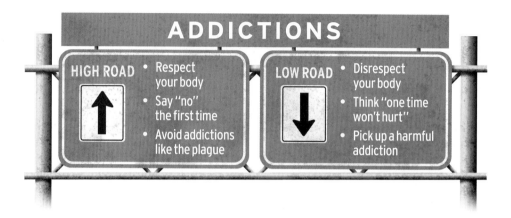

If you're on the high road (no pun intended) and free of addictions of any kind, rejoice and be glad that you don't have to deal with the baggage that goes with it. If you're experimenting and haven't made up your mind about the road you want to take, I hope you'll consider what's been said and put all your heart into staying clean. If you're already hooked on something, please change course before it's too late. It's your call.

By the time you turn 20 and graduate from your teens, if you are free of addictions, you will have a huge advantage. You will be in control of your body and your life. You will have achieved a huge accomplishment and deserve a prize.

CONGRATULATIONS!
YOU ARE ADDICTION FREE!

● ● ● COMING ATTRACTIONS ● ● ●

Do you own a Barbie doll? Keep reading and discover what Barbie would be like if she were real. Don't stop now. You've only got one more decision to read about.

BABY STEPS*

1. In the wheels below, write the names of the people who would be impacted if you picked up a serious addiction. If you already have one, write the names of those you're impacting now.

2. Draw a picture, create a collage, or write down words describing how you'd like your future family to be. Don't let any addictions get in the way of that dream.

3. Think about someone you know who is addicted to drugs. What kind of impact has it had on their life?

4. Go to your favorite Internet search engine and type in: "How to avoid drugs" or "How to overcome an addiction." There's a ton of good information out there.

5. Using one of the 5 Nos, role-play how to say "no" to peer pressure in front of a mirror.
   - *Be Direct*
   - *Use Humor*
   - *Blame It on Your Parents*
   - *Suggest an Alternative*
   - *Get Up and Go*

---

6. Make a list of the things that give you a natural high.

7. Post this reminder on your locker, mirror, planner, or journal:

"Does this fit with who I want to be?"

Ask yourself this question each time you face a tough decision.

8. Make a list of people and things that inspire you. Spend time with them. Feed the good wolf.

People that inspire me:

Things that inspire me (books, movies, magazines, music, pictures):

9. If you have an unhealthy addiction, get help now. Talk with a trusted adult, see a counselor, read up on the topic, or visit the Help Desk. Don't wait one day longer.

10. List three good reasons for avoiding porn.

SELF-WORTH

Top 10

Things You Oughta Know About Self-Worth...

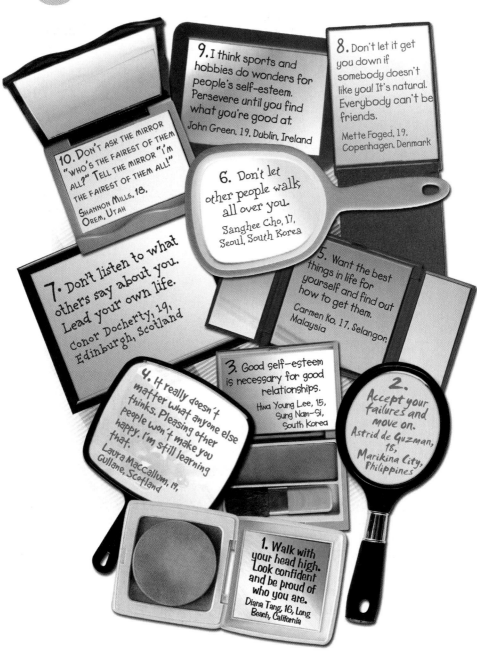

9. I think sports and hobbies do wonders for people's self-esteem. Persevere until you find what you're good at.
John Green, 19, Dublin, Ireland

8. Don't let it get you down if somebody doesn't like you! It's natural. Everybody can't be friends.
Mette Foged, 19, Copenhagen, Denmark

10. DON'T ASK THE MIRROR "WHO'S THE FAIREST OF THEM ALL?" TELL THE MIRROR "I'M THE FAIREST OF THEM ALL!"
SHANNON MILLS, 18, OREM, UTAH

6. Don't let other people walk all over you.
Sanghee Cho, 17, Seoul, South Korea

7. Don't listen to what others say about you. Lead your own life.
Conor Docherty, 19, Edinburgh, Scotland

5. Want the best things in life for yourself and find out how to get them.
Carmen Ko, 17, Selangor, Malaysia

4. It really doesn't matter what anyone else thinks. Pleasing other people won't make you happy. I'm still learning that.
Laura MacCallum, 19, Gullane, Scotland

3. Good self-esteem is necessary for good relationships.
Hwa Young Lee, 15, Sung Nam-Si, South Korea

2. Accept your failures and move on.
Astrid de Guzman, 18, Marikina City, Philippines

1. Walk with your head high. Look confident and be proud of who you are.
Diana Tang, 16, Long Beach, California

> Our greatest fear is not that we are inadequate. It is our
> light, not darkness, that most frightens us. We ask
> ourselves, "Who am I to be brilliant, gorgeous, handsome,
> talented, and fabulous?" Actually, who are you not to be?

— Marianne Williamson

Two sisters, only a year apart, were having fun on the swings at recess when a new girl joined them. After a few minutes playing together, the new girl pointed to the older sister and asked, "How come you're so pretty," and then to the younger sister, "and you're so ugly?"

Though the third girl was a complete stranger, her words were devastating to the younger sister's self-esteem, and caused conflict and comparisons between the two sisters for years to come.

Whoever said "Sticks and stones will break my bones, but words will never harm me" was a total idiot! Unkind words can crush you. So can a lot of other stuff, like flunking a test or surviving the divorce of your parents. Building healthy self-esteem is no walk in the park, that's for sure.

Just what do I mean by self-esteem? Self-esteem is your opinion of yourself. It goes by other names, including self-image, self-confidence, or self-respect. I like the term *self-worth* best because I think it says something the other terms don't. What is your self-worth? Get it?

Although how you esteem yourself may RiSE and FALL

WHAT YOU'RE REALLY WORTH NEVER CHANGES.

And just how much are you worth? More than you can probably imagine. As the Yiddish saying goes, "All of us are crazy good in one way or another."

What you do about your self-worth is the last of the most important decisions you'll ever make as a teen. To take the high road, you need to catch sight of your best self, build your character and competence, and learn to like yourself, flaws and all. Of course, you're always free to choose the low road by fixating on the opinions of others, doing nothing to improve yourself, and being hypercritical of your imperfections.

Having a healthy sense of self-worth doesn't mean you're full of yourself, it simply means you've got ample self-confidence and that you're okay with who you are.

Healthy self-worth can help you:

- *Withstand peer pressure*
- *Try new things and get to know new people*
- *Deal with disappointment, mistakes, and failure*
- *Feel loved and wanted*

Then again, poor self-worth may lead you to:

- *Cave in to peer pressure*
- *Avoid trying new things*
- *Fall apart during tough times*
- *Feel unloved and unwanted*

Maxwell Maltz put it this way: "Low self-esteem is like driving through life with your hand brake on." The good news is: no matter what you may think of yourself today, you can build your self-worth simply by thinking and acting a little differently. It's not rocket surgery.

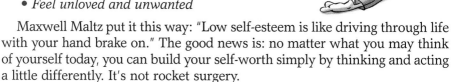

SELF-WORTH CHECKUP

So, how's it going now? Try this short checkup.

CIRCLE YOUR CHOICE	NO WAY!				HECK YES!
1. I generally like myself.	1	2	3	4	5
2. I have confidence in myself.	1	2	3	4	5
3. I'm okay with how I look.	1	2	3	4	5
4. I can handle rude or mean comments.	1	2	3	4	5
5. I have good skills and talents.	1	2	3	4	5
6. I finish what I start.	1	2	3	4	5
7. I am happy for others when they succeed, even those closest to me.	1	2	3	4	5
8. I regularly push myself to try new things and expand my comfort zone.	1	2	3	4	5
9. I see myself as a winner.	1	2	3	4	5
10. I have accomplished some important things in my life.	1	2	3	4	5
TOTAL					

You're on the high road. Keep it up!

 You're straddling the high and low roads. Move to higher ground!

 You're on the low road. Pay special attention to this chapter.

The truth is, all teens struggle with self-worth at some time and in some way, even those who seem supremely confident. This chapter has three sections. In **The Social Mirror and the True Mirror** we'll discuss why it isn't healthy to obsess about other people's opinions of you. **Character and Competence** will show you a practical approach to building self-worth. Finally, **Conquering Your El Guapo** gets into how to handle the thorns of life that so easily afflict us.

The Social Mirror and the True Mirror

Have you ever been to an amusement park where they have those "crazy" mirrors? It's hilarious to see yourself looking two feet tall, or your face and body all contorted or elongated. We laugh because we know it isn't true. The question is: When it comes to how you feel about yourself, which mirror are you looking at, the crazy one or the real one?

You see, there are two mirrors to choose from. One I call the *social mirror*, the other the *true mirror*. The social mirror is a reflection of how other people see you. The true mirror is a reflection of the real you.

The social mirror is based on how you stack up compared to others. It may lead you to think things like, "I'm better looking than she is" or "He's smarter than I am." In contrast, the true mirror is based on your potential and your personal best.

The social mirror is external—you look outside yourself for the definition of who you really are. The true mirror, on the contrary, is internal—you look inside for your self-definition.

·THE SOCIAL MIRROR·
- *What others say about you (image)*
- *Based on comparisons to others*
- *External*
- *Comes from the media*
- *Where you are today*

·THE TRUE MIRROR·
- *The real you*
- *Based on your personal best*
- *Internal*
- *Comes from conscience and self-awareness*
- *Your potential*

Think about what happens if your self-image comes from the social mirror—the reflection of how others see you. You begin to think that your reflection is the real you. It becomes your label and you get comfortable with it. You forget that you're even looking into a crazy mirror. Author Stan Herman wrote about the social mirror in this way:

Ed said
When men found the mirror
They began to lose their souls
The point, of course, is that
They began to concern themselves
With their images rather than
Their selves

Other men's eyes are mirrors
But the most distorting kind
For if you look to them you
    can only see
Reflections of your reflections
Your warping of their warpings

To figure out which mirror you're looking at, try this experiment. In the social mirror, write down how others would describe you. By others, I mean society in general, friends, teachers, family, neighbors, and so on.

In the true mirror, write down how you would describe the *real you.* The real you represents your best self and your potential. Consider how someone who fully believes in you, like your mom, dad, or grandma, would answer this question. If you believe in God, consider God's opinion of you.

A 17-year-old high school senior named Keli'i completed the experiment this way:

THE SOCIAL MIRROR
(How would others describe me?)
- *Stuck-up*
- *Ugly*
- *Mean*
- *Reserved*
- *Unpopular*

THE TRUE MIRROR
(How would I describe the real me, my best self?)
- *Fun-loving*
- *Kind*
- *Outgoing*
- *Confident*
- *Secure*

Give it a try by answering the questions below.

·THE SOCIAL MIRROR·

(How would others describe me?)

- _____
- _____
- _____
- _____
- _____

·THE TRUE MIRROR·

(How would I describe the real me, my best self?)

- _____
- _____
- _____
- _____
- _____

Now look at the two lists, and ask, in which mirror do I see myself—the social mirror or the true mirror? If you're like most teens (and adults), your self-image comes more from the social mirror than the true mirror. In other words, your opinion of yourself is made up of the opinions of others.

In some cases, others may already see the best in you, and looking in the social mirror is basically the same as looking in the true mirror. If so, lucky you! But in most cases, our opinions of ourselves come far too much from how others see us and far too little from who we really are.

CRACKS IN THE SOCIAL MIRROR

Looking to the social mirror is bad news for several reasons:

The social mirror is unrealistic. Somehow the media has sold everyone the lie that *looks are everything*. And we've bought it! Our culture proclaims that if you are good-looking, skinny, or buff, you can have it all—popularity, boyfriends, girlfriends, success, and happiness. "It is amazing how complete is the delusion that beauty is goodness," said Russian author Leo Tolstoy. The problem is that the images of how we're supposed to look come from movies and magazines that feature unrealistic models of perfection.

LUCKY COW   *MARK PETT*

Writer Georgia Beaverson states:

Television and other media venues have put our teens between a rock and a hard place. What makes up the rock? Impossibly buffed men. Women whose looks are perfection. Athletes who never seem to lose. Clothes, money, success, and sex are the name of the game. And what is the hard place for teens? In a word, reality!

What's seen as normal and desirable keeps getting thinner and thinner. Girls are surrounded by 12- and 13-year-old underweight models who are dressed up to look like women. Boys are bombarded with tan, incredibly ripped, and perfectly dressed men. It's estimated that only about 5 percent of women have the ultra-long and skinny body types possessed by most models. And yet that's the kind of body every girl wants and the only one that seems to be acceptable.

The media's influence is so strong we begin to think we ought to look like a Barbie doll, but could anyone? Adiosbarbie.com talks about what this would mean:

If Barbie were a real person, she would be 5'9" tall, have a neck twice the length of a normal human's neck, and weigh 110 pounds, only 76 percent of her healthy weight. Her measurements would be 38-18-32, and her feet would be too small to support her when she walks.

Similarly, young boys are supposed to have muscles popping out all over their bodies like the GI Joe Extreme action figure. If GI Joe were life-size, he would have a 55-inch chest and a 27-inch bicep. In other words, his bicep would be almost as big as his waist and bigger than most competitive body builders.

Ridiculous! No wonder we feel inadequate when we compare ourselves to the models in magazines or on TV. *"Perfect looks, perfect hair, perfect plot, perfect ending. Are these Hollywood teens anywhere close to the real you?"* asks writer Todd Hertz. I think not.

The social mirror is always changing. If your self-perception comes from how others see you, you'll never feel stable, because opinions, fads, and fashion are always changing. It's hard to keep up. You'll start to feel like Alice in Wonderland.

"Who are you?" said the caterpillar. Alice replied, rather shyly, "I hardly know, Sir, just at present—at least I know who I was when I got up this morning, but I think I must have changed several times since then."

The fashion magazines can never seem to make up their minds. They'll include an article on why you should be happy with the body you were born with and then, on the opposite page, run an ad on improving your looks through plastic surgery. So, which is it?

As one girl told me, "Most teenagers are trying to keep up with the trends. You create a lot of stress because you want to be like this person, but you want to be yourself as well."

The social mirror isn't accurate. You are so much more than the opinions of others. You are so much more than how you look on the outside. You have beauty and potential that no one recognizes, not even you.

Beware of the social mirror.

MIRROR, MIRROR, ON THE WALL

Every day you choose to look at the social mirror or the true mirror. Every day you choose to focus on your flaws or your qualities. Let's take a look at three common mirror moments.

THE GETTING READY MOMENT. Every time you look in the mirror to get ready for the day or that hot date you can:

Compare yourself to the latest teen celebrity and hate the way you look.

Be comfortable with how you look and focus on your better features.

THE FEELING INSECURE MOMENT. When you're with a group of friends and you feel insecure (as we all do sometimes) you can:

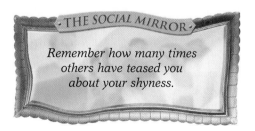

Remember how many times others have teased you about your shyness.

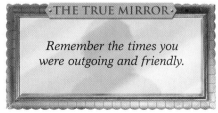

Remember the times you were outgoing and friendly.

THE COURAGE MOMENT. When you're scared to death about trying something new, like trying out for a sports team, you can:

·THE SOCIAL MIRROR·

*Think about
how much more talented
everyone else is.*

·THE TRUE MIRROR·

*Focus on your strengths
and the price you've paid to
be prepared.*

Getting your cues from the true mirror will give you power. Getting your cues from the social mirror will suck it out of you. The choice is yours. Remember what teen advisor Julia DeVillers said: "You can't live your life worrying that the world is staring at you. When you let people's opinions make you self-conscious you give away your power...The key to feeling confident is to always listen to your inner self—the real you."

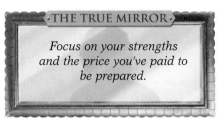

MIRROR, MIRROR, ON THE WALL, WHO'S THE FAIREST ONE OF ALL?

YOUR FACE IS TOO FAT, YOUR NOSE IS TOO BIG, AND THAT SNOW WHITE CHICK IS WAY BETTER LOOKIN' THAN YOU.

RELAX, YOU LOOK JUST FINE, ESPECIALLY THOSE CUTE DIMPLES OF YOURS. JUST BE YOUR BEST SELF. YOU GO, GIRL!

Character and Competence

Imagine. You've just been told you have a heart problem and you *may* need surgery. You have two doctors to choose from. The first, Dr. Good, has a great reputation for being an honest person, someone who cares deeply about his patients. The problem is he's never performed heart surgery before.

Your second choice, Dr. Able, has a great reputation for being a skilled heart surgeon. The only problem is that he's dishonest and is known to perform operations just for the money, even if his patient doesn't need it.

So, who will it be? Dr. Good, a great guy with no skills, or Dr. Able, a skilled guy but a liar?

What you'd really want is a doctor who is both honest and skilled, a doctor with both character and competence.

The two ingredients that make a good doctor, character and competence, just happen to be the primary ingredients that are essential to healthy self-worth. Let's define them.

Character is who you are, the qualities you possess. The scout law is a good definition of character. A scout is trustworthy, loyal, helpful, friendly, courteous, kind, obedient, cheerful, thrifty, brave, clean, and reverent.

Competence is what you're good at, your talents, skills, and abilities. We admire people who are competent, who have know-how and expertise, whether it be fixing a car, playing the violin, hitting a golf ball, memorizing names, or solving a quadratic equation.

Study the diagram below to see in which box you'd place yourself.

THE CHARACTER AND COMPETENCE SQUARE

CHARACTER

	LOW	HIGH
COMPETENCE / HIGH	**SQUANDERERS** **Characteristics** • Talented • Arrogant • Selfish	**STARS** **Characteristics** • Leader • Honest • Courageous
COMPETENCE / LOW	**PILES** **Characteristics** • Lazy • Dishonest • Negative	**HI-POs** **Characteristics** • Steady • Honest • Lacking courage and initiative

Squanderers (low character, high competence) are people with great talents but no backbone or moral fiber. I call them *squanderers* because they are wasting their talents. They're in a position to do so much good but don't because they think only of themselves. As an example, think of the many high profile athletes who are bad examples to the kids who adore them.

Piles (low character, low competence) have real issues. They don't care about other people nor do they care much about themselves. Just what is a pile? A pile just sits there, does nothing constructive, and isn't going anywhere. They need a life makeover. Enough said.

Hi-Pos or high potentials (high character, low competence) are good, honest people, but haven't yet challenged themselves to expand their abilities. Because they have a foundation of character, however, they have high potential of becoming a star. So many teens are in this box. They've got their act together; they just need to push themselves a little more.

Stars (high character, high competence) have solid skills and are good people. These people have worked hard to develop their talents but not at the expense of others. They're not perfect but they're trying.

Luckily, there are a lot more Hi-Pos and Stars than Piles and Squanderers. Furthermore, everyone has the capability of becoming a star. First, decide that you want to make a change and then build your character and competence one stone at a time, as explained below.

THE SELF-WORTH ARCH OF TRIUMPH

Years ago, while driving into Paris, I came upon one of the most beautiful sights I'd ever seen: L'Arc de Triomphe, or The Arch of Triumph. It's a beautiful Roman arch about fifty yards high and just as wide. It was decreed to be built by Napoleon, the great emperor, almost two hundred years ago. Around this arch is a gigantic roundabout, seven lanes deep, that's legendary for its traffic accidents. While gazing at this spectacular arch, I got stuck in the middle of the roundabout. The local French drivers had no sympathy for me—yet another dumb American tourist—but shook their fists and used nasty French words I couldn't understand. But you should have seen that arch!

The process for building character and competence and ultimately self-worth is found in the architecture of the arch, or what I call The Self-Worth Arch of Triumph. On one side you have the foundation stones of character: integrity, service, and faith. On the other side you have the foundation stones of competence: talents and skills, accomplishments, and physical health. At the top you have the keystone, smart decisions, which holds the whole thing together.

THE FOUNDATION STONES OF CHARACTER

Although there are many things that build character, the three essentials are integrity, service, and faith.

 Integrity is another word for honesty, with a twist. It means being true to what you know is right and being honest with everyone, including yourself. As Shakespeare wrote: "To thine own self be true." You don't cheat on tests, you don't lie to your parents about what you did last night, you don't talk nice to someone's face and rip on them behind their back. People with *integrity* are whole or complete, like an *integer* in your math book. They know where they stand and stand there.

How is integrity a source of self-worth? Having it leads to inner peace. And if you have inner peace you can handle most anything, even mean girls, heart-wrenching breakups, and major embarrassments. Talk show host Dr. Laura said this: "Don't worry so much about your self-esteem; worry more about your character. Integrity is its own reward."

Now, if you're like I was and most other teens are, you'll make mistakes and have to work on this integrity thing. No one's perfect. So, if you mess up, make up. Never try to cover up a mistake. It only makes things worse. NBA coach Rick Pitino said:

"Lying makes a problem part of the **FUTURE;** truth makes a problem part of the **PAST.**"

In 1974, the 37th president of the United States, Richard M. Nixon, was charged in the Watergate scandal. He went on national TV and denied any involvement, saying, "I am not a crook." Later the truth came out. He knew what was going on and tried to cover his rear end. The nation was so upset that he was forced to resign, in disgrace. Greater than the mistake was the cover-up. People are quick to forgive mistakes, but slow to forgive a cover-up.

When I was about eight, my parents tell me I set a fire in the window well of my neighbor's house, just for fun. Well, the fire got out of control and almost burned down his house. As you can imagine, my neighbor, Mr. Beckham, was furious and I earned a bad reputation around the neighborhood for being a troublemaker.

To help me redeem myself, my dad taught me about what he called the *four-fold*. A four-fold means that when you make a mistake, you make up for it times four. So I cleaned Mr. Beckham's window well. I cleaned his yard, and I did a couple of other things to make up for the fire. If you can believe it, Mr. Beckham grew to actually like me and my reputation in the neighborhood was restored. That's how four-fold works.

So when you slip up, apply the four-fold. If you told a big fat lie to your parents, make it up to them times four. Maybe that means you do the dishes one night, clean the car, write a sorry note, and never lie again.

Fixing up instead of covering up—that's what integrity is all about.

SERVICE "The service we render others is the rent we pay for our room on earth," said Wilfred Grenfall. When you really think about it, we have so much to be grateful for. Ponder this:

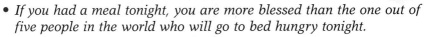

- *If you are reading this book right now you are better off than nearly one billion people who cannot read.*

- *If you have a place to stay, food in the refrigerator, and clothes on your back, you are wealthier than nearly three billion people who live on less than two dollars a day.*

- *If you can attend a church meeting this week without fear of harassment, arrest, torture, or death, you are luckier than more than two billion people.*

- *If you had a meal tonight, you are more blessed than the one out of five people in the world who will go to bed hungry tonight.*

Because we have been given much, we too should give. It should come as no surprise that when you give, you get. Jose from Andress High School wrote about a time when he was challenged by a teacher to help the homeless.

I went out and bought a couple things from McDonald's and went driving around with my friend and we found a homeless man on the streets. So I got out and walked over and offered him the food. He was so grateful. I sat and talked to him for a while and then I left. It made me feel good just knowing that the man was not hungry before he went to bed that night.

This reminds me of this saying I once heard: "Service is like wetting your pants. Everyone can see what you've done, but only you can feel the warmth!" The great thing about serving and volunteering is there are limitless ways to do it: adopting a pet, being a Big Brother or Sister to at-risk kids, tutoring at an inner city school, reading to kids in a hospital, supporting the veterans, joining a service club, speaking out against drugs, or just going out of your way to be nice to those who need it. You get the picture.

The irony is that when you try to build someone else's self-worth, you build your own. Author Nathaniel Hawthorne put it this way,

"Happiness is like a butterfly. The more you chase it, the more it will elude you. But if you turn your attention to other things, it comes and sits softly on your shoulder."

My niece Shannon learned this firsthand when she left her comfortable home as a young adult to volunteer at an orphanage in Romania for several months. Here's an excerpt from one of her letters:

When we went to the orphanage for the first time, I experienced true culture shock. I walked in the room and saw all the babies lying in their cribs, staring off into space. There were some that were three to a crib. It was very difficult to see beautiful babies just wasting away in their cribs, and I wanted to hold every one of them and never let them go.

I remember the first time a special baby named Denisa fell asleep in my arms. I didn't want to put her down because I knew this may have been the first time she had fallen asleep in someone's arms instead of alone in her cold, hard, metal crib. As I watched her sleep, I could feel the beauty of her spirit, and I realized then that God knew and loved Denisa as I did.

Another time I was putting a few two-year-olds to bed and was holding two of them, but another one was crying and wanted to be held. I couldn't hold three, so I scooted my chair over by his crib so I could comfort him too. I started singing "Edelweiss," a song my dad used to sing to me when I was little. Almost immediately he stopped crying and listened to my singing, which really wasn't very good, and a beautiful spirit came into that orphanage room in far-off Romania, so far from my home.

I came to love these children who would put their arms out to be held and run to me, calling me mama. Every day, I prayed that they would someday have a better life than they do now. How grateful I was that I had left my selfish life for a few short months to bring them mere moments of contentment and love. I can never repay them for what they gave me and how they changed my life forever.

Like a drop in a pond, the good you do will ripple forth long after you're gone. When Shannon returned home from Romania, she put on slide shows in schools and churches encouraging others to work in an orphanage. As a result, several girls from her area volunteered to serve in Romania. She was happy to know that her babies were still being looked after.

If I can stop one heart from breaking,
I shall not live in vain;
If I can ease one life the aching,
Or cool one pain,
Or help one fainting robin
Unto his nest again,
I shall not live in vain.

— Emily Dickinson

FAITH Faith means believing in something you can't see. It comes in all varieties. You can have faith in yourself, faith in others, or faith that through hard work good things will happen. For example, you have faith that by cutting out junk food and exercising you will lose weight. You have faith that through making smart choices around school, friends, and drugs today, you will have a brighter future. Faith causes you to act. Without it, there's nothing to hope for.

There's yet another kind of faith that's increasingly important to many teens—faith in spiritual things.

Did you know that your brain is hard-wired to connect spiritually? Babies yearn to be held and teenagers hunger for meaning and spirituality. At least that was the conclusion of 33 experts from the nonpartisan Commission on Children at Risk, which researched why kids today are in crisis. In their report, "Hard-wired to Connect," they concluded that our brains are yearning for spiritual meaning, and listed spiritual and religious development as one of the ten marks of an ideal community. Interesting, huh?

TEEN SPIRIT

Of course, everyone believes differently and that's okay. But study after study has shown that faith or religious involvement of some sort can build self-worth in teens. Why's that? Faith can:

- *help you connect to something bigger than yourself*
- *provide you with standards to live by*
- *help you overcome negative peer pressure*
- *give you a sense of identity and belonging*

Over the last several years, I've received hundreds of mission statements from teens all over the globe and I'm always amazed by how often faith, God, church, and other similar things are mentioned. In fact, research shows that faith is the second biggest influence in your lives, second only to parents. Hmmmm.

I'm reminded of an unforgettable scene from the movie *Signs* on the topic of faith, where Graham, the reverend, asks his brother Merrill whether or not he believes in miracles.

GRAHAM: *People break down into two groups...Are you the kind who sees signs, sees miracles? Or do you believe that people just get lucky?*

MERRILL: *I was at this party once. I'm on the couch with Randa McKinney. She was just sitting there looking beautiful, staring at me. I go to lean in and kiss her...and I realize I have gum in my mouth. So I turn, take out the gum, stuff it in a paper cup next to the sofa, and turn around. Randa McKinney throws up all over herself. I knew the second it happened it was a miracle. I could have been kissing her when she threw up. That would have scarred me for life. I may never have recovered.*

I'm a miracle man.

So, what about you? Do you believe in miracles or do you believe people just get lucky? Or as Albert Einstein put it,

"THERE ARE TWO WAYS TO LIVE YOUR LIFE. ONE IS AS THOUGH NOTHING IS A MIRACLE. THE OTHER IS AS THOUGH EVERYTHING IS A MIRACLE."

As for me, I'm a miracle man. I believe God loves all his children and knows each of us by name. I believe he hears and answers prayers. For me, completing this book was a miracle; I never could have done it without divine help. I can relate to Martin Luther, the great religious reformer, who said: *"I have so much to do today I'll have to spend an extra hour on my knees."*

Here is a part of a letter written by a courageous young girl named Nicki Jean Jones, whose faith was put to the test in her battle with cancer.

To all my beloved family and friends:

Over the last 16 months, I have had the opportunity to better prepare myself to meet my Heavenly Father. I have come to realize that no matter what you go through or are tested with in this life, with God you don't have to do it alone.

I decided that instead of feeling sorry for myself that I would count the blessings that I have received instead. Not only do I still have one good leg, I have two good arms and hands. I have eyes that can see, and ears that can hear, and a mouth that can communicate with the world. I have come to realize that my true beauty lies within, and that the Lord judges me by what's in my heart.

*I want you to know that I have beaten my cancer! You might argue with that because of the outcome: It has taken my leg, momentarily caused me to lose my hair, and in the end, be the very thing that has taken my life, but it still has not beaten me because it cannot take my smile, it cannot take my beliefs, and it absolutely cannot break my spirit. And therefore, **I HAVE WON!***

When I look back on this, I would not change a thing because what I have gained from this cancer is far more precious than anything I've lost.

In closing, I would like to say that I love you all so very much, that I will always be with you, and I promise to put in a good word for all of you!

All my eternal love, Nicki

I wish I could say that Nicki's cancer is now in remission, but she died shortly after this was written. Truly, she had cancer, but cancer did not have her! Even in her last days, she inspired her friends and family to live on a higher plane. Her faith was her anchor.

THE FOUNDATION STONES OF COMPETENCE

I attended a lot of assemblies as a teen where the speaker said something like, "You are a wonderful human being. Feel good about yourself!" And I'd walk away feeling no different. Hearing someone tell you to like yourself because they said so won't do squat, if you do nothing different. Although character is vital to healthy self-worth, there's more to it than that. What builds self-worth faster than anything else is finding and developing a talent or skill of some kind. This is competence, and there's no substitute. The foundation stones of competence include talents and skills, accomplishments, and physical health.

The longer I live the more I'm convinced that everyone is born with unique talents and skills.* But they won't just happen to you—you have to happen to them. I remember breaking my arm as a kid. When I got my cast off, my arm had been transformed into this hairy shriveled-up thing. Such is life. If we don't push ourselves to try new things, we weaken and wither. To grow, we must expand our comfort zone and move into the courage zone. How? Through pushing ourselves, trying out, taking chances, failing and rising again, and exploring new summits. Competence, like a muscle, can only be developed through resistance.

Melody learned about the confidence-boosting effects of stretching oneself.

---

*To show off your talents in film, computer animation, art, writing, poetry, and more, go to www.6decisions.com.

To audition for the All-State Choir in Kentucky you have to sing in a quartet. The first time my choir teacher called me to sing in front of the class I was nervous, my heart beat wildly, my palms sweat, and my legs shook. Since then I have sung more than twenty times in front of the class. I've worked to expand my comfort zone so I no longer become nervous. My audition is tomorrow evening, and now I have confidence in myself. I know I will be fine.

Think about your own life. Are you wasting the talents you've been given? Or are you continually pushing yourself and learning new things? I know of one ninth grader, Roxy, who has become an excellent designer and seamstress and can make just about anything on her sewing machine. Although she's proud of her sewing skills, Roxy says, "No one thinks sewing is cool." Well, who's to say what's cool? Personally, I think anything you can excel at is cool, whether it be sewing, writing essays, organizing things, speed reading, teaching children, or building Web sites.

As a boy I was scared of speaking in front of people. To help conquer my fear I signed up for a speech class in seventh grade. The first time I had to speak in class, I was terrified. But it got better each time. Over the next four years I took speech and debate classes to help me develop my speaking skills. Although I never fully got over my fear, I improved as a speaker and it boosted my confidence.

I'm familiar with a blind boy from Tibet named Tashi Pasang, who could not have had a worse start in life. When he was only 11 years old, his father brought him to a town called Lhasa and swapped him for a sighted child because he was such a burden. Tashi was repeatedly robbed and beaten up by the other street children. Somehow, he survived his very first winter on the streets by begging and wrapping himself in plastic bags to keep warm.

Eventually, some kind Tibetans found him and took him to a school for disadvantaged kids. There, despite being blind, Tashi pushed himself to develop his talents and skills. To everyone's amazement, he now reads, writes, and speaks three languages: Tibetan, Chinese, and English. He uses a computer with a speech synthesizer. And he recently received an official medical masseur license from the Chinese government.

Now, after five years, he plans to return to his home village and assure his parents that he is alive and well and that he bears no bad feelings toward them. And you thought your problems were bad.

Through the charity of caring people, and with the ability to read, write, and speak three languages, Tashi is equipped to make something of his life. Without those skills he wouldn't have a chance. You see, in today's world, it's not enough just to be a great guy. You've gotta be competent.

ACCOMPLISHMENTS Great power comes from accomplishing something you set your mind to. In the legends, when a knight defeats an enemy in battle, he absorbs the strength of that enemy. So it is when we overcome a weakness, resist a temptation, or achieve a goal we've set. We absorb the strength of the challenge into our being and become stronger. For one, an accomplishment might mean getting straight As, for another it means making the drill team, and for another it's overcoming a weakness, like cleaning up your language.

Sometimes our accomplishments are different than we expect. Tanner, from Northridge High School, always had the goal of becoming the state wrestling champion like his older brother. After years of hard work, Tanner became recognized as one of the top wrestlers around. Finally, it was his chance to prove himself in the match that would qualify him for the state tournament.

During the championship round, however, Tanner severely dislocated his elbow and his dreams of becoming the state champ were shattered. He was sick about it, until he received a letter from his older brother, who wrote:

Tanner,

It feels good being a state champion, but not everyone is gonna remember you for that. But they will remember you for the way you prepared. You gave all you could give before you actually wrestled for state, and that's what really matters. You left everything you had on the mat.

Tanner was deeply touched. To top it off, during the state tournament, the entire team each wore an elbow brace to honor him. It was then that Tanner realized he'd actually accomplished what he had set out to do in the first place.

There's always a gap between where we are and where we'd like to be. Sometimes the gap is small. Sometimes it's huge. Whatever your gap, stay positive, keep closing the gap, and beware of the perfectionist inside you who is never pleased. Closing the gap even a little is an accomplishment to be proud of.

GREAT GAP CANYON

WHERE I
AM NOW

WHERE I
WANT TO BE

PHYSICAL HEALTH As a kid, I loved pop, doughnuts, and chips of every kind. Consequently, I got called *fatso* a lot. I'd ask, "Mom, do you think I'm fat?"

"No, you're not fat," she'd say. "You're husky." And I'd walk away grinning. "Yeah, I'm not fat. I'm husky."

MAYBE I SHOULD LAY OFF THE TWINKIES.

During the summer before I started eighth grade, my dad sent me on a four-day survival trek, to toughen me up. I hated it. Basically, eighty or so of us hiked about fifty miles over a four-day period while eating nothing but weeds. The leaders made us do all sorts of crazy things like rappel off cliffs, cross raging rivers, and kill and eat a cute little lamb. Poor thing.

From this I lost about ten pounds. When I came back, my mom's friend said, "Hey, Sean, you're sure lookin' skinny." It was the first time in my life that someone had told me that. I was thrilled! It was the jump start I needed.

So, I went home and got ahold of my mom's eating guide, which, even today, is based on solid principles of nutrition. It separated all the food groups and had little check boxes on the number of servings you were allowed to eat each day. I remember it exactly.

FOOD GROUP	DAILY SERVINGS				
Grains (bread, rice, cereal, pasta, etc.)	☐	☐	☐	☐	☐
Fruits (any sort)	☐	☐	☐		
Vegetables (any sort)	☐	☐	☐	☐	
Dairy (milk, cheese, yogurt, etc.)	☐	☐	☐		
Proteins (chicken, fish, beef, beans, etc.)	☐	☐			
Fats (butter, oil, etc.)	☐	☐	☐		
Water	☐	☐	☐	☐	☐

After watching what I ate for a few days I realized I was living on bread, meat, and fat, and that I seldom ate fruit, veggies, or dairy. I was hardly drinking any water either. What a shocker! So, I started following the program religiously. Every night, before bed, I'd check off what I had eaten that day. I was still eating a lot of food, just different kinds of foods, like fruits and veggies. I also started lifting weights and running. My body changed quickly and the extra weight I was carrying just melted away in a matter of months. Suddenly, I felt so much better and more in tune with my body. To my surprise, I even went from being one of the slower players to the fastest player on my eighth grade football team.

As I discovered for myself, getting in shape physically is a competence that needs to be learned through trial and experience. If learned at a young age, it will serve you for life. Don't ever underestimate the impact of physical health on emotional health.

Here are ten commonly agreed upon principles of nutrition that will improve your health every time:

Today's specials

1. Eat Breakfast

2. Don't try fad diets. They're unsustainable. You'll temporarily lose weight, but gain it all back and more in the long run.

3. Eat at least five servings of fruits and vegetables daily. Eat a variety. All kinds are good. ✱

4. Eat whole grains, like oatmeal, brown rice, and whole wheat, in place of processed grains, like enriched flour, store-bought muffins, and white rice.

5. Limit your intake of sugar, processed foods, and fried foods, like pop, sugar cereals, and French fries.

6. Get at least two servings of protein each day from meat, chicken, fish, eggs, beans, or soy products.

7. Get at least two servings of dairy each day from string or cottage cheese, yogurt, frozen yogurt, or milk.

8. Eat some healthy fats each day (fish, nuts, olive oil, sunflower oil, canola oil).

9. Spread out your calories. You're better off eating smaller meals throughout the day than eating one big meal at one sitting.

10. Drink LOTS of water. ✱

In addition to sound nutrition, exercise is also essential. Have you heard of endorphins? They're powerful chemicals in your brain that do two things: elevate mood and kill pain. Guess how you get them? Exercising. Isn't that amazing? Hey, who needs drugs when you can get a natural endorphin high at any time for free?

Everyone thinks they don't have time to exercise. In reality, you don't have time *not* to. Exercise will make you feel better, look better, and live longer (not that you're worried about that yet). For a balanced exercise program, *Time* magazine health experts recommend you do these four things:

CLEAR YOUR MiND: *Yoga, Pilates, or some sort of stretching, breathing, or meditation relaxes the body, protects against injuries, and enhances circulation. Do it three times a week to reduce stress.*

EXERCISE YOUR HEART: *Swim, power walk, cycle, jog, kickbox, or do an aerobic exercise that significantly increases your heart rate. It benefits your heart, lungs, and circulatory system, as well as burns calories and body fat. Do it three to five times a week for 20 to 60 minutes.*

BUILD YOUR MUSCLES: *Weight lift, do calisthenics or any sport that makes you flex muscles repetitively. Weight lifting makes the body burn more calories, and increases bone mass. Do it two to three times a week for 20 to 40 minutes.*

TAKE A BREAK: *Strength training and other strenuous exercises tear down muscle fiber. During periods of rest, muscles repair and rebuild themselves; avoid weight training the same muscle group two days in a row.*

If you play competitive sports, you'll usually be doing all of the four suggested activities above regularly, and have some fun in the process.

As a rule of thumb, one pound of weight is equal to 3,500 calories. So, if you want to lose a pound of weight in a week, you'd have to burn 500 calories more than you're taking in each day (500 calories × 7 days = 3,500 calories).

Learn about sound nutrition and exercise. Get in shape and watch how it improves your social, mental, and spiritual sides. I'm not talking about obsessing over your looks and I'm not talking about being thin. (You can be a large person and still be healthy, by the way.) I'm talking about getting healthy. It's how you feel on the inside, not what you look like on the outside that really counts.

SMART DECISIONS

THE KEYSTONE

Fourteen-year-old Leah shared how she had just begun junior high and was having a rough time. It seemed that everyone was so into looks and clothes and popularity. She didn't feel accepted and was often made fun of because she was overweight.

A few months later she found some friends and life got much better. But it wasn't long before Leah's friends began going in a different direction than Leah wanted to go. They dressed sleazy, used rough language, and were experimenting with addictive substances.

One night, while roaming around with her friends, Leah looked at them and thought: "My friends look like sleazebags. Is that how I look?" She called her mom to come pick her up. That night she made the gutsy decision to stop hanging out with these friends.

The next few weeks were rough for Leah. Her old friends turned on her when she'd no longer hang out with them. She'd often eat her lunch in the bathroom stall because it was too embarrassing to eat alone in the lunchroom.

But Leah hung on, and in a matter of a few months she'd made some new friends who shared her standards and brought out the best in her. One of her old friends also left the old group and started hanging out with Leah instead. Leah grew in confidence and began finding her way. What a difference one smart choice can make!

So, which comes first? Do you make good decisions because you have high self-worth or do you have high self-worth because you make good decisions? Yes. It works both ways. It's sort of like asking, "Which came first, the chicken or the egg?"

Smart decision-making is the keystone of the Self-Worth Arch of Triumph. *If you do this one right, all the other building blocks seem to fall into place.* Funny thing is, building healthy self-worth, the sixth most important decision you'll ever make, is the result of being smart about the previous five decisions. Here's how smart choices boost self-worth.

HIGH ROAD DECISIONS	HOW IT BOOSTS YOUR SELF-WORTH
Do your best in school	• You'll learn more and develop stronger skills • Your parents will nag you less
Choose true friends and be a true friend	• Your friends will bring out the best in you • You'll make friends more easily

Get along with your parents		• You'll have more peace at home • You'll get more support from your parents
Date intelligently, respect your body, and save yourself		• You'll enjoy a good reputation • You won't worry about STDs, pregnancy, or emotional trauma
Avoid addictions		• You'll feel better physically • You'll be in control of your life

The social mirror of the world tells you that self-worth comes from good looks and popularity. The truth is, healthy self-worth comes from character, competence, and smart choices. As Dumbledore says in *Harry Potter and the Chamber of Secrets,*

> *"It's our choices, Harry, that show what we truly are, far more than our abilities."*

Conquering Your El Guapo!

One of the great movies of all time is *The Three Amigos*, in which a classic battle between the good guys and a crazy villain named El Guapo takes place. In one scene, one of the amigos is trying to inspire the villagers to stand up to El Guapo, by saying, "In a way, all of us have an El Guapo to face someday. For some, shyness might be their El Guapo. For others, a lack of education might be their El Guapo. For us, El Guapo is a big dangerous guy who wants to kill us."

When it comes to self-worth, all of us have our El Guapo to conquer. What's yours? Here are three common ones:

- *How do I build self-worth if I think I'm not good-looking?*
- *How can I cope when I constantly get called names, put down, and teased?*
- *How can I get out of this depression I'm in?*

HOW DO I BUILD SELF-WORTH IF I THINK I'M NOT GOOD-LOOKING?

This question was sent to me from a teen from Israel named Rotem. I'll answer by telling the story of another citizen of Israel who felt just like Rotem when she was a teen. Her name was Golda Meir.

I was never a beauty. There was a time when I was sorry about that, when I was old enough to understand the importance of it and, looking in any mirror, realized it was something I was never going to have. Then I found what I wanted to do in life, and being called pretty no longer had any importance. It was only much later that I realized that not being beautiful was a blessing in disguise. It forced me to develop my inner resources. I came to understand that women who cannot lean on their beauty and need to make something on their own have the advantage.

Golda Meir became the first female prime minister of Israel, and is considered one of the great leaders of all time. So, how did Golda build her self-worth? She found out what she wanted to do with her life, and suddenly being pretty wasn't that important. You can do likewise. Once you get a sense of what you want to do with your life—your goals, dreams, and purpose—you'll be energized by it and won't obsess about your looks.

Virtually every teen I know wishes they were better-looking or could change something about themselves. I hear stuff like:

"My nose is too big." *"I've got a fat face."*

"I've got stubby fingers." *"I'm too short."*

"MY EARS STICK OUT." "I'm too tall."

In one survey by TRU.com, teens were asked: What are the top things you would change about yourself if you could?

WHAT WOULD YOU CHANGE ABOUT YOURSELF?

1. BETTER LOOKING
2. BETTER STUDENT
3. MORE CONFIDENT
4. BETTER ATHLETE
5. HAVE A BOYFRIEND/GIRLFRIEND
6. MORE POPULAR
7. HARDER WORKER

The New You

It's no surprise that being better-looking was the top response. While not fixating on your looks, strive to look your best and enhance the natural features you were blessed with. Notice what colors look best on you, practice good hygiene, and find a hairstyle that suits you. Appreciate your finer features. After all, everyone is beautiful in their own way—sparkling blue or rich brown eyes, a delicate chin, high cheekbones, a cute nose, a prominent nose, elegant ears, graceful fingers, broad shoulders, muscular legs, long eyelashes, full lips, or buns of steel.

Author Susan Tanner, who was once an insecure teen with a bad case of acne, never forgot the lesson her mother taught her. "You must do everything you can to make your appearance pleasing, but the minute you walk out the door, forget yourself and start concentrating on others." This is good advice for all of us.

Remember, if you always look to the social mirror, you'll always feel inadequate. If you look to the true mirror, you'll realize that inner beauty is more important than the outer kind.

Audrey Hepburn was one of the most glamorous Hollywood actresses from my parents' time and was famous for her beauty and style. She often quoted these beauty tips.

Beauty Tips

For attractive lips,
Speak words of kindness.
For lovely eyes,
Seek out the good in people.
For a slim figure,
Share your food with the hungry.
For beautiful hair,
Let a child run his or her fingers through it once a day.
For poise
Walk with the knowledge that you'll never walk alone.
People, even more than things, have to be restored,
Renewed, revived, reclaimed, and redeemed;
Never throw anybody out.
The beauty of a woman is not in the clothes she wears,
The figure that she carries, or the way she combs her hair.
The beauty of a woman must be seen from in her eyes
Because that is the doorway to her heart, the place where love resides.

— Sam Levenson

Reprinted by permission of SIl/Sterling Lord Literistic, Inc., Copyright © 1973 by Samuel Levenson

Author Neal Maxwell observed:

"Wouldn't it be interesting if what was on the inside of a person were revealed on the outside? Then we would know who the truly beautiful people of the world are."

You'll Be Dead Before You're Thin Enough

In our quest to look and feel good, please don't take things to the extreme.

...I tried this vomiting business...I thought I could make it whatever I wanted. When I ate something on my "bad" list, I could get rid of it. I had this irrational fear of starting to eat and not being able to stop and just becoming huge. I figured if I reached a certain weight, I would feel secure enough and would be able to stop. The strange thing was the number on the scale was never low enough...

This is how someone who suffers from an eating disorder thinks. An eating disorder is defined as an eating habit which hurts you physically and mentally. The three most common ones are *anorexia nervosa* (starving yourself), *bulimia nervosa* (binge eating then throwing up), and *binge eating disorder* (uncontrollable binge eating). Did you know that tens of thousands of teens have died or will die because of them? In fact, anorexia nervosa has one of the highest death rates of any psychological disorder.

Millions of teens have an eating disorder. You probably know someone who does. Maybe you've got one yourself. They're found among boys and girls, rich and poor, children as young as three and adults as old as ninety. They're most common among teen girls. Often an eating disorder can go unnoticed for years. When it is finally recognized, denial usually follows, and the disorder goes untreated. There are many contributing factors, including family problems, depression, sexual abuse, or an obsession with being thin.

HEALTH EXPERTS ESTIMATE THAT 5 TO 20 PERCENT OF THOSE WITH ANOREXIA NERVOSA WILL DIE FROM IT. FRIGHTENING!

As a teen with a future, you need to have a strong, healthy body. You can't afford memory loss, disorientation, constipation, deterioration of muscles, slow irregular heartbeats that lead to heart attacks, or any other symptom that goes with anorexia. Don't let yourself get suckered into this unnatural, unhealthy lifestyle. Eating disorders are hard to shake and can stay with you for life. There are natural and healthy ways to lose weight if that's your desire.

If you've got a disorder right now, go to your parents, the family doctor, or a local support group for help. Or visit the Help Desk in the back of the book for some credible resources.

 ## HOW CAN I COPE WHEN I CONSTANTLY GET CALLED NAMES, PUT DOWN, AND TEASED?

Sixteen-year-old Reese was on a roll this time. At least, *he* thought so. He was telling his friends the long version of how he got lost skiing and ended up on the Olympic jump site, where no one was allowed, when Brad cut him off.

"Reese!" he yelled. "Shut up! We don't care about your dumb story! You know what? You talk too much!"

Everyone laughed. Reese acted like it didn't bother him, but he died inside that day. He felt like such a fool and wondered how many of the stories he'd told in the past were annoying, too.

After that, he started being extra careful about anything he said around these friends. He didn't call to see if they wanted to hang out for fear of bugging them, and soon they stopped calling him, too. He kept thinking, "If they want to do something, they'll call me." They never did. Eventually, these friendships ended and his self-worth took a huge hit.

This kind of thing happens all the time, doesn't it? A rude comment. An unkind word. Gossip. And it hurts! We should all be a lot more careful with our tongues.

I remember talking to a middle-school girl who hated school. I asked her why. In tears she said, "It's because, on B-days, I've got all these rude girls in my classes that are mean and call me all sorts of names. I just can't stand it anymore."

What can you do if it's happening to you? Just ask anyone who has gone through it and survived. They'll all tell you the same thing. Bridget from Joliet Township High School shared how she learned to cope with mean words.

In junior high, I wouldn't stand up for myself very much. If someone told me, "I don't like your shoes," I wouldn't say anything. I'd just sit there. Then I got into high school. I started hanging out with people that were a positive influence, like Michelle. She does not care what other people say about her. She is who she is. If you don't like her, too bad. I learned you have to stand up for yourself and be confident in who you are. Now if somebody says, "I don't like this about you," I have nerve enough to stand up for myself and deal with it.

That's smart counsel. In any case, if you knew how little time other people actually spend thinking about you, you wouldn't care so much about what they think.

 ## HOW CAN I GET OUT OF THIS DEPRESSION I'M IN?

Depression is such an overused word I get depressed even thinking about it. Just what does it mean?

The American Heritage Dictionary defines depression in two ways:
1. Low in spirits; dejected. 2. Suffering from psychological depression.

Rachel experienced the first kind, low in spirits.

My entire life right now stresses me out. I am always anxious, depressed, or agitated. It's like my feelings won't make up their mind! It really worries me because it affects the people I'm around sometimes. Like when I'm at home and I'm in a bad mood, I tend to take it out on my family, which isn't right because it's not their fault.

Everyone experiences this first kind of depression, the normal ups and downs of life, or what many call *the blues.* Lots of stuff can make us feel this way: you break up with your girlfriend or boyfriend, your parents announce you're moving, or it's Sunday night, and you haven't started your homework. Now, that's depressing! But usually that feeling doesn't last more than a few days.

The second kind of depression, when you suffer from psychological or clinical depression, is much more serious. And, despite what some ignorant people may think, it's not something you can just wish away and it's not a sign of personal weakness. This kind of depression is caused by stuff like the death of a friend or family member, loneliness, stress, sexual abuse, chemical imbalance, substance abuse, or family problems. According to the National Alliance on Mental Illness (NAMI), the symptoms of this kind of depression include:

- *Big changes in sleep, appetite, and energy*
- *Lack of interest in activities that were once a lot of fun*
- *Feelings of sadness, guilt, worthlessness, hopelessness, and emptiness*
- *Regular thoughts of death or suicide*

If you have any of these symptoms, please know that they can be treated successfully through counseling, nutrition, exercise, medicine, or a combination of any of these. Surprisingly, however, less than half of depressed people actually get help.

All of us get physically sick from time to time from a cold or the flu. Sometimes we go to a doctor and take medication. We talk openly about it and say things like, "I feel awful."

We can also get emotionally sick or depressed. Something terrible happens. The chemicals in our brain misfire. We lose hope. But unlike physical sickness, we don't talk about the mental kind. There's this stigma. We hesitate to go to a doctor or take medication, mistakenly thinking we can treat it ourselves. Mental health expert Sherri Wittwer summed it up well:

"There is no shame in having a mental illness.
Mental illness is no different than any other illness such as asthma or diabetes.
What we do know is that treatment works, recovery is possible, and there is hope."

A courageous young guy named Jake Short who suffered from a bipolar disorder, or manic depression, shared how his life was a living nightmare until he got treatment.

School was very hard for me from the beginning, and I struggled just to learn. I didn't interact with any of the kids. One night in third grade, my parents were helping me write sentences for spelling words. I couldn't do it no matter how hard I tried. I was so upset and anxious I just cried. Even though I was only eight, I ran away from home that cold, snowy night and wandered around for a long time. I finally was so cold I came home. My mom was crying and asked me what would make me feel better. I told her "just to be dead." They knew then that something was really wrong with me.

This began years of being treated for different problems such as social phobias, ADD, severe anxiety, and depression. My life was full of therapy and medication.

In fifth grade and sixth grade, I started to get worse. I would run away from school, cut myself, and hide from everyone. I knew something was really wrong, but no one could help me. My parents were frantic. My doctor just kept upping my medication doses, and I would stay awake all night because I was so afraid to have to wake up and go to school. I still couldn't do any homework and would cry and roll around on the floor holding my head yelling, "That black thing is in me again!"

Finally I was taken to a treatment facility, and my new psychiatrist correctly diagnosed me as bipolar. It was such a relief to finally know what was wrong with me all those years. He took me off all my meds and started me on new ones. After I had been on them for a while, I started to feel better and do better little by little. School was still a challenge, but it was bearable as I began to improve and get my life back.

I started to do things I'd never done before like speaking in front of people. When I was 13, I even spoke at the Capitol to the legislators where a bill was being debated on mental health. Because of my story, the bill passed. I will continue speaking out on mental health and doing whatever I can to help people like myself. My illness is no different than someone who has diabetes. My chemical imbalance is just in my head and theirs is in their pancreas.

If you have thought about suicide or wonder if it matters if you live or not, please listen to me:

There is someone out there who loves you. Please hold on for dear life. Things are never as dark as they seem. Talk with someone immediately and let them know how you're feeling, in the same way you'd talk to them if you had a terrible flu. "I'm feeling really sick. Can you help me?"

Dido wrote a song about dealing with pain with a promise of hope to come. Here's a part of it:

"I'm comin' round to open the blinds
You can't hide here any longer
You need to rinse those puffy eyes
You can't last here any longer

And you probably don't want to hear tomorrow's another day
Well I promise you you'll see the sun again
And you're asking me why pain's the only way to happiness
And I promise you you'll see the sun again..."

SEE THE SUN
Words and Music by DIDO ARMSTRONG ©2003 WARNER/CHAPPELL MUSIC LTD (PRS)
All Rights Administered By WB MUSIC CORP. All Rights Reserved. Used by Permission.

We could go on and on with all kinds of El Guapos, like dealing with the death of a family member, trying to rise above poverty, or coping with a major physical setback. But we won't because the solution is usually the same for each of them.

FOCUS ON WHAT YOU CAN CONTROL, LOOK TO THE TRUE MiRROR, AND DON'T LOSE HOPE.

ACRES OF DIAMONDS

Several years ago Russell Conwell gave a speech, "Acres of Diamonds," in which he told the story of a farmer named Ali Hafid who lived in ancient Persia. Not being content with what he had, Ali sold his farm and left his family to look for diamonds. For the next several years, he wandered through Palestine and Europe until he reached the coast of Spain. Penniless, heartsick, and weary after years of searching, Ali drowned himself in the ocean. Later, it turns out that the farm he sold was the very site of Golconda, the greatest diamond mine in the history of the world. If Ali had stayed home and dug in his own fields, he would have found acres of diamonds.

That's how I feel about each and every one of you reading this book. I believe you have tons of natural ability, acres of diamonds as it were, already within you, and that you don't need to look anywhere else. Just dig in your own fields.

There's a great scene from *The Lion King* that makes this same point. After Mufasa, the king of the forest, is killed, Simba, his son, is supposed to become the next king. But, feeling responsible for the death of his father, Simba runs away and spends the next several years goofing off with his irresponsible friends. Soon, he forgets his great responsibility and heritage. One night Simba sees his father, Mufasa, in a vision.

> **MUFASA:** *Simba, you have forgotten me.*
>
> **SIMBA:** *No, how could I?*
>
> **MUFASA:** *You have forgotten who you are and so forgotten me. Look inside yourself, Simba. You are more than what you have become. You must take your place in the Circle of Life.*
>
> **SIMBA:** *How can I go back? I'm not who I used to be.*
>
> **MUFASA:** *Remember who you are, you are my son and the one true King. Remember who you are. Remember. Remember. Remember…*

I hope you too will remember who *you* really are. I hope you'll remember the great things you've done in the past, like the times you've followed your heart, achieved a goal, or were extra nice to someone. I hope you'll remember the dreams and hopes you have for the future. I hope you'll remember that you're part of the great human family, as well as part of a direct family.

When all is said and done, your family may be the best source of self-worth you have available. Perhaps you're thinking, "Are you crazy? I can't stand my siblings and my parents are always nagging me." I admit that some families are dysfunctional, but most are pretty good. And even though your mother or sister may annoy you, they're blood, and, in a life-and-death situation, they'd do anything for you. Latoya from Paterson, New Jersey, told me, "Sometimes boys make you feel like you're special and you're the only one they care about. A lot of girls feel like they need that. But my mother loves me and my father loves me, so there's no gap to fill."

One of the hottest things on the Web today is tracing your pedigree. In the chart below, see if you can identify three generations of your ancestors. Put in your name first, followed by your parents, grandparents, then great-grandparents. If you get stuck, ask your parents or grandparents for help.

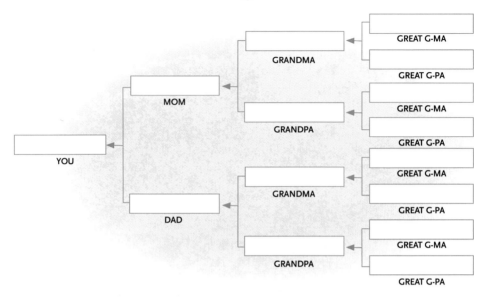

How well do you know your lineage? Can you tell any stories about your grandparents or great-grandparents? What were they like as teens? I'll bet each of you has someone in your lineage whom you can look to as a great role model.

Getting to know your extended family will give you a sense of identity, belonging, and worth. Like Simba, you will see that you are part of something much bigger than yourself. You will also see the great impact that one person can have for good and bad upon generations.

LET YOUR LIGHT SHINE

At the start of this chapter I quoted author Marianne Williamson. This is the second half of that quote.

"You are a child of God. Your playing small does not serve the world. There is nothing enlightened about shrinking so that other people won't feel insecure around you. We are all meant to shine, as children do. We were born to make manifest the glory of God that is within us. It is not just in some of us; it is in everyone. And as we let our own light shine, we unconsciously give other people permission to do the same."

Although some teens seem to have been born with a great deal of self-worth, most have to work at it. It may take years before you'll get a sense of what you're capable of doing. You don't just wake up and say, "Wow. I'm glad I'm me." But I promise you it *will* happen. Your true worth has nothing to do with your looks or popularity. It has everything to do with the fact that you're a human being, a child of destiny, with amazing potential. No one is worth more or less than anyone else. We're all equal and we're all worth a ton! That's why there's never a need to compare yourself to a brother, sister, or friend, and feel inferior or superior. So what if you have braces, so what if you have acne, so what if you're socially awkward. You'll turn out just fine. Never let the social mirror strip you of your unique gifts, as R. Buckminster Fuller, the great inventor, warned:

"All children are born geniuses; 9,999 out of every 10,000 are swiftly, inadvertently degeniusized by grown-ups."

How will you know if your self-worth is improving?

- *You'll worry less about what other people think of you.*
- *You'll give more service.*
- *You'll bounce back more quickly when you have a setback.*
- *You'll feel more at peace.*
- *You'll be happy for the successes of others, like Cody in this story.*

Kiefer couldn't wait to tell his friends! He had worked so hard for three years, and now he was named "All-State!" He couldn't believe it! He held the newspaper in his hand where he found his name among the others and read it over and over just to make sure it was true.

Suddenly, his friend Brett grabbed it out of his hands. "Hey, is this the All-State team? Who made it from our school?" Kiefer smiled shyly, waiting for Brett to see his name.

"WHAT!** You made All-State, Kiefer?"* *Brett asked, his face crunched up in disbelief. "Are they serious? Why'd they choose **YOU?"

"I don't know," was all Kiefer could say, the smile gone from his face. He felt like an idiot and was deeply hurt by his friend's response. He hadn't expected that.

*However, a few minutes later, Cody had just heard the news and exploded with excitement down the hall! "**YEAH! ALL-STATE,** Kiefer! That's awesome! **YOU DESERVE IT, MAN!**" Cody picked Kiefer up and shook him, both of them with huge smiles. They celebrated as true friends, one genuinely happy for the other.*

THE EVERY DAY CHOICE

Remember, having self-worth is a choice you make every day. I read this in the Dear Harlan column of the Deseret Morning News:

Dear Harlan:

I'm a college junior who needs advice on how to handle being unattractive. I am overweight and have been working to lose that weight—with some success. I've got extensive stretch marks from being fat and acne (which I'm treating with help from a dermatologist). I have some acne scarring on my face and on my chest.

I have never been on a date. It would be nice to not be dismissed as a potential partner. How do I handle these feelings?

Signed, Mask-Wearer

Dear Mask-Wearer:

I did a little research this weekend (at the mall) and witnessed dozens of couples with bad skin, love handles and stretch marks in love. The conclusion: stretch marks aren't holding you back—it's you! You're so used to dismissing yourself that you never give anyone a chance.

Here's how you turn this around: work to accumulate great qualities. Add one good quality each month (work out, get involved, volunteer, learn to listen, etc.). In 12 months you'll have 12 more good qualities, and so on. The more good qualities you accumulate, the more you can smile about.

You are attractive. You are worthy of the best. Love yourself today—others will learn how to love you tomorrow and forever.

So, which road is it going to be, the high or the low? I'd recommend taking the high road by looking to the true mirror, building character and competence, and accepting yourself as a work in progress.

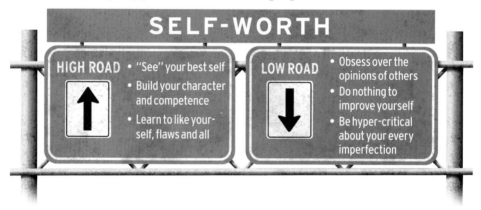

Building a healthy self-worth doesn't mean you won't ever get hurt or feel insecure. It simply means that you have a strong immune system that can fight the germs life sends your way. Be like a peach. Peaches are sweet and delicious on the outside, but have a solid pit on the inside. We shouldn't be afraid to give and receive love, to be open and vulnerable. We may get hurt from time to time but we can deal with it, because we have a solid, unflappable core beneath, a core that can't be broken.

I hope to see you on the high road soon!

● ● ● **COMING ATTRACTIONS** ● ● ●

The final chapter is all about pirates and hobbits. (Weird combination, wouldn't you say?) It's also really short. Three more pages and you're done. Congrats!

BABY STEPS*

1. Make a copy of Audrey Hepburn's favorite "Beauty Tips" and post it on your mirror.

2. The next time someone calls you a name, respond with Pee-wee Herman's famous line, "I know you are, but what am I?" Be prepared to get smacked when you do this.

3. Make a list of your best talents and skills. Now add one more thing to that list you'd like to develop.

   New talent or skill I want to develop:

   _____

   _____

4. The next time you mess up, try the four-fold principle. Make up for your mistake times four.

5. For five days in a row, do one small act of service for someone who needs it. Check the boxes as you complete them and watch how good you feel.

   ☐ Day 1   ☐ Day 2   ☐ Day 3   ☐ Day 4   ☐ Day 5

6. What is the most significant accomplishment of your life? Record how it made you feel when you accomplished it.

   _____

   _____

7. Hold a day of integrity. For one whole day, be totally honest in all your dealings. Don't lie, cheat, exaggerate, or gossip. Keep all your commitments. See how whole it makes you feel.

---

* To keep an online journal of your Baby Steps progress, go to www.6decisions.com.

8. Name five things that you believe or have faith in.

1. _____

2. _____

3. _____

4. _____

5. _____

9. For three consecutive days, count how many servings of fruits and vegetables you eat. If you're not getting five or more, make adjustments to your diet.

Servings of fruits and veggies

Day 1 _____

Day 2 _____

Day 3 _____

10. Think through the first five most important decisions you'll ever make: School, Friends, Parents, Dating & Sex, and Addictions. Which one are you struggling with most? Make up your mind to start making better decisions today in that area.

STICK TO THE CODE

It's Worth Fighting For!

There's a great scene from the movie *Pirates of the Caribbean* that you can't forget. When everything seems to be falling apart, one of the pirates asks Captain Jack Sparrow what they should do. The Captain (who is less than admirable but does have one good line!) simply responds:

"STICK *to the* CODE!"

The pirate completely understands, **"Aye, the code!"**

Although I'm sure Captain Sparrow had a different code in mind, stick to the code in this book means that you make smart decisions about each fork in the road you face and stick to what you know is right, even when it's hard or unpopular. And if you get off track, you get back on fast.

I wish I could tell you that everything in life will be peachy from here on out. But you and I know better. You will have depressing days and bad hair days.

PARDON MY PLANET   **BY VIC LEE**

SOMETIMES I'M JUST SO OVERWHELMED WITH THE VASTNESS OF THE UNIVERSE.

I MEAN, THINK ABOUT IT . . . BILLIONS OF GALAXIES, EACH HOSTING *BILLIONS* OF PLANETS.

I CAN'T HELP THINKING THAT OUT THERE, SOMEWHERE, THERE'S SOMEBODY THAT'S AS UPSET ABOUT THEIR NEW HAIRCUT AS I AM.

© King Features Syndicate

At times it may seem that everything is falling apart. In such situations, "Stick to the code." Listen to your conscience, the common sense inside you that makes you feel guilty when you're mean to a friend and warm when you're nice to your mom. It will lead you down the right path. You know what I'm talking about. Aye matey, the code!

For years, people have debated, "Do your genes make you who you are? Or does your environment or upbringing make you who you are?" My answer is neither.

CHOICE MAKES YOU WHO YOU ARE.

Although genes and upbringing deeply influence you, you are you because of your choices. Choice rules!

So remember, there are six key decisions you will make during your teen years that can make or break your future. And you are free to choose your path. Hopefully, after reading this book, you'll be more prepared than ever to answer these questions:

1. What am I going to do about my education?

2. What type of friends will I choose and what kind of friend will I be?

3. What kind of relationships will I build with my parents?

4. Who will I date and what will I choose to do about sex?

5. What will I do about smoking, drugs, pornography, and other addictive things?

6. What am I going to do about building my self-worth?

PLEASE CHOOSE WISELY
YOUR VERY LIFE IS AT STAKE

Choosing the high road will help you become happy and healthy today, and ready for your twenties, thirties, and beyond. By ready I mean: all set, fully prepared, standing by, geared-up, equipped, organized, good to go. Who wouldn't want that?

Some of you might be thinking, I wish I had this book years ago. I've already blown some of these decisions. Well, it's **never too late** to learn from your mistakes and get back on track. I repeat, whether you're 15 or 19 or 25, it's never too late to change course. If you do, your past trials can actually become a blessing to you and others.

Of course, you're better off sticking to the high road from the start. After all, smart people learn from their own mistakes while really smart people learn from the mistakes of others. If you're on the high road already, reach out and help others do the same, instead of judging them. Be a good influence to a friend who may be flunking out of school or getting into drugs. Who knows, you just might be the lifesaver they need.

STICK *to the* CODE!

There's a lot of hate, violence, and depressing stuff going on in this world of ours and it's easy to hang your head and get down. But take heart, there is good and beauty all around. I'm reminded of the dialogue between Frodo and Sam in *The Lord of the Rings* trilogy when they are both exhausted and about to lose hope.

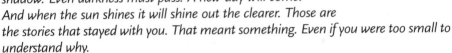

SAM: *"It's like in the great stories, Mr. Frodo. The ones that really mattered. Full of darkness and danger they were. And sometimes you didn't want to know the end. Because how could the end be happy? How could the world go back to the way it was with so much bad happening? But in the end, it's only a passing thing, this shadow. Even darkness must pass. A new day will come. And when the sun shines it will shine out the clearer. Those are the stories that stayed with you. That meant something. Even if you were too small to understand why.*

"But I think Mr. Frodo, I do understand. I know now. Folk in those stories had lots of chances of turning back only they didn't. They kept going. 'Cause they were holding on to something."

FRODO: *"What are we holding on to, Sam?"*

SAM: *"That there's some good in this world, Mr. Frodo. And it's worth fighting for!"*

I second the motion. There is some good in this world and it is worth fighting for. I also firmly believe that you are good and that you are worth fighting for. Even more, I think you're the finest generation of teens that has ever lived. That's why I wrote this book.

Well, here we are at the end of all things. I congratulate you on finishing the book (or did you just look at the cartoons?). I leave you with my most excellent wishes for success in life. Keep reading books. It's brain food, you know. And never forget the words of P. J. O'Rourke,

"Always read stuff that will make you

look good if you die in the middle of it."

THANK-YOUS

A fellow author once asked me, "So, who was your ghostwriter?" I was offended. "A ghostwriter?" I said. "Why would I use a ghostwriter?"

The fact is, I love to write and wrote all 100,749 words of this book on my IBM ThinkPad. That said, as every author knows, it takes an army to amass a book. So I would like to thank that army who made this book possible.

Thank you, Annie Oswald, for leading this project from start to finish. Your passion for helping teens and wanting to make a difference shone through every day. Thanks for collecting stories, conducting interviews, setting up focus groups, compiling research, finding awesome quotes, getting permissions, giving straight feedback, and doing 101 other things. Everyone tells me regularly how much they love working with you. So do I.

Thanks to Cynthia Haller, my sister. Thank you for writing beginning drafts of the Friends, Dating & Sex, and Self-Worth chapters. You were inspired! Your fingerprints and influence are all over this book and you contributed more stories than anyone. Truly, you are a great writer. Without you, this book wouldn't be half as good.

Thanks to the entire team at The FaQtory for the layout, illustrations, images, color, and the overall look and feel of the book. Specifically thanks to Ray Kuik, creative director; Bob Gair, art director; Jasper Jonker, project manager; and Eric Olson, illustrator. It was a riot working with you guys. Although you're Canadian, you're geniuses. Brilliant work!

Thank you, Mark Pett, for thinking up the majority of the cartoons in this book and for contributing several illustrations and comic strips. Your humor is one of a kind and brought comedic relief to some very intense subjects. I hope every paper in the country picks up your excellent comic strip, *Lucky Cow*.

Thank you, Rebecca, my lovely wife, for your steadfast support and for never complaining over a three-year period. At last, it is finished! And I can start taking out the garbage again.

Thank you, Jean Crowther, for your outstanding editorial assistance at the last hour. I will forever recommend you to others.

Thank you, Maria, my sister, for reviewing and giving great input on every chapter (except Dating & Sex because it embarrassed you so much).

Thank you, Deborah Burkett, Deb Lund, and Greg Link for your great help on gathering endorsements and marketing the book.

Thank you, Dominick Anfuso, Wylie O'Sullivan, and the other key players at Simon & Schuster, for your patience and your belief in the project.

Thank you, Jan Miller and Shannon Miser-Marvin from Dupree-Miller (my book agent), for suggesting I do this book in the first place.

A big thanks to the many schools—and the administrators, teachers, and students within them—who participated in focus groups, did interviews, and gave input. Specifically, thanks go to:

- Gary DeLuca and the students of Allen East High School in Ohio.

- Sherri Stinson and the students of the Community Career Center of Metro Nashville Public Schools.
- Jennifer Williams, Susan Warline, Norm Emmets, Erica Gillespie, and the students of Hilliard Darby High School in Ohio.
- Tony Contos, Marie Blunk, Cathe Ghilain, Susan Graham, Kelly Manning-Smith, Emily Petronio, and the students of Joliet Township High School in Illinois.
- Liz Whitsom and the students of Warren Central High School in Kentucky.
- Dave Barrett and the students of Millington Central High School in Tennessee.
- James Lynch and the students of Snyder Middle School in Pennsylvania.
- Jennifer Suh and the students of Daewon Foreign High School in South Korea.
- David Downing, Mrs. Van Dine and her multicultural literature class, and the students of Millikan High School in Long Beach, California.
- Kay Cannon and the students at Northridge High School in Layton, Utah.
- Denise Hodgkins and the students of Utah Valley State College 7 Habits classes, especially: Ben Hicks, Amanda Pledger, Sophia Iacayo, Martin Palmer, Rachel Turner, Brandon Beckham, DeAnna Stock, Michelle Chappell, Kimberly Schultz, Curtis Walker, and Jason Ormond.

Thank you, Kristin Bloodworth, Reverend Barbara Roby, and teen members of the Braddock Street United Methodist Church in Winchester, Virginia, for conducting a key focus group on a sensitive subject. In particular, thanks to Lindsey Shrimp, Frankie Welton, Erin Gardner, Eric Fisher, Rachel Carson, Chris Gardner, Danielle Brown, Glen Carson, Taylor Hoffman, Heather Gronlund, Taylor Hodges, Willy B. Hawse, Amber Brill, and Nick Adams.

A big thanks to the students of Utah Valley High School, who showed up at my home early on Saturday mornings off and on for two years to participate in focus groups. In particular, thanks to Dane Andersen, Cameron Bench, Nicolas Blosil, Charles Bohr, Jarrett Burge, McKinlee Covey, Tyler Davis, Elise Fletcher, Jake Glenn, Joey Gunnell, Hank Hillstead, Celeste Huntsman, Aaron Jaynes, Ellen Jaynes, Justin Karoly, Janna Mills, Shannon Mills, Chris Moon, Cody Naccarato, Shannon Nordin, Chelsey Olsen, Metta Oswald, Cameron Robinson, Natalie Robison, Jessica Sagers, and Keli'i Wesley.

Thanks to all the FranklinCovey international offices, who contributed in various ways.

Thank you, Vickie-Jean Mullins and Florida Department of Health (greattowait.com) for providing great information.

Thanks to the many other adults who offered feedback, editorial help, stories, and more, including Greg Fox, Luison Lassala from Ireland, Doug Hart from Palestine, Sainbayar Beejin and his classmates from Mongolia, Barbara Muirhead, Heather Seferovich, my mom (Hi, Mom!), and my sister Catherine.

Thanks to the many other teens from all over the world who contributed advice, stories, and interviews.

Help Desk

SCHOOL

- **If you're trying to find a great scholarship for college,**
go to www.scholarshipcoach.com or pick up Ben Kaplan's book How to
Go to College Almost for Free

- **Worried about the ACT/SAT?**
Go to www.saab.org or Google "Free ACT/SAT Tests" for practice tests,
preparation tips, and tons of other ideas

- **If you're looking for some great study tips,**
go to www.academictips.org or www.homeworktips.about.com

- **Want to know your learning style?**
Visit http://homeworktips.about.com/od/homeworkhelp/a/lstyleqz.htm
or go to www.engr.ncsu.edu/learningstyles/ilsweb.html

- **If you're trying to decide what to major in,**
go to www.lifebound.com or pick up Carol Carter's book Majoring in the
Rest of Your Life: Career Secrets for College Students

FRIENDS

- **If you're looking for fun things to do with friends,**
go to http://kidshealth.org/teen/ or visit www.bored.com

- **If you're looking for ways to deal with troubled friends,**
go to www.health.org/govpubs/phd688

- **If you're struggling with how to resist negative peer pressure,**
go to www.abovetheinfluence.com

- **For a great book about the power of friends,** read Holes by
Louis Sachar

PARENTS

- **If you're suffering abuse from a parent or any other person,**
call the National Child Abuse Hotline: 1-800-25-ABUSE or go online to
www.ChildHelpUSA.com

- **Want help with an alcoholic or addicted parent?**
Go to www.al-anon.alateen.rg or call 888-4AL-ANON

- **Need some tips and help on how to get along with your parents?**
Go to http://teenadvice.about.com/cs/parentstalkto/ht/parentrelateht.htm

- **Want to know more about your family history?**
Go to www.usgenweb.org or www.familysearch.org

DATING & SEX

- *Not sure how to get out of an abusive relationship?*
  Call 1-800-999-9999 or visit www.ndvh.org

- *Looking for some great date ideas?*
  Go to www.bygpub.com/books/tg2rw/dating-ideas.htm

- *Do you need to know more about STDs?*
  Go to www.cfoc.org or www.familydoctor.org/children.xml

ADDICTIONS

- *If you're addicted to tobacco, drugs, or alcohol and need help,*
  call the Center for Substance Abuse Treatment Referral Line at
  1-800-662-HELP (4357) or visit www.health.org/govpubs/rpo884/ or
  call Alateen: 1-888-425-2666 or visit http://www.al-anon.alateen.org/ or
  http://www.freevibe.com/drug_facts or www.teens.drugabuse.gov/facts

- *If you want to know more about alcohol and drug prevention,*
  visit www.health.org

- *If you're addicted to porn and want out,*
  go to www.porn-free.org

SELF-WORTH

- *If you can't pull yourself out of the funk you're in,*
  go to http://www.copecaredeal.org/, or information is also available
  from the Substance Abuse and Mental Health Services Administration
  by calling toll free: 1-800-662-4357 or www.familydoctor.org/children
  .xml, check out the Teens section

- *For tips on common teen health conditions and staying healthy,*
  go to www.familydoctor.org/children.xml

- *If you think you might have an eating disorder,*
  go to www.edap.org, or www.familydoctor.org/children.xml

- *If you're interested in losing weight in a healthy way,*
  go to www.mypyramid.gov or www.familydoctor.org/children

- *Want to volunteer but don't know where to start?*
  Go to www.pointsoflight.org or www.dosomething.org

- *Want help staying away from destructive decisions?*
  Go to www.sadd.org or www.abovetheinfluence.com

- *To find out about IQ, EQ, Personality type, Aptitude, and all kinds of*
  cool things about you, go to www.2h.com/index

BIBLIOGRAPHY

THE 6 BIG ONES

Hinckley, Gordon B. *Standing For Something.* New York: Crown, 2000.

Frost, Robert. *The Road Not Taken.* New York: Owl Books, 2002.

7 HABITS CRASH COURSE

Reavis, George H. "The Animal School." Public domain.

DECISION 1

U.S. Department of Labor, Bureau of Labor Statistics, www.bls.gov. Public domain, 2005.

Kaplan, Ben. *How to Go to College Almost for Free.* New York: HarperCollins, 2001.

DECISION 2

"Popular" from the Broadway musical *Wicked*
Music and lyrics by Stephen Schwartz
Copyright © 2003 Stephen Schwartz
All rights reserved. Used by permission.

Wiseman, Rosalind. *Queen Bees and Wannabes.* New York: Three Rivers Press, 2003.

Keith, Kent M., *The Silent Revolution: Dynamic Leadership in the Student Council.* Cambridge, MA: Harvard Student Agencies. Copyright © 1968 Kent M. Keith, renewed 2001.

DECISION 3

"Stay Together For The Kids," words and music by Tom DeLonge, Mark Hoppus and Travis Barker.
Copyright © 2001 EMI APRIL MUSIC INC. and FUN WITH GOATS
All Rights Controlled and Administered by EMI APRIL MUSIC INC.
All Rights Reserved International Copyright Secured. Used by Permission.

DECISION 4

Anderson, Kristen. *The Truth about Sex by High School Senior Girls.* Copyright © 2001 Kristen Anderson.

Bearman, Peter S., James Moody, and Katherine Stovel. "Chains of Affection: The Structure of Adolescent Romantic and Sexual Networks." *American Journal of Sociology* 110(2004): 44-91.
Copyright © 2004 by The University of Chicago. All Rights Reserved. Used by Permission.

Meeker, Meg, M.D. *Epidemic: How Teen Sex Is Killing Our Kids.* Washington, D.C.: LifeLine Press, 2002.

Florida Department of Health. www.greattowait.com. Copyright © 2006. All Rights Reserved.

DECISION 5

Golding, William. *Lord of the Flies.* New York: Riverhead, 1999.

Phil S. *The Perfect Brightness of Hope.* Copyright © 2002 Perfect Brightness LLC.

DECISION 6

Levenson, Sam. *In One Era & Out the Other.* New York: Simon & Schuster, 1981.

"See The Sun," words and music by DIDO ARMSTRONG
Copyright © 2003 WARNER/CHAPPELL MUSIC LTD (PRS)
All Rights Administered By WB MUSIC CORP.
All Rights Reserved. Used by Permission.

"Help Me Harlan." Deseret Morning News. Copyright © King Features Syndicate.

Herman, Stanley M., *Authentic Management*, Addison Wesley.
Copyright © 1977.

STICK TO THE CODE

Tolkien, J. R. R. *The Return of the King.* Boston: Houghton Mifflin, 1999.

OTHER

Below are a few books that heavily influenced the author:

Fox, Lara, and Hillary Frankel. *Breaking the Code.* New York: New American Library, 2005.

Bytheway, John. *What I Wish I'd Known in High School.* Salt Lake City: Deseret Book, 1994.

Harris, Joshua. *I Kissed Dating Goodbye.* Oregon: Multnomah Publishers, Inc., 1997.

INDEX

ABOUT FRANKLINCOVEY

Sean Covey is Chief Product Architect at FranklinCovey. At FranklinCovey, our mission is to enable greatness in people and organizations everywhere. We believe the outcomes of great organizations include:

- *Achieving sustained superior financial performance*
- *Creating intensely loyal customers*
- *Developing a winning organizational culture*
- *Making a distinctive contribution*

Through a balanced focus on individual effectiveness, leadership development, and processes that drive focus and execution, we believe organizations can achieve these outcomes—predictably and measurably.

At FranklinCovey (NYSE:FC), we provide consulting and training, productivity tools, and assessment services to global clients in a wide range of industries. Our clients include 90 percent of the Fortune 100 and more than 75 percent of the Fortune 500, as well as thousands of small-to-midsize companies around the world. We also work extensively with numerous government and educational institutions. Organizations and individuals access our products and services through corporate onsite consulting and training, licensed client facilitators, public workshops, catalogs, Web sites, and a network of retail stores.

FranklinCovey has more than 2,000 associates providing professional services and products in 28 languages, in 39 offices, and in 95 countries worldwide.

To learn more about FranklinCovey products and services, please call 1-888-868-1776 or 1-801-817-1776 or go to www.franklincovey.com or www.7habits4teens.com.

Services and Products

- *xQ survey and debrief (to help leaders and organizations assess their ability to focus and execute on their top priorities)*
- *The 4 Disciplines of Execution consulting services*
- *The 7 Habits of Highly Effective People Signature Program*
- *Focus: Achieving Your Highest Priorities workshop*
- *The 4 Roles of Leadership workshop*
- *Business Acumen: What the CEO Wants You to Know workshop*
- *The FranklinCovey Planning System*
- *PlanPlus for Outlook (planning and scheduling software)*
- *Writing Advantage, Presentation Advantage, and Meeting Advantage workshops*
- *And more*

Let FranklinCovey Help Your School Achieve Greatness

When people talk about "good" schools, it seems the same descriptions come up time and time again: high-quality education, good teachers, effective administrative leadership...but how does a school move from simply being good to being great?

Through our deep involvement with thousands of schools, districts, and communities, we understand many of the challenges educators face—student achievement, creating a winning culture, shifting social expectations, and parent/community involvement. With a broad spectrum of proven programs designed to improve results in all these areas, FranklinCovey can help you make your school not just good, but great.

> **"I don't know of any other programs more powerful than FranklinCovey's."**
> **—Dr. Pedro Garcia, Metropolitan Nashville Public School District**

PROVEN PRINCIPLES. PROVEN PROCESSES. PROVEN RESULTS.

By taking a holistic, inside-out approach FranklinCovey's Education Services has dramatically improved results in schools all over the world, including:

- *Increasing Academic Performance Index scores by 18 percent over three years*
- *Decreasing drop-out rates from 20 percent to 4.7 percent over four years*
- *Significantly increasing the number of students in advanced-placement and college-prep classes*
- *Improving attendance and graduation rates*

Imagine what FranklinCovey can do for your school.

THE HALLMARKS OF A GREAT SCHOOL

FranklinCovey's Education Services delivers the outcomes of a great school, including:

- **Sustained superior performance**—*Great schools constantly improve test scores, graduation rates, and college attendance.*
- **Winning culture**—*Great schools have teachers and administrators who would rather work at that school than anywhere else.*

- **Distinctive Contribution**—*Great schools graduate students who are academically strong and emotionally well adjusted, students who are prepared to make a difference in society.*
- **Customer Loyalty**—*Great schools create loyalty among students, parents, the community, and other key stakeholders.*

FranklinCovey can help you build a foundation of greatness through:
- *Effective students*
- *Effective teachers and administrators*
- *Focus and execution on the school's most important goals*

GREAT SCHOOL

FOCUS AND EXECUTION

- xQ™ Organizational Assessment
- The 4 Disciplines of Execution™

EFFECTIVE TEACHERS/ ADMINISTRATORS

- The 7 Habits of Highly Effective People®: Signature Program
- The 7 Habits for Managers™
- The 4 Roles of Leadership™

EFFECTIVE STUDENTS

- The 7 Habits of Highly Effective Teens™
- The 6 Most Important Decisions You'll Ever Make™

PUT YOUR SCHOOL ON THE PATH TO GREATNESS

For more information about the programs listed above or to learn how FranklinCovey's Education Services can help your school achieve unprecedented results, call toll free 1-800-272-6839. For international callers, please call 001-801-342-6664. Or visit www.franklincovey.com or www.7Habits4Teens.com.

Covey Classics

A Covey classic: a generally older movie watched so many times by the Covey family that lines are used frequently in everyday conversation; often bizarre; not always award winning, but who cares; addictive in nature; must-see movies

Back to the Future (series)
Beauty and the Beast (Disney)
Ben-Hur
A Christmas Story
Christmas Vacation
Dances with Wolves
Dead Poets Society
Dirty Rotten Scoundrels
Ever After
First Knight
Fletch
Groundhog Day
Heaven Can Wait
Home Alone
The Incredibles
Indiana Jones (series)
The In-Laws (1979)
A Knight's Tale
Life Is Beautiful
The Lion King
A Little Princess
The Lord of the Rings (series)
The Man from Snowy River
Meet the Parents
My Fair Lady

Nacho Libre
Napoleon Dynamite
Now You See Him, Now You Don't
Overboard
Pirates of the Caribbean
The Princess Bride
Quigley Down Under
Remember the Titans
Rocky (series)
Seems Like Old Times
Shanghai Noon
Signs
Spies Like Us
Star Wars (series)
The Ten Commandments
They Call Me Trinity
Three Amigos
Tommy Boy
A Walk to Remember
What About Bob?
What's Up, Doc?